The Jurisp...

WILLIAM...

Studies in American Constitutionalism
General Editors: Gary J. Jacobsohn and Richard E. Morgan

The Jurisprudence of Justice

WILLIAM J. BRENNAN, JR.

The Law and Politics of "Libertarian Dignity"

David E. Marion

ROWMAN & LITTLEFIELD PUBLISHERS, INC.
Lanham • Boulder • New York • Oxford

ROWMAN & LITTLEFIELD PUBLISHERS, INC.

Published in the United States of America
by Rowman & Littlefield Publishers, Inc.
4720 Boston Way, Lanham, Maryland 20706

12 Hid's Copse Road
Cummor Hill, Oxford OX2 9JJ, England

British Library Cataloging in Publication Information Available

Library of Congress Cataloging-in-Publication Data
Marion, David E., 1948–
    The jurisprudence of Justice William J. Brennan, Jr. : the law and
politics of "libertarian dignity" / David E. Marion.
        p.   cm.
    Includes bibliographical references and index.
    ISBN 0-8476-8566-7 (cloth : alk. paper). — ISBN 0-8476-8567-5
(pbk. : alk. paper)
    1. Brennan, William J. (William Joseph), 1906–   .
2. Constitutional history—United States.   I. Title.
KF8745.B68M37   1997
347.73'2634—dc21   97-20407
                                                              CIP

ISBN 0-8476-8566-7 (cloth : alk. paper)
ISBN 0-8476-8567-5 (pbk. : alk. paper)

Printed in the United States of America

♾ ™ The paper used in this publication meets the minimum requirements of
American National Standard for Information Sciences—Permanence of Paper
for Printed Library Materials, ANSI Z39.48—1984.

Contents

Introduction

Alexander Hamilton's description of a judicial branch that lacks independent "force" and "will" has long ceased to be considered an accurate characterization of the federal judiciary. Indeed, most Americans would quarrel with the claim that these are qualities even to be desired in any judicial department, whether national or state. Toleration of an independent judicial "will" is the flip side of general popular acceptance of policy making by judicial officials. No special expertise in the law is needed to understand that one of the great changes that has occurred since the founding is the enlarged role that the courts now play in shaping the American way of life. For this reason, a strong case can be made that the preferences and beliefs of judicial officials merit greater public attention today than was true at the founding.

One way to gain an appreciation for the place and role that the judiciary now occupies in the governmental system is to study the opinions of jurists who have exercised a formative influence over the modern court. Whether the test is length of service, authorship of majority opinions, or personal reputation, few jurists in the twentieth century stand out as prominently in the field of constitutional law as Justice William J. Brennan Jr. This book attempts to make a contribution to the already growing scholarship devoted to Brennan's jurisprudence. Unlike some other works that compare his positions on legal controversies with that of selected colleagues or delve into behind-the-scene-negotiations and discussions, the objective of this book is to reconstruct the teaching that Brennan conveyed in the opinions he made a part of our "public" discourse and to subject that teaching to both strict constitutional and broad political scrutiny. Informing this study is the assumption that the legal opinions he allowed to carry his name represented his best efforts (whether the product of much or little negotiation) at influencing public opinion and government policy. The examination of Brennan that follows offers support for the twin claims that he might be seen as the most important liberal jurist of the twentieth century and that a careful review of his opinions will not only result in a heightened appreciation for his defense of "libertarian dignity," but should supply some important insights into the impulses that define the modern American psyche.

Beginning early in his tenure with notable majority opinions in the obscenity area in *Roth* v. *United States* (1957), malapportionment in *Baker* v. *Carr* (1962), and general freedom of "expression" in *New York Times* v. *Sullivan* (1964) and *Freedman* v. *Maryland* (1965), Brennan's record of major opinions rivals that of any justice since John Marshall. As *Roth, Baker, Sullivan*, and *Freedman* established important standards for evaluating governmental policies, so during the middle and concluding periods of his service Brennan's majority opinions set out standards for determining the boundaries of legitimate action in controversial cases dealing with public employee liability (*Bivens* v. *Six Unknown Named Agents of the Federal Bureau of Narcotics* [1971]), gender classification (*Frontiero* v. *Richardson* [1973] and *Roberts* v. *United States Jaycees* [1984]), affirmative action/reverse discrimination (*Johnson* v. *Transportation Agency, Santa Clara County* [1987] and *Metro Broadcasting* v. *FCC* [1990]), and symbolic expression (*Texas* v. *Johnson* [1989]). Whether in majority opinions such as these, or in his much publicized concurring and dissenting opinions submitted in *Abington School District* v. *Schempp* (school prayer [1963]), *Paris Adult Theatre I* v. *Slaton* (access by consenting adults to X-rated movies [1973]), *CBS* v. *Democratic National Committee* (network's refusal to air political ads [1973]), *Regents of the University of California, Davis* v. *Bakke* (public sector quota program [1978]), and *Cruzan* v. *Missouri Department of Health* (right to die [1990]), Brennan's jurisprudence gives concrete expression to an important dimension of the modern mind, that is, to the belief that through deliberate exertions of the human will it is possible to overcome the tragic dimensions of existence and perfect the American republic of rights.

Brennan's vision of a society guided by the principle of "libertarian dignity," the realization in the modern state of a high degree of autonomous individualism, separates him from the Holmesian and New Deal liberals of the first half of the twentieth century. Although there is ample evidence that his thinking was critically influenced by the work of both the Progressives and the New Dealers, Brennan's opinions seek to supply a corrective to the blemishes that tarnished the legacy of the political and judicial liberals who preceded him. New Deal-style coalitional politics, for example, left openings for electoral and governmental restraints on rights that were visible in the continuation of segregationist practices in the 1950s and in some of the excesses of the modern administrative state. It is impossible to read the corpus of his judicial writings without being struck by the depth of Brennan's commitment to freeing people from the constraints of "collective" society, whether rooted in nature, tradition, history, or majoritarian preferences, so that they may define themselves in the image of their own choosing. When looked at in its entirety, Brennan's project represents the most extensive and carefully developed judicial effort of this century to bring about a permanent improvement in human affairs by "completing" the American Revolution that had proclaimed the primacy of individual rights on behalf of all mankind. If the defining feature of modern culture is the enhancement of self through expressive activity, ideally resulting in complete individual differentiation, then it might also be argued that Brennan left behind the closest thing that we have to a jurisprudence of modernity.

For people familiar with modern natural rights theory or with the attraction of the principles of equality and individual liberty in democratic times, the appearance on the Supreme Court of a justice committed to advancing the ends articulated by Brennan could hardly have been unanticipated. To say that his thoughts on freeing up people to enjoy the maximum of self-expression and self-determination are not remarkable for our time, however, is not to prove that there is nothing problematical about his objectives or the means he employed to achieve them. The aim of the present study is to subject Brennan's opinions to the kind of scrutiny that befits writings intended to shape public opinion and policy or, more generally, the way of life of a people. Unless good governance is taken for granted in modern republics such as the United States or is simply to be left to chance, responsible democratic citizenship requires a careful and serious examination of the thoughts and actions of individuals such as Justice Brennan who actively participate, or seek to participate, in the process of shaping a way of life for a community. This book looks to make a provocative contribution to such an exercise.

Countless students, colleagues, and friends have engaged me in a career-long debate on the possibilities and limitations of political life. To the hundreds of students who have endured my almost endless questions about the "lessons" to be drawn from the Court's rulings in cases such as *Marbury, McCulloch,* and *Brown,* and to the colleagues and friends who have shared their own thoughts on the American founding and U.S. constitutional history, I can only admit to having taken more than has been given. To them must go much of the credit for the persuasive parts of this book. For the unpersuasive parts, the responsibility is entirely mine. It would be remiss of me, however, not to single out several people for a special expression of gratitude. My colleagues in the Political Science Department at Hampden-Sydney College, Roger Barrus, John Eastby, Jim Pontuso, and Joe Lane, are at least "spiritual" co-authors of this work. To them, as well as to Joseph Goldberg, James Simms, Stephen Baron, Morton Frisch, Gary Glenn, George Romoser, John Kayser, and the late Martin Diamond and Herbert Storing, I am indebted for giving me a practical lesson in the real meaning of Aristotelian friendship that cannot be repaid in a few words or one deed. John Dinan provided many useful suggestions for improving the first three chapters. The final round of editing was guided almost entirely by Robert Faulkner's provocative reflections on the thesis of the book and my interpretation of the case material. Taylor Reveley III, who clerked for Justice Brennan at the end of the 1960s, was generous with both his time and his reflections on my thesis. Jane Mahne provided invaluable technical assistance and always with extraordinary patience and graciousness. I am grateful to the editors of *Polity* for permission to draw on my 1995 essay ("Justice William J. Brennan and the Spirit of Modernity") that gave birth to this book. The staff at Rowman & Littlefield, especially Stephen Wrinn and Robin Adler, guided the manuscript through the various phases of publication with great professionalism and in the spirit of real friendship. Finally, Dianne and the boys, Eric, Stephen, and John, have put up with a great deal from "Dad" for more years than this book has been in progress. It is to them and to the memory of my parents that I dedicate this political and constitutional study of William Brennan's jurisprudence.

Chapter One

JURISPRUDENCE AS HIGH POLITICS

I have no quarrel, therefore, with the doctrine that judges ought to be in sympathy with the spirit of their times.
—Benjamin Cardozo, *The Nature of the Judicial Process* (1921)

Sensitivity to one's intuitive and passionate responses, and awareness of the range of human experience, is therefore not only an inevitable but a desirable part of the judicial process, an aspect more to be nurtured than to be feared.
—William J. Brennan, Jr., Cardozo Lecture (1987)

If William Brennan had "no inkling of [his] impending appointment" to the United States Supreme Court until the morning of its announcement on September 29, 1956, President Dwight Eisenhower surely had no more knowledge of the formidable influence that his new nominee would exercise over the Court and the nation during the next thirty-four years.[1] With his sights fixed more on reelection than on any transformation of the Court, Eisenhower believed that the selection of an Irish Catholic and moderate Democrat would be a "politically appeal[-ing]" move.[2] He was expecting the appointment to be well received in the Northeast with its heavy Catholic population and among Eisenhower Democrats who would be reassured by the apparently nonpartisan action of the World War II hero. He surely did not anticipate paying any great price for his decision.

It would not be long, however, before Brennan would have Eisenhower regretting the decision that he made in the heat of the 1956 political campaign.[3] By most estimates, the man he elevated to the highest court in the land would become the most important liberal jurist of the second half of the century, and by some accounts of the entire century. His contribution would take the form of mounting a defense of

1

principles and practices designed to make individual autonomy in matters having to do with the pursuit of a way of life the defining quality of
American society.

In its lead story on the White House announcement, the *New York
Times* reported that Brennan seemed to be "immensely pleased about
his appointment."[4] Perhaps the fifty-year-old nominee had some "inkling" of what he would do with the power that he was about to be
handed. This son of an Irish immigrant would craft a jurisprudential
philosophy whose goal seemed to be nothing less than to finish the work
of the Progressives and New Dealers and, in that way, to bring about the
completion of the American republic of rights that had its origins in the
Declaration of Independence. Admittedly, there is little evidence that
Brennan entered upon his duties as did Ronald Reagan with a self-
appointed mission to complete the work begun in 1776 with the Declaration and in 1787 with the Constitution. But if self-governance was the
immediate objective of the signers of the Declaration, by at least the
mid-1960s Brennan was providing clear signals in his opinions that he
believed the time had come to go all the way to the far end of the
American Revolution by contriving a liberal democratic state where
each person can experience the full pleasure of their own existence as a
free, equal, and autonomous human being. Here is the core principle of
Brennan's jurisprudence of "libertarian dignity."

The Brennan family story is quintessential American fare. A graduate of the University of Pennsylvania and Harvard Law School, William
Brennan Jr. could draw inspiration from a father who, after his arrival
from Ireland in 1890, rose from laboring as a coal shoveler in a brewery
to become a city commissioner and director of public safety in Newark,
New Jersey. After graduating among the top ten students in his class at
Harvard Law School, the younger Brennan found his way to the New
Jersey Supreme Court following a successful tour of duty during World
War II that earned him promotion to the rank of colonel in the U.S.
Army. Curiously, it was Republican chief executives who provided
Brennan with the most significant appointments of his professional career: first Governor Driscoll of New Jersey in 1950 and then Eisenhower. By the time he announced on July 20, 1990 that he would retire
from the bench for reasons of failing health, his authorship of trailblazing
First and Fourteenth Amendment decisions had made him the leading
liberal jurist in the country. Among other things, it was Brennan who
formulated the now famous "malice rule" that has shielded the media
since the mid-1960s from the chilling effect of libel suits. He is commonly identified as the principal architect of the modern overbreadth

doctrine that has been effectively used to protect fundamental freedoms in governmental regulatory cases. It is also Brennan who is credited with reinvigorating judicial enforcement of school desegregation, after it had languished for a dozen years following *Brown* v. *Board of Education,* with his decision in *Green* v. *County School Board.*[5] From affirmative action to gender discrimination to general freedom of expression and self-determination, Brennan's opinions chartered new ground for post–New Deal America.

One hundred years after William senior's arrival from Ireland, not only could the Brennan family boast that one of its own had served on the highest court in the land, it could say with the editors of the *New York Times* that it had given the country "an influential shaper of the Constitution."[6] The younger Brennan's reputation was solidified with conferral of the Medal of Freedom, the nation's highest civilian award, by President Bill Clinton on November 30, 1993. In tributes to Brennan, Justice Thurgood Marshall called him "irreplaceable" while Justice Byron White bluntly declared that Brennan would be remembered "as among the greatest Justices who have ever sat on the Supreme Court."[7] Much earlier, Chief Justice Earl Warren had asserted in the *Harvard Law Review* that "it would be difficult to name another Justice who wrote more important opinions in his first ten years" than Brennan.[8] Perhaps the best evidence of his stature by the time of his retirement is the common appearance of the phrase "Brennanesque reasoning" in the literature of constitutional law.[9]

The U.S. Supreme Court that Brennan joined in 1956 was still reeling from the political effects of the *Brown* school desegregation decision of 1954 and would soon encounter more trouble in 1957 when it announced in *Yates* v. *United States* that officials of the Communist Party were protected by the Constitution when they taught the advisability of overthrowing the government. With the country still adjusting to the unsettling effects of *Brown*, the *Yates* decision produced the most significant court crisis since Franklin Roosevelt's threat to pack the Court in 1936. That decision, coming after *Brown* had forced many communities to alter long-entrenched school practices, prompted several members of Congress to introduce legislation designed to curtail the Court's authority to hear cases involving segregationist practices and subversive activity. Although none of the bills received sufficient support to become law, the threat of retaliatory action could easily have reinforced any reservations that Brennan had about relying principally on legislative or executive officials to secure rights or redress grievances. And, in fact, the reaction of many members of Congress to the *Brown* and *Yates* decisions led some prominent scholars to defend precisely the type of judicial activism that would become a defining characteristic of Brennan's jurisprudence of libertarian dignity.[10] By coincidence, it was also during Brennan's first full year on the Court that Justice Felix Frankfurter, his former law professor and now colleague, published an essay that invited justices to "pierce the curtain of the future" and to "give shape and visage to mysteries still in the womb of time." The great jurists were really "legal philosophers" according to Frankfurter.[11] This high-toned view of the judicial role coincided well with the approach to constitutional interpretation with which Brennan would come to be associated. Like Eisenhower, Frankfurter would eventually quarrel with Brennan's handling of a number of major constitutional controversies, lamenting that his former student had gone too far with the advice to be creative.[12] Leaving the merits of these reservations for later consideration, it is sufficient to note at this point that Brennan was joining a Court that was being pushed from both the inside and outside to reconsider in the most dramatic way since the 1930s its place and role in the American political order.

While it may have been Eisenhower's intention to add to the bloc of judicial moderates on the Court, Brennan did not wait long to signal his sympathy with a liberal form of judicial activism. At the time of his appointment, the term "liberal" had come to be associated with New Deal thinking. Classical or Lockean liberalism set out to advance the safety and happiness of the people by limiting governmental authority and subordinating it to private rights. New Deal liberalism reflected the conviction that comfortable preservation or the advancement of safety and happiness required the toleration of a broader range of governmental action than was common in eighteenth- and nineteenth-century liberal thought. The thinking of the legal and political liberals associated with the Progressive and New Deal movements supplied the critical foundation for the jurisprudential philosophy that Brennan would come to identify with a fully completed democratic state. Two key figures in shaping at least the legal dimensions of the movement from nineteenth-century liberalism to New Deal liberalism were Justices Oliver Wendell Holmes and Benjamin Cardozo. In their writings on and off the Court, both justices accommodated and legitimated the Progressive belief that society is open to perfection through deliberate human action. What this finally meant in practice for the Progressives was that the collective wisdom of all citizens should invigorate and give direction to society through mechanisms that provide direct popular involvement in governance. This idea was given concrete expression with the advocacy of the initiative, referendum, and recall and in the New Deal defense of policy making rooted heavily in coalitional politics rather than constitutional interpretation and tradition. By the 1950s, however, even the friends of this movement had to admit that New Deal–style politics had failed to satisfy its great objectives. Brennan's project would be to supply a corrective to address the deficiencies that had surfaced by the 1950s. By the time of his retirement in 1990, he had crafted a rights-oriented jurisprudence that reflected the modern conviction that every person should be able to experience the fullest possible control over their way of life and, thereby, gain the greatest possible pleasure from their own existence. Brennan the jurist had become inseparable from Brennan the "philosopher" of libertarian dignity.

Jurisprudential Midwifery: Begetting the Jurisprudence of Libertarian Dignity

Considering what the Brennan family had been able to accomplish in the course of a single generation, there was no reason for William Brennan Jr. to quarrel with the vision of a fully consummated democratic society set out by either the Progressives or the New Dealers. There was nothing in his background to provoke him to question the belief that a democratic society should seek to free people of all manner of fears, promote toleration of diverse opinions, and subscribe to a broad definition of civil liberties. If there were problems with the efforts of these liberal reformers, they had to do more with misjudgments about processes and insufficient boldness than with the substance of their objectives. Not only were the grand objectives of the Progressives and New Dealers not realized by mid-century, but their efforts ended up creating new obstacles for the attainment of their ends. Brennan's jurisprudence is best understood as an attempt to correct the defects that accompanied coalition-style majoritarian politics and the appearance of bureaucratic institutions that had the potential to interfere with the attainment of the promises of the liberal reformers. New Deal coalitional politics, for example, had not resolved the problem of racial segregation or malapportionment. At the same time, Brennan worried about the emergence of a new threat to individual freedoms in the form of the bureaucratic state with its powerful regulatory agencies that, as the German theorist Max Weber had predicted, are disposed to focus more on efficiency than on the protection of personal liberties. In short, the project of the political and judicial liberals of the first half of the century would turn out to be both incomplete and too modestly defined for Brennan.

Born on April 25, 1906 in Newark, the youthful Brennan would have been hard-pressed to avoid contact with reformist rhetoric, whether directed at corporate America or at party politics. As a young law student at Harvard in 1929–31, and earlier as an undergraduate economics major at the University of Pennsylvania, Brennan would have found it virtually impossible to stay clear of heated debates on the proper scope of governmental regulatory powers. Nor could he easily have avoided discussions of the merits of sociological jurisprudence, which elevated the social good above attention to language and/or precedent. His legal career was in its infancy when Franklin Roosevelt outlined his New Deal for post-Depression America. In short, the world Brennan knew for his first three decades was defined in large part by the arguments of figures such as Woodrow Wilson, Oliver Wendell Holmes, Benjamin Cardozo, and Franklin Roosevelt. Even a cursory reading of Brennan's legal writings on and off the bench supplies ample evidence of the influence of these figures on his thinking and scholarship.

Without doubt, the dominant liberal reformer of the first decades of the century was Wilson. Democratic government represented for him the culmination of all political development. By the 1880s, Wilson dismissed the exercise of defending democracy as superior to all other governmental forms as a thing of the past. The unrivaled benefits of the liberal democratic orders that were based on modern European political thought were a matter of historical record. Here is "end of history" reasoning long before the end of the Cold War.[13] For Wilson, the really important political undertaking that remained for America was to create the perfectly efficient democracy. Above all else, he believed that this required the people to be treated as the true sovereign body not just in theory but in practice. This, indeed, is the dominant theme of *The New Freedom*, the book that anticipated Wilson's presidency: "the deepest conviction and passion of my heart is that the common people, by which I mean all of us, are to be absolutely trusted."[14] Wilson freely proclaimed himself to be "among those who believe so firmly in the essential doctrine of democracy that I am willing to wait on the convenience of this great sovereign, provided I know that he has got the instrument to dominate whenever he chooses to grasp it."[15] Holding to the position that the state really reveals its character in its laws, and that the laws ought to reflect a fluctuating public will, Wilson concluded that rightly constituted democratic states should be malleable and historical, not fixed and permanent. Hence his assertion that a "good" government is one that is "amenable from day to day to public opinion," and capable of accommodating changing preferences.[16] To cite once more from *The New Freedom*: "political liberty is the right of those who are governed to adjust government to their own needs and interests." By extension, "government must have a machinery of constant adaptation."[17] In effect, the end of real political history coincides with the appearance of the truly free society that efficiently implements the will of a self-conscious and self-directing people. This is messianistic thinking that anticipates a "new world order" that marries political populism with scientific management thinking. Those who assist in bringing about this end, according to Wilson, will deserve no less recognition than Abraham Lincoln and those who helped him preserve the Union at the time of the Civil War.[18] Indeed, it is important to note that Wilson's defense of democratic government rests on a vision of a social order that had not yet fully matured when he was writing on such themes as administration and congressional government or even when he served as president. Hence alongside public expressions of faith in the common man can be found rather striking comments about the ignorance and foolishness of the people.[19] The people were still in need of the guidance of a progressive leader capable of transforming them into the kind of citizen body needed for efficient democracy to exist. There is no doubt he believed that a perfected American democratic order was right around the corner and that his leadership could serve as the catalyst needed to move the United States to the last stage of its historical development.

The implications of Wilson's arguments would have been significant for a self-described liberal such as Brennan whose position on the Supreme Court required that he regularly balance competing appeals to individual rights and to government interests. In the context of Wilsonian thought, the perfection of the democratic state requires an openness to all preferences and a corresponding toughness on the part of the people when it comes to tolerating or withstanding the expression of unorthodox or even heretical opinions by others. The liberation of opinion and preferences from historical or traditional standards of legitimacy facilitates the expansion of personal liberty or freedom. But to successfully reach this point, a society must effectively domesticate desire or passion and spiritedness. That is to say, the people must be conscious of the good that comes from reining in spiritedness at the same time that they must exercise self-discipline with regard to their own wants and those of their fellows. Wilson could be comfortable in asserting that decisions about which preferences ought to prevail are best made in accordance with the dominant will of the community because he believed that an enlightened people would arrive at positions only after a careful airing of competing opinions on any given issue. If there was no preordained economic or fiscal policy that defines a good democracy for Wilson, there surely was a process of decision making that he identified with a perfected democratic order. It is a process that creates fewer obstacles to the expression of public sentiments than were believed necessary by Founders such as James Madison who insisted on the need for "devices of prudence" that would work to "refine and enlarge" the public's views. As will become evident, for Brennan the right process would include access to an independent judiciary that is committed to accommodating diverse and changing preferences, especially regarding personal lifestyles. This, in turn, requires that the hold of history, tradition, and nature on society be relaxed, if not entirely suspended.

The jurisprudential analogue to Wilson's political reasoning was provided during the same period by Oliver Wendell Holmes. Elevated from the Massachusetts Supreme Court to the Supreme Court of the United States by Theodore Roosevelt, Holmes interpreted the Constitution in a way that accommodated the work of the Progressives. The Constitution, in his view, establishes processes of governance that stand apart from endorsements of particular economic or social policies and practices. In his now famous dissent in *Lochner* v. *New York*,[20] in which he supported a state law regulating the hours of bakers, Holmes protested that the Constitution did not enact Herbert Spencer's theory of "social statics" or mandate any specific economic arrangement.[21] Justice Rufus Peckham, writing for the majority in *Lochner*, overturned the New York regulation for violating freedom of contract and the right of persons to freely pursue a profession. The Constitution, emphatically countered Holmes in dissent, leaves the people free to embrace paternalism, capitalism, or socialism, depending on their preferences.[22]

The principal constitutional concern for Holmes was to ensure that the people are given the opportunity to express freely their opinions and choose a preferred program of governmental action; hence his especially vigorous defense of freedom of speech and press in federal and state seditious activity cases such as *Abrams* v. *United States*[23] and *Gitlow* v. *New York*.[24] In effect, Holmes argued for the deconstitutionalization of economic and social questions while insisting on preserving the constitutional inviolability of such asserted requisites of democracy as freedom of speech. The Constitution for Holmes is silent on substantive issues of economic or social policy that are held to be separable from the procedures of democratic government. But if the Constitution is silent on which economic program to follow, it loudly proclaims the necessity of judicial protection for the advancement of preferences in the "marketplace of ideas." A boisterous, indeed even an adversarial, marketplace of ideas is essential to progressive democracy for Holmes. Hence the now famous declaration in his *Abrams* dissent:

When men have realized that time has upset many fighting faiths, they may come to believe even more than they believe the very foundations of their own conduct that the ultimate good desired is better reached by free trade in ideas—that the best test of truth is the power of the thought to get itself accepted in the competition of the market, and that truth is the only ground upon which their wishes safely can be carried out. That at any rate is the theory of our Constitution. It is an experiment, as all life is an experiment.[25]

The convergence of the interests of democracy and the rule of knowledge that appears in this quotation is typical of Wilsonian thinking. Wilson domesticated G.W.F. Hegel's historicist philosophy for the American people by arguing that the perfectly efficient democratic state represented the last stage of historical development or the final rule of reason in history as well as the victory of perfect freedom within the modern administrative order. Toleration, not spiritedness, emerges as the great social virtue. Abstracting from the reservations about direct popular government expressed by founding-era figures such as Chief Justice John Marshall, Holmes cast the judicial role in terms that were compatible with a Wilsonian democracy that gives full scope to the prevailing will of the day.[26]

The practical consequences of Holmes's reading of the Constitution were important to both the Progressives and the New Dealers. Whether to regulate production or hours and wages came to be treated as an electoral question, not an issue to be decided by constitutional construction. Here is an invitation to build coalitions in support of desired policy goals. When it comes to economic or social policies, electoral power replaces the kind of reflection on permanent constitutional principles that was characteristic of the reasoning of justices such as Peckham. It is in this spirit that Holmes asserted in his *Lochner* dissent that, with few exceptions, "the word liberty in the Fourteenth Amendment is perverted when it is held to prevent the natural outcome of a dominant opinion. . . ."[27] Here is good Wilsonian rhetoric that would be fertile soil for liberal reformers, whether political or judicial, who believed that the Constitution must accommodate even the most profound social changes. Indeed, it would not be long before the opening created by Holmes for legitimating economic and social policies electorally rather than constitutionally would be used to full advantage by Franklin Roosevelt.

The distinctiveness of Holmes's fundamentally open-ended approach to substantive policy issues becomes even clearer when it is contrasted with the reasoning of Chief Justice Marshall, whose jurisprudence also left considerable room for the exercise of governmental power, especially by the national legislature during the first decades of the republic. A classic example of Marshall's application of the underlying principles of the Constitution to substantive policy matters appears in *Fletcher* v. *Peck*, a decision that overturned a seemingly reasonable attempt by the Georgia legislature to reverse a prior tainted transaction involving the sale of state land.[28] For Marshall, constitutional protection for vested property rights may supersede otherwise reasonable exercises of legislative will. But where Marshall looked to the architectonic principles of the Constitution for guidance in such cases, principles that were presumed to be the product of reasoned reflection on the natural rights of individuals, the Progressives with jurists such as Holmes at their side sought legitimacy from the will of popular majorities. This was the new formula for completing the American political order that the reformers believed was initiated as a constitutional republic, but not a pure democracy.

Another major judicial figure of Brennan's formative period who helped to legitimize "progressivism," and whose contribution to American law would later earn high marks from Brennan, was Benjamin Cardozo.[29] First as the author of several important legal treatises and addresses and later as Holmes's replacement on the Supreme Court, Cardozo provided reform-minded jurists with a defense of judicial decision making that paid attention to "social utility."[30] His influential treatise, *The Nature of the Judicial Process*, published shortly after World War I during the period when Holmes and Louis Brandeis were faulting their conservative brethren for defeating such progressive legislation as the federal child labor law, championed the view that the "great generalities of the constitution have a content and a significance that vary from age to age."[31] Without dismissing the value of history or precedent, Cardozo emphasized that judges might properly take "some compelling sentiment of justice" or a "semi-intuitive apprehension of the pervading spirit of our law" as their guide when deciding "where to go."[32] While a valiant attempt is made to preserve some respect for history and precedent, his treatise finally points jurists to the overarching importance of meeting the contemporary demands of social justice. In a sentence that is as short as it is revealing, he observed that "The final cause of law is the welfare of society."[33] Promoting social justice and the "welfare of society" emerge as the decisive tests of a responsible judiciary. Here, again, is jurisprudential support for the labors of the political reformers of the period. Significantly, Cardozo would lend his own support to the efforts of the New Dealers while serving on the Supreme Court. Writing in dissent in a 1936 commerce clause case, *Carter* v. *Carter Coal Co.*, he reminded his colleagues that the commerce power "is as broad as the need that evokes it."[34] Such reasoning from a member of the Supreme Court must have been music to Roosevelt's ears. It is just this form of reasoning that Brennan would later employ when interpreting both the powers of the national government and what he called "the majestic generalities" of the Constitution. For Brennan, Cardozo legitimated reliance on passion as well as reason in judicial decision making.[35] As will become increasingly clear later in the chapters on Brennan's interpretation of the First and Fourteenth Amendments, what he meant by sensitivity to the passions of the day really amounted to a decidedly modern form of compassion rooted in the conviction that each person should be able to enjoy the full pleasure of their own existence. To facilitate such pleasure, he believed that governmental action must be attentive to the preferences and needs of everyone, especially Wilson's "common man."

On New Deal Ends and Means: Rethinking the American Republic

The influence of figures such as Wilson, Holmes, and Cardozo on liberal intellectuals notwithstanding, the seminal events of the century for reformers took the form of the policies and arguments of the New Dealers. If the public's view of Madison's republic had undergone a transformation by the 1950s when Brennan was appointed to the Court, this was due largely to the changes wrought by Franklin Roosevelt and his "Brain Trust." The theme that government exists to protect the people from "bitter wrongs" and tragedies that might interfere with the full enjoyment of personal freedoms was writ large in New Deal–style liberalism. The attainment of happiness for the many, and not merely protection for the pursuit of happiness, became the measure of the respectability of government.[36] The companion goal to Wilson's desire to see that World War I was the war to end all bloody struggles was the conquest of domestic problems such as those associated with the Depression. The objective of New Deal liberals was to leave the people with no remaining great fears. Ideally, fear itself would be eliminated as a significant feature of human life. In this connection, New Deal liberalism shifted attention away from the concern of persons such as Justice Peckham for preserving a way of life that made its peace with obstacles to general human happiness (for example, due process principles that leave the economy fundamentally unregulated) and toward finding out how best to mobilize public opinion and interest group support behind an agenda that was designed to eliminate or conquer the remaining sources of deprivation and intimidation. As the following chapters will reveal, this shift away from a fixed view of the American way of life along with the sanctification of the achievement of happiness through facilitative government action is writ large in Brennan's jurisprudence.

The 1937 report of the President's Committee on Administrative Management or Brownlow Report—the most significant administrative document of Franklin's Roosevelt's presidency—exposes the transformation in thinking that had occurred between the framing of the Constitution in 1787 and 1937. One hundred and fifty years after the Constitutional Convention, the executive is now cast principally as a political leader, or to use the language of the report, the "leader of [the] people," whose aim ought to be to raise "the level of the happiness and dignity of human life." This language conveys the New Deal vision of the means and ends of democratic government.[37] In an observation that anticipates Brennan's conviction that government should be prepared to facilitate social reform, the report declares that "there is much bitter wrong to set right in neglected ways of human life." There is here, as in the writings of Wilson, the distinct presumption that proper exertions of human will can correct such "bitter wrong[s]."[38] Political leaders are responsible for identifying these ills and then for mobilizing both the public will and the administrative machinery needed to correct them. Not surprisingly, it was to the executive branch that the New Dealers looked for leadership.

The concern of the Founders that excessively inflating the authority of one department might lead to unchecked or unreflective government was replaced by the assertion that society benefits from a visible magnification of the authority of the president.[39] If "industrialism" and other social and economic activities were to "serve humanity," to borrow from New Deal Brain Truster Harold Ickes's *The New Democracy*, then it was most likely to occur through executive management of public affairs.[40] In line with this thinking, the Brownlow Report tended to treat governmental activities in managerial terms, for example, fiscal management and personnel management.[41] Appeals by Roosevelt to a broad reading of the Constitution's general welfare clause issued from the same reasoning.

For New Dealers such as James Landis, the objective was to put "disinterested expertise" to work to promote "social regulation."[42] If nothing else, the Depression had revealed that comfortable preservation could not be taken for granted even in the best democratic society of the day. To the extent that freedom from want and economic exploitation could be guaranteed, then liberal democracy as a political form should be protected from these potential threats to its well-being. Here, after all, was the source of the discontent that Marxists predicted would lead the proletariat to bring down capitalist states. If economic sufficiency could be guaranteed for all the members of the community at the same time that pluralist politics protected political liberty, then Wilson's project could be completed, at least at home in the United States. Landis, and other associates of Roosevelt such as Frankfurter, believed that a combination of professional ethics, properly arranged administrative procedures, effective public scrutiny, and presidential oversight of government affairs would allow the country to merge the benefits of modern science and technology with the principles of democratic governance. Insofar as New Dealers were given to occasional expressions of unhappiness with the bureaucracy, it was a product of the perception that agencies were abusing their independence and not the result of a quarrel over the utility of applying modern administrative means to achieve desired political ends. It is in this vein that the Brownlow Report characterized independent regulatory commissions as constituting a "headless 'fourth branch' of government, a haphazard deposit of irresponsible agencies and uncoordinated powers."[43] The possibility that administrative action might not be connected in any obvious way to constitutional principles was not the source of their consternation. The impatience with the bureaucracy that was shown by Roosevelt and his aides arose from the conviction that this part of the government was not adequately serving public needs as articulated by elected officials and their political assistants. Holmes, after all, had invited his contemporaries to worry less about the constitutional legitimacy of economic policies and more about the political viability of these policies and finally their effective implementation. Not surprisingly, a by-product of the heightened attention given to ends was a casualness about means. Witness in this regard Roosevelt's willingness to mobilize federal workers to participate in electoral politics, sometimes at the expense of fellow Democrats. This controversial practice was one of the reasons for passage of the federal Hatch Act in 1939 that barred federal Civil Service personnel from participating in most forms of partisan political activity.[44] Perhaps the best example of impatience with processes that obstructed favored reforms was Roosevelt's attack on the Supreme Court that culminated in his ill-advised Court-packing plan in the mid-1930s. Interestingly, it would be to an independent and activist judiciary that Brennan would look to complete the task of raising "the level of the happiness and dignity of human life."

In sum, the liberal thought that helped shape Brennan's thinking wedded the moralistic and communitarian idealism of theorists such as Jean-Jacques Rousseau and Immanuel Kant with modernity's faith in science in a fashion that invites people to expect more of government than did Founders such as James Madison and George Washington.[45] This body of thought played on the desire of the people for solutions to social and economic problems that had been considered intractable barriers to comfortable self-preservation for the many. Needless to add, post-Depression America was ripe for the reformist rhetoric and the promised action of the New Dealers. If the Wilsonian liberals were apostles of change, the later New Deal liberals had become defenders of an accepted faith in the beneficent powers of government.

The Post-*Brown* Supreme Court

From Reagan Republicans to Ted Kennedy Democrats, few Americans at the end of the twentieth century dispute the claim that by the time of Brennan's ascendancy to the Court in the mid-1950s, the New Deal had already reshaped the collective thinking of the American people about the means and ends of modern democratic government. By comparison, a relatively modest number of people understand that the country experienced a judicial revolution in 1937 that substantially redefined by the middle 1950s the way the judiciary handled cases involving individual freedoms and the economic regulatory powers of the nation and the states. After repeated clashes with Roosevelt, the Court in 1937 adopted a deferential approach in cases involving the use of the national commerce power as well as the authority to tax and spend to promote the general welfare. By the mid-1940s, New Dealers could be confident that the Court would no longer challenge economic policies that had the backing of the people and their representatives.[46] By contrast, the post-1937 Court gradually developed an aggressive approach to the review of all governmental action that restrained non-economic individual rights. In short, where the Court had painstakingly protected general economic liberties, including especially property and contract rights, and offered only modest protection for personal rights of the non-economic variety prior to 1937, the very opposite results began to take shape quickly after 1936. If this flip-flop was a recognized feature of American law by the time of Brennan's appointment to the Court, its full implementation still had not yet come by the mid-1950s. This was especially true in the area of judicial protection for non-economic freedoms.

The reversal that came in the period following 1936 represented a vindication of the arguments that Holmes had been making in his dissents in cases such as *Lochner, Abrams,* and *Gitlow.* Indeed, on several occasions the Court openly admitted that these dissents had acquired the status of majority opinions.[47] In keeping with Holmes's deconstitutionalization of economic issues, the justices employed the most deferential reasoning when assessing the permissibility of state and federal legislation regulating commercial activities. In the words of Justice William O. Douglas in *Williamson* v. *Lee Optical,* a case involving state regulation of activities relating to eye care: "The day is gone when this Court uses the Due Process Clause of the Fourteenth Amendment to strike down state laws, regulatory of business and industrial conditions, because they may be unwise, improvident, or out of harmony with a particular school of thought."[48] If the people found themselves at odds with such regulatory legislation, then Douglas admonished them not to recur to the courts but to the polls. So far did the Court retrench from its old activist posture in these cases that the U.S. Congress came to believe that it was free to use the commerce power to regulate any activity that might minimally be connected with the health and vitality of the national economic system. This was especially visible in the decision to use the commerce power alongside the Fourteenth Amendment to legitimate the federal Civil Rights Act of 1964, legislation principally designed not to promote interstate commerce or preserve the health of the national economy but to eradicate a social evil. As expected, the Court easily upheld Congress's action.[49] This part of the revolution of 1937 was well entrenched by the time Brennan joined the Court.

The second dimension of the turnabout of 1937—the heightened commitment to protecting non-economic individual rights—was not as well grounded by 1956. Although it was increasingly the case that the Court by the mid-1950s would apply strict scrutiny to government action that limited First Amendment freedoms as well as enforce federal Bill of Rights guarantees such as protection against illegal searches and seizures against state action, national and state authorities could still count on more than occasional judicial deference when their actions burdened non-economic liberties. Thus in 1951 the Supreme Court upheld Smith Act convictions gained by the Truman Administration against eleven leaders of the American Communist Party for teaching and advocating the necessity of overthrowing the government of the

United States and for organizing the Communist Party to advance this end.[50] Justices Douglas and Hugo Black did not see how these convictions could be reconciled with First Amendment principles, but their arguments were unpersuasive in 1951. Additionally, the Court was still stingy in its application of federal due process guarantees to state action.[51] The right to counsel in all criminal prosecutions as well as protection against compelled self-incrimination and access to a jury trial in cases involving serious offenses had not yet been incorporated into the Fourteenth Amendment as limits on state action. In short, the national government and the states still enjoyed considerable freedom to regulate in the name of self-preservation and self-defense. There was evidence of growing judicial impatience with some practices that burdened non-economic liberties, but serious trimming of these practices had to wait until the 1960s.

At least in the area of non-economic freedoms, the Court was still in transition at the time Eisenhower elevated Brennan in 1956. The *Brown* decision of 1954, however, did signal the Court's willingness to become more aggressive in challenging prevailing practices and norms that constituted important barriers to the full enjoyment of civil rights by all people, irrespective of race and eventually of gender as well. To appreciate the significance of this development it is useful to remember that there were still many people at the time of *Brown* who believed that Congress, not the courts, was principally responsible for enforcing the terms of the Fourteenth Amendment.[52]

In reasoning that would produce criticism even from some people who were sympathetic with the results in *Brown*, Chief Justice Warren relied on the asserted ambiguity of both the language of the Fourteenth Amendment and the intentions of its proponents as justification for a decision that seemed right for the country in the mid-1950s.[53] Rather than being construed as grounds for judicial self-restraint or silence, constitutional ambiguity became an opening for judicial activism in the service of a societal good, in this case school desegregation. Here is a judicial analogue to the casualness about means that marked some of the political efforts of the New Dealers. If the end of promoting social welfare didn't trump strict constitutional reasoning, Warren at least indicated that it could tip the balance in the direction of worrying more about achieving desirable ends than about deviating from rigid constructions of language or precedents.[54]

With its decision in *Brown*, the Warren Court put political authorities on notice that tradition and history would no longer carry sufficient weight to immunize from judicial scrutiny practices that restrain individ-

ual liberties of the First or Fourteenth Amendment variety. Any doubts
about the Court's willingness to challenge state government intransi-
gence were dispelled in *Cooper* v. *Aaron*, a 1958 case that produced a
unanimous, no-nonsense directive to Arkansas officials in the area of
school desegregation.[55] This decision came one year after the Court
warned the Eisenhower Administration that it would not merely defer
to the federal government's efforts to immobilize the American Communist Party by imprisoning its leaders for advocating seditious action.[56]
Within less than a decade after *Brown*, the Court signaled that heightened scrutiny would apply to government personnel practices, including
the use of loyalty oaths, as well as to obscenity regulations, school prayers, and legislative districting schemes.[57] The role that Brennan came to
play in bringing about these changes was not inconsiderable. It was to
Brennan that Warren turned when it came to drafting the per curiam
opinion for the Court in *Cooper* v. *Aaron* and a majority opinion in *Baker*
v. *Carr*, the monumentally important 1962 decision declaring that state
malapportionment cases were no longer to be avoided on the grounds
that they involved nonjusticiable political questions. Brennan's opinion
in *Baker* later earned Warren's designation as a "historic" decision destined to affect virtually every American. Two years after *Baker*, Brennan
announced for the Court that laws designed to shield government officials from attacks that might damage their reputation and credibility
would have to survive the difficult "malice" standard.[58] With the help of
Brennan, the post-*Brown* Court significantly reduced the constitutional
weight assigned to claims raised on behalf of self-defense and self-preservation by state and federal officials.

The ideas and developments identified above form an important
dimension to the study of Brennan's opinions. Drawing on that part of
modernity that holds that the human condition both should and can be
perfected through determined action, Brennan's jurisprudence represented an effort to advance individual rights and personal dignity by
correcting the deficiencies that remained unresolved despite a half-cen-
tury of liberal reform thought and action. Brennan clearly saw that the
failures of coalitional politics could be dramatic for particular groups or
individuals. Rights can go unprotected or, worse still, be positively
abused due to majoritarian politics that neglects minority interests or
plays on the tension between majority and minority interests in a mean-
spirited fashion.[59] Minority interests and individual rights also might suffer as a result of narrowly self-interested or misguided action by any of
the numerous agencies spawned by the Progressives and New Dealers.
In addition, the movement in the direction of a national state, focused

on the advancement of group interests, carries the possibility of washing away the ground of private rights and individual freedoms. In the multiplicity of ways that have been documented by scholars such as Theodore Lowi, New Deal–style politics revealed itself to be less than perfect.[60] The politics of the new welfare state turned out to carry "costs" that even its friends could not disregard. In short, the work of Wilson, Holmes, Franklin Roosevelt, and Cordozo was incomplete.

To anticipate arguments that appear in the next several chapters, over a period of thirty-four terms Brennan set out a body of legal thought designed to address the deficiencies of the system that Progressives and New Dealers, both of the political and judicial stripe, had done so much to shape. In some revealing remarks penned at the end of the 1980s, he spoke of the importance of continuing the long "struggle" against inequities so that all groups could "partake of the abundance of American life."[61] By the time of his retirement, Brennan would come to be closely identified with the vindication of individual and group rights against political and administrative impediments that coexisted with, and in many instances were a product of, the practices and thinking of his liberal predecessors. His aggressive commitment to the advancement of individual rights accounts for designations such as "liberal activist," "social humanist," and "liberal legalist." He has even been classified as a postmodern "deconstructionist."[62] If a label is desired, however, none appears to be more suitable than his own claim to be a proponent of "libertarian dignity."[63] Here is a distinctive label that permits so-called "Brennanesque" reasoning to be appropriately set apart from the thinking of earlier "social humanists" and "liberal activists."

When viewed in its totality, Brennan's legal writing, informed by the ideal of libertarian dignity, represents an effort to complete the American republic of rights by universalizing the achievement of human dignity through passionate self-assertiveness by all. Establishing the conditions for just such human activity is the real end of the American founding, or more fundamentally of the American Revolution, for Brennan.[64] In the context of his jurisprudence, America will fully earn its claim to be the paradigmatic "city upon a hill" when it no longer tolerates practices that result in people being profoundly unhappy or constrained in their ability to shape a way of life for themselves. Libertarian dignity is achieved when persons can experience the full pleasure of their own existence. Anything that does not affirm the full worth of a person as an autonomous being becomes constitutionally suspect. In keeping with the optimism of twentieth-century progressive thought, there is the presumption that all people can be content with being recognized as the equal of all other people and that the liberation of passion or desire in the form of the virtually free choice of lifestyles need not come at the expense of order or stability. Brennan's is a facilitative jurisprudence that challenges the strict rule of rationality that can overwhelm the passions by demanding reasoned justifications for actions, while at the same time it values the opportunity for continuous innovation opened up by modern science. It is a jurisprudence that can be tough and hard-hitting in the service of establishing a niche in the modern bourgeois state for virtually unbounded toleration of the idiosyncrasies of a highly heterogeneous population. Hence the frequency with which he exhibited passionate intolerance whenever his colleagues failed to embrace his toleration of unpopular or untraditional practices.[65]

The search for a social order in which the legal system and ideally every institution affirm the full worth or dignity of all persons, which presumably would demand either the rule of universal "reason" or the peaceful toleration of an almost infinite range of preferences, has occupied some of the greatest minds of modernity. If equalizing dignity or each person's sense of personal worth is the dominant passion and goal in the modern liberal state, then it is possible to argue that Brennan's legal writing represents the quintessential jurisprudence of modernity. Insofar as his writings publicly celebrate the wisdom of liberal democratic principles while seeking ways to fine-tune democracy to minimize the possibility that people might be left unhappy or dissatisfied, it might be said that Brennan had embarked on an "end of history" project. For good theoretical and practical reasons, his opinions deserve serious consideration by persons interested in the direction of the American republic, and of modern democracy itself. The account of his jurisprudence that follows will seek to establish the accuracy of the interpretation offered above while submitting his legal thought to a level of scrutiny befitting the importance that his opinions have acquired in American constitutional law.

Notes

1. *New York Times*, Sept. 30, 1956, 1:1.
2. *New York Times*, July 22, 1990, 22:2. A careful review of the events surrounding Brennan's appointment to the Court appears in Stephen Wermiel, "The Nomination of Justice Brennan: Eisenhower's Mistake? A Look at the Historical Record," 11 *Constitutional Commentary* 515–37 (Winter 1994–95), especially 521–22.
3. Henry Abraham, *Justices and Presidents* (New York: Oxford University Press, 1974), 246. Perhaps the best examination of the allegation that Eisen-

hower regretted his appointment of Brennan to the Court can be found in Wermiel, 535–537. In fact, ample evidence of Brennan's "liberalism" and his commitment to reforming the judicial system in order to improve "fairness and compassion in the law" was available to Eisenhower at the time the appointment was made. See ibid., 516–518.

4. *New York Times*, Sept. 30, 1956, 1:1.

5. 391 U.S. 430 (1968).

6. *New York Times*, July 22, 1990, IV, 18:1.

7. Thurgood Marshall, "A Tribute to Justice William J. Brennan, Jr.," 104 *Harvard Law Review* 1 (1990); Byron White, "Tribute to the Honorable William J. Brennan, Jr.," 100 *Yale Law Journal* 1113 (1991).

8. 80 *Harvard Law Review* 2 (1966).

9. See, for example, Nina Totenberg, "Tribute to Justice Brennan," 104 *Harvard Law Review* 38 (1990).

10. See C. Herman Pritchett, *Congress versus the Supreme Court, 1957–1960* (Minneapolis: University of Minnesota Press, 1961); also Walter F. Murphy, *Congress and the Court* (Chicago: University of Chicago Press, 1962). For Brennan's thoughts on the jurisprudence of "libertarian dignity" see his "Address to the Text and Teaching Symposium," in *The Great Debate: Interpreting Our Written Constitution* (Washington, D.C.: Federalist Society, 1986), 22–23. Hereafter cited as Georgetown Address.

11. Felix Frankfurther, "The Supreme Court in the Mirror of Justices," 105 *University of Pennsylvania Law Review* 781 (1957), cited in Henry Abraham, *Justices and Presidents*, 44.

12. For Frankfurter's thoughts on Brennan's legal scholarship, see Stephen J. Friedman, "William J. Brennan," in *The Justices of the United States Supreme Court 1789–1969*, ed. Leon Friedman and Fred L. Israel, 4 vols. (New York: Bowker, 1969), IV: 2851.

13. A careful exploration of the "end of history" thesis can be found in Francis Fukuyama, *The End of History and the Last Man* (New York: Avon Books, 1992).

14. Woodrow Wilson, *The New Freedom* (Englewood Cliffs, N.J.: Prentice Hall, 1961), 109.

15. Ibid., 231.

16. Arthur S. Link, ed., *The Papers of Woodrow Wilson* (Princeton: Princeton University Press, 1966), 4: 62. Hereafter cited as *Wilson Papers*.

17. *New Freedom*, 4, 6.

18. In a July 4 address at Gettysburg in 1913, Wilson assigned great weight to the project on which he had embarked: "We have harder things to do than were done in the heroic days of war, because harder to see clearly, requiring more vision, more calm balance of judgment, a more candid servicing of the very springs of right." *Wilson Papers*, 28: 24.

19. Wilson's administrative thought is perhaps best presented in his centennial year essay, "The Study of Administration," 2 *Political Science Quarterly* (June 1887). The importance of proper education of the citizenry to the attainment of the goals of the progressive movement is one of the subjects covered in Herbert Croly's *The Promise of American Life* (New York: Macmillan, 1909). This much cited book was one of the principal works of the Progressive period.

20. 198 U.S. 45 (1905).

21. Holmes, who came to be identified with the belief that society ought to be open to continual progress through the clash of opinions and ideas, challenged in *Lochner* the argument that the Constitution might be grounded in the social thought presented by Herbert Spencer, an English theorist who also believed in progress as a natural phenomenon that could be interrupted by governmental regulations that emanated from an unwillingness to accept change on nature's terms.

22. 198 U.S. at 75.

23. 250 U.S. 616 (1919). The *Abrams* case was brought under the Espionage Act of 1917.

24. 268 U.S. 652 (1925). The *Gitlow* case came to the Supreme Court in the form of a challenge to New York criminal anarchism law.

25. 250 U.S. 616, 630 (1919). Holmes's dissent in *Abrams* anticipated his now famous dissent in *Gitlow* v. *New York*. It is indicative of the movement away from judicial deference in the area of governmental regulation of non-economic rights that occurred after 1937 that Chief Justice Fred Vinson confirmed in *Dennis* v. *United States*, a 1951 Smith Act case that upheld the convictions of high-level officers of the American Communist Party, that the Court had come to recognize Holmes's position as reflecting the proper reading of the First Amendment.

26. Marshall's thoughts on the advantages of representative government over direct democracy are well summarized in Robert K. Faulkner, *The Jurisprudence of John Marshall* (Princeton: Princeton University Press, 1968), 116.

27. 198 U.S. 45, 75 (1905).

28. 6 Cranch 87 (1810). An excellent treatment of Marshall opinion in the *Fletcher* case, and of his jurisprudence in general, can be found in Faulkner, 196.

29. See Brennan in 10 *Cardozo Law Review* 3 (1988); also Brennan, 42 *Rec. A.B. City of New York* 950, 953 (1987), cited in Norman Dorsen, "Tribute to Justice William Brennan," 104 *Harvard Law Review* 15, 21, and nn. 49, 51 (1990).

30. Three notable works by Cardozo that appeared in the 1920s include *The Nature of the Judicial Process*, *The Growth of the Law*, and *The Paradoxes of Legal Science*.

31. Benjamin Cardozo, *The Nature of the Judicial Process* (New Haven: Yale University Press, 1921), 17.

32. Ibid., 43.

33. Ibid., 66.

34. 298 U.S. 238 (1936).

35. For Brennan's thoughts on Cardozo's contribution to American jurisprudence, see William J. Brennan Jr., "Reason, Passion, and 'The Progress of the Law,' " 10 *Cardozo Law Review* 3–23 (1988).

36. Morton J. Frisch, *Franklin D. Roosevelt: The Contribution of the New Deal to American Political Thought* (Boston: Twayne, 1975), 110.

37. United States, Executive Department, *Report of the President's Committee on Administrative Management* (Washington, D.C.: U.S. Government Printing Office, 1938), 1, 2 (hereafter cited as Brownlow Report); also John A. Rohr, *To Run a Constitution* (Lawrence: University of Kansas Press, 1986), 129, 145.

38. Brownlow Report, 2.

39. For an excellent examination of the modern argument for limited government and hidden executive power see Harvey C. Mansfield Jr., *Taming The Prince* (New York: Free Press, 1989).

40. Harold Ickes, *The New Democracy* (New York: Norton, 1934), 77, 121.

41. See Rohr, 138.

42. James O. Freedman, *Crisis and Legitimacy* (Cambridge: University Press, 1978), 45.

43. Cited in Rohr, 152; also James Q. Wilson, *Bureaucracy* (New York: Basic Books, 1989), 72.

44. For a useful discussion of the origins of the Hatch Act see Frisch, 87.

45. Brennan's advocacy of greater use of the social sciences during his judicial service in New Jersey is noted in Paul L. Murphy, *Constitution in Crisis Time: 1918–1969* (New York: Harper and Row, 1972), 321, n. 31.

46. Representative of this trend are the decisions in *United States* v. *Darby*, 312 U.S. 100 (1941) and *Wickard* v. *Filburn*, 317 U.S. 111 (1942).

47. See Chief Justice Fred Vinson's opinion in *Dennis* v. *United States*, 341 U.S. 494, 507 (1951).

48. 348 U.S. 483, 488 (1955).

49. *Katzenbach* v. *McClung*, 379 U.S. 294 (1964) and *Heart of Atlanta Motel, Inc.* v. *United States*, 379 U.S. 241 (1964).

50. *Dennis* v. *United States*, 341 U.S. 494.

51. For example, *Adamson* v. *California*, 332 U.S. 46 (1947) and *Irvine* v. *California*, 347 U.S. 128 (1954).

52. Reflecting on the arguments offered by the Justice Department on behalf of the schoolchildren in *Brown,* Justice Robert Jackson mused aloud that "realistically the reason this case is here is that action couldn't be obtained from Congress." Cited in Alexander Bickel, *The Supreme Court and the Idea of Progress* (New York: Harper, 1970), 7.

53. One of the most significant commentaries on *Brown* that found weaknesses with Warren's reasoning was offered by Herbert Wechsler of Columbia Law School. He advanced the merits of a "neutral principles" rather than a fact-based attack on school segregation. See Herbert Wechsler, "Toward Neutral Principles of Constitutional Law," 73 *Harvard Law Review* 31–35 (1959).

54. The claim that the Court might legitimately worry more about ends than means appears early in Justice Harry Blackmun's majority opinion in *Roe* v. *Wade* where he asserts that it is more important to note that at least five justices agree that a right to privacy exists than to be concerned about the reasoning used by those justices to reach this conclusion. 410 U.S. 113 (1973).

55. 358 U.S. 1 (1958). In their collective opinion, the justices declared that the interpretation of the Fourteenth Amendment found in *Brown* represented "the supreme law of the land" and hence was directly "binding on the states" (ibid., 18).

56. *Yates* v. *United States*, 354 U.S. 298 (1957).

57. See *Schware* v. *Board of Bar Examiners*, 353 U.S. 232 (1957); *Roth* v. *United States*, 354 U. S. 476 (1957) *Engel* v. *Vitale*, 370 U.S. 421 (1962) and *Abington School Dist.* v. *Schempp*, 374 U.S. 203 (1963); also *Baker* v. *Carr*, 369 U.S. 186 (1962).

58. *New York Times* v. *Sullivan,* 376 U.S. 254 (1964).

59. William J. Brennan Jr., "The Role of the Court—The Challenge of the Future" (1965), in *An Affair with Freedom: William J. Brennan, Jr.,* ed. Stephen J. Friedman (New York: Atheneum, 1967), 567.

60. See Theodore J. Lowi, *The End of Liberalism* (New York: W.W. Norton, 1969); and Theodore J. Lowi and Benjamin Ginsberg, *Poliscide* (New York: Macmillan, 1976).

61. Brennan, "Color-Blind, Creed-Blind, Status-Blind, Sex-Blind," 14 *Human Rights* 1, 36.

62. Regarding these designations, see Leonard W. Levy, *Original Intent and the Framers' Constitution* (New York: Macmillan, 1988), 372; also Leonard W. Levy, *Against the Law: The Nixon Court and Criminal Justice* (New York: Harper and Row, 1974), 39; and Kermit L. Hall, *The Magic Mirror* (New York: Oxford University Press, 1989), 310.

63. William J. Brennan Jr., "The Role of the Court—The Challenge of the Future," in *An Affair with Freedom: William J. Brennan, Jr.,* 331; William J. Brennan Jr., Georgetown Address, 18.

64. William J. Brennan Jr., "Reason, Passion, and 'The Progress of the Law,' " 10 *Cardozo Law Review* 11.

65. See, for example, Brennan's charge in *FCC* v. *Pacifica Foundation* that the majority was guilty of lending its power to the enforcement of "the dominant culture's inevitable efforts to force those groups who do not share its mores to conform to its way of thinking, acting, and speaking." (438 U.S. 726, 777 [1978] {Brennan dissenting}). It is worth noting that Brennan does not grapple in his dissent with the fact that all societies seem naturally propelled to act in this fashion in their pursuit of self-preservation or in the name of self-defense and that legitimacy in modern democratic states is generally associated with the principle of majority rule. As will become evident in the chapters that follow, the objectives of his jurisprudence of libertarian dignity require that Brennan challenge the rule of history, tradition, nature, and majoritarian preferences.

Chapter Two

THE JUDICIARY AND THE ADVANCEMENT OF LIBERTARIAN DIGNITY

. . . that branch which is to act ultimately, and without appeal, on any law, is the rightful expositor of the validity of the law, uncontrolled by the opinions of the other co-ordinate authorities. It may be said that contradictory decisions may arise in such case, and produce inconvenience. This is possible, and is a necessary failing in all human proceedings. Yet the prudence of the public functionaries, and authority of public opinion, will generally produce accommodation.

—Thomas Jefferson (1815)

Let us not forget that the integrity and efficiency of the judicial process is *the first essential* in a democratic society. The confidence of the people in the administration of justice is a prime requisite for free representative government. The public entrusts the legal profession with the sacred mission of dealing with the vital affairs that affect *the whole pattern of human relations*. . . . (Emphasis added)

—William J. Brennan, Jr. *Modernizing the Courts* (1957)

It is common for people familiar with William Brennan's jurisprudence to point first to his opinions in individual rights cases when summarizing his contribution to American constitutional law. Considering the impact and notoriety of his opinions in First and Fourteenth Amendment cases such as *Regents of the University of California, Davis v. Bakke*[1] and *Johnson v. Transportation Agency, Santa Clara County* (affirmative action/reverse discrimination),[2] *Texas v. Johnson* (flag burning),[3] *Freedman v. Maryland* (prior restraint/freedom of expression)[4] and *Cruzan v. Missouri Department of Health* (right to die),[5] it is neither surprising nor entirely unwarranted to think first of his labors in these areas of the law. It is a mistake, however, to believe that an appreciation of these opinions alone will supply a comprehensive understanding of Brennan's jurisprudence. It is only when the full range of his legal scholarship is examined,

25

including his thoughts on the rules governing judicial decision making (for example, matters of jurisdiction and justiciability), that the true character of his understanding of the American constitutional order and the role of the judiciary in that system emerges. Although often dwarfed by his handling of heavily publicized First and Fourteenth Amendment controversies, in many important respects his thoughts on the scope of the power of the judiciary and on the oath of office taken by judicial officials reflect the real foundational pillars of his jurisprudence as much as his construction of such language as "freedom of speech" and "equal protection of the laws."

As already noted, Brennan's activism was an outgrowth of the deep-seated belief that it is not possible simultaneously to accept the deficiencies, some in the form of unchecked majoritarian politics, of Holmesian or New Deal liberalism and be faithful to the Constitution. Remaining faithful to the Constitution for Brennan involves an unwavering commitment to address practices that fail to meet the standards of what might be termed the comprehensive constitutional doctrine: rights should be construed broadly and protected fully and all injuries warrant proper redress even against majoritarian preferences and entrenched historical practices and values.

What cannot be overlooked is the central role assigned the judiciary by Brennan not only when rights and personal interests are in need of protection but whenever guidance is needed to determine how best to adjust competing claims in cases involving "the whole pattern of human relations." His willingness to cast judges as active participants in the process of adjusting the meaning of the Constitution to suit the times is a hallmark of his jurisprudence. Here is the context for his defense of an expansive rather than narrow interpretation of the federal habeas corpus power and of rules of justiciability such as "standing" requirements that affect when and how the courts may use their authority.[6] A generous view of the role of the judiciary as adjudicator, educator, and overall guardian of society permeates his legal thought.[7] The product of this reasoning is a judicial department that is both open to the fullest number of claimants and poised to provide maximum direction to public officials and private citizens. Brennan helped the Court take a giant step in this direction with his opinion in *Baker* v. *Carr*, a 1962 Tennessee malapportionment case that opened the door to judicial review of challenges to state management of electoral schemes.[8]

The Political Questions Doctrine Redefined

In what Earl Warren would later identify as a "historic" decision destined to "affect the lives of all the people," Brennan ruled in *Baker* v.

Carr that state malapportionment suits did not warrant automatic dismissal by judges on the grounds that they involved nonjusticiable political questions.[9] The repercussions of this declaration continue to reverberate within courtrooms as evidenced by several controversial 1990s cases involving judicial review of the legality of race-driven districting.[10] Until 1962, the federal courts routinely dismissed attempts to litigate challenges to state districting schemes. Writing a plurality opinion in *Colegrove* v. *Green* in 1946, Felix Frankfurter announced that people having problems with the way electoral districts have been drawn should seek redress through electoral or legislative processes.[11] It was his conviction that the judiciary ought to stay clear of what could best be described in his judgment as a "political thicket."[12] This was the advice heeded by the lower court in *Baker*.

The persistence of malapportionment and racial segregation demanded resolution, according to Brennan, if the country was to satisfy the high principles of democratic egalitarian governance that he associated with the Constitution. His task was to get around the claim that the judiciary was barred from inquiring into the legitimacy of state apportionment decisions. To reach his end, Brennan redefined the terms of the political questions doctrine, a long-standing rule of justiciability that could be traced back to John Marshall's observation in *Marbury* v. *Madison* that "Questions, in their nature political . . . can never be made in this court."[13] Brennan effectively reconstructed the term "political" to comprehend much less than what it had been construed to cover during the century and a half that had elapsed between *Marbury* and *Baker*.

If the Warren Court is now synonymous with an expansion of federal judicial authority, Brennan's opinion in *Baker* contributed much to this reputation. In language that legitimated wide-open judicial supervision of governmental activity, Brennan matter-of-factly declared that the Supreme Court alone is responsible for "[d]eciding whether a matter has in any measure been committed by the Constitution to another branch of government, or whether the action of that branch exceeds whatever authority has been committed. . . ."[14] The constitutional responsibility to discharge this "delicate" work is invested by Brennan in the Court with all the characteristics of a moral obligation. The assertion of a power to act was matched with an equally firm insistence on a responsibility to act. Against this backdrop, Brennan set himself up to determine whether the apportionment of electoral seats is a matter that properly falls within the jurisdiction of the courts or one to be left to a "political" department. His answer was unequivocal: "We have no question decided, or to be decided, by a political branch of government coequal with this Court."[15] The common denominator for nonjusticiable politi-

cal questions cases became the presence of a separation of powers component. If there was no separation of powers element to a case, then
there could be no political questions doctrine problem rendering the
case nonjusticiable. To confirm this conclusion he summarized six situations that create justiciability difficulties under the political questions
doctrine, all of which he confidently declared were connected to the
principle of separation of powers:

> Prominent on the surface of any case held to involve a political ques-
> tion is found a textually demonstrable constitutional commitment of
> the issue to a coordinate political department; or a lack of judicially
> discoverable and manageable standards for resolving it; or the impossi-
> bility of deciding without an initial policy determination of a kind
> clearly for nonjudicial discretion; or the impossibility of a court's un-
> dertaking independent resolution without expressing lack of the re-
> spect due coordinate branches of government; or an unusual need for
> unquestioning adherence to a political decision already made; or the
> potentiality of embarrassment from multifarious pronouncements by
> various departments on one question.[16]

With separation of powers identified as the irreducible component of all
these examples of political questions, "political" action taken by state
officials lost much of the immunity to national judicial scrutiny that it
had enjoyed, since state–nation clashes are federalistic in nature and,
hence, distinguishable from issues having to do with interdepartmental
checks and balances. When Brennan finished, quarrels involving different levels of government were no longer "political" in the way that
quarrels between different branches of the national government were
held to be "political."

That the courts may take cases involving "political" action by state
officials, however, represented only part of the message conveyed by
Brennan in *Baker*. What emerged from his opinion was an uncompromising directive to lower courts to act whenever possible to protect
rights and redress grievances: "They [the courts] will not stand impotent
before an obvious instance of a manifestly unauthorized exercise of
power."[17] State officials were put on notice that the management of
electoral affairs, as with the assignment of children to public schools, is
subject to constant judicial oversight. The cover that had been provided
by federalism was shrinking to the size of a fig leaf. It was not mere
coincidence that at the same time that the political questions doctrine
was being narrowed in a way that gave little cover to American federal-

ism the Court was giving an expansive interpretation to the national commerce power, thereby arming Congress to regulate an increasing array of activities within the states.[18]

Although Brennan was satisfied that he had merely sharpened, through clarification, the political questions doctrine as a rule of justiciability, his reasoning does not necessarily support his reduction of the doctrine to separation of powers controversies. Thus, for example, it is possible to argue that "judicially discoverable and manageable standards" might not be available to federal judges because some matters fall outside the powers and responsibilities of the national government. Standards may be unavailable as a result of the fact that the Founders created a federal system based on the theory of limited government. That is to say, the principle of separation of powers need not account for all the times when "discoverable and manageable" standards for decision making are unavailable to federal judicial officials. Viewed in this light, one of the "rules" identified by Brennan does not necessarily comport with his conclusion that cases fall under the political questions doctrine, and thus are nonjusticiable, only because they have a separation of powers component to them. It should quickly be noted that this is not the same as saying that the "rule" itself is wholly indefensible. The claim that cases should fall under the political questions doctrine if there are no judicially discoverable and manageable standards makes good sense. But this rule can also cover matters left by the Founders to the states and their courts as opposed to the federal government and its courts. The important point is that Brennan narrows the doctrine beyond the bounds required by his own summary of the occasions when the doctrine restricts judicial action. This difficulty was not lost on Frankfurter who seized on it in dissent as evidence of the degree to which the Court had allowed the preoccupation with achieving a specific end to blind it to sound and prudent constitutional reasoning.

Frankfurter and John Marshall Harlan, who also dissented, fully understood the largest implications of the *Baker* decision. Brennan had dramatically opened the judicial forum to a new and potentially large group of claimants who heretofore were left to seek relief through electoral and legislative means. Access to the judiciary was a way to level the playing field consistent with the principle of egalitarian dignity. He was directly challenging Frankfurter's assumption that "there is not under our Constitution a judicial remedy for every political mischief, for every undesirable exercise of legislative power."[19] The Court was entering the dangerous zone of governance on the basis of "will" for Frankfurter, for only by identifying its own set of standards for a true democracy could the Court decide malapportionment cases on their merits. Harlan was equally critical in his summary of the consequences of the decision:

> Those observers of the Court who see it primarily as the last refuge for the correction of all inequality or injustice, no matter what its nature or source, will no doubt applaud this decision and its break with the past. Those who consider that continuing national respect for the Court's authority depends in large measure upon its wise exercise of self-restraint and discipline in constitutional adjudication, will view the decision with deep concern.[20]

What Frankfurter and Harlan considered to be dangerous about Brennan's reasoning was just what he considered to be a necessary addition to the work of the liberal reformers who preceded him. Not surprisingly, *Baker* represented only an early shot in his campaign to lower barriers to judicial decision making and increase the judiciary's participation in overseeing the way of life of the people. For Brennan, this was both compelled by constitutional principles and necessary to the achievement of a completed democratic state, that is, a society that respects in theory and practice the principle of libertarian dignity. If a strong dose of judicial activism was needed to achieve this goal, then for Brennan the end clearly justified the means. That the public was ready to use the judiciary to challenge state districting schemes was amply demonstrated by the flood of malapportionment suits that quickly followed on the *Baker* decision. The results fit well with Brennan's desire to wed the courts to the people in a common effort to check not only the mistakes of government officials, but the hubris that he saw reflected in practices that confine the pursuit of preferred lifestyles. The results also confirmed Frankfurter's fear that the availability of judicial devices for overriding political decisions could erode the commitment of the people to toil at electoral politics, which by traditional thinking would be bad for political democracy. Brennan's failure to attend more closely to the effects of his *Baker* decision on what might be called the duties of democratic citizenship is the flip side of his untroubled devaluation of the political significance of governmental forms such as federalism. James Madison's governmental arrangements were no less immune to the voraciousness of Brennan's principle of libertarian dignity than traditional interpretations of due process of law. The regime of libertarian dignity draws both life and legitimacy from an all-consuming commitment to expand the realm of individual choice and self-construction.

Storming the Barricades

Baker represented only one episode in what was a career-long campaign by Brennan to ensure the widest possible access to the judicial forum. The Court, in fact, was still engaged in sorting out the ramifications of *Baker* when Brennan invited a new set of claimants to bring their grievances to federal judicial authorities. Writing for the majority in *Dombrowski* v. *Pfister*, a 1965 case arising out of the threat of enforcement of subversive activities laws by Louisiana authorities against members of a civil rights organization who argued that the statutes were overly broad and vague, Brennan declared that federal judges possess the power to supply declaratory relief in advance of the completion of state proceedings when constitutional rights are in danger of being curtailed or impaired as a result of suspect governmental action.[21] This judgment stood in contrast to the verdict of the District Court that federal authorities must abstain from intervention in such cases pending final action by the state courts. For Brennan, the risks involved in holding to a narrow view of the federal judiciary's power to provide equitable relief in cases where substantial rights such as freedom of expression are threatened offset all other considerations, including the potential for damage to the federal system set up by the Constitution. Where the District Court concluded that abstention represented the appropriate response in cases such as *Dombrowski*, Brennan urged preemptive federal review as a protection against unjustifiable infringements of rights: "abstention and the denial of injunctive relief may well result in the denial of any effective safeguards against the loss of protected freedoms of expression, and cannot be justified."[22] Once the unjustified impairment of freedom of expression was cast as an "irreparable injury," then the deferential stance championed by Harlan, who urged his colleagues to show greater sensitivity for state interests and prerogatives, was made to ring rather hollow. Harlan bluntly summarized what he considered to be the results of Brennan's reasoning in *Dombrowski* as far as state interests were concerned: "In practical effect the Court's decision means that a State may no longer carry on prosecutions under statutes challengeable for vagueness on 'First Amendment' grounds without the prior approval of the federal courts."[23] If Brennan wasn't entirely blind to the federal dimensions of the political system, he did appear to be deaf to the appeals of Harlan in *Dombrowski*. Brennan would later be equally untouched by the pleas of Justices Lewis Powell and Antonin Scalia that he assign greater weight to political considerations in opinions that he wrote for the Court in two cases involving patronage-related confinements of First Amendment rights.[24] Where Oliver Wendell Holmes deconstitutionalized economic and social policy, and thus indirectly elevated the importance of political and electoral decision making, Brennan left political processes with minimal constitutional weight when they clashed with rights interests. The possibility that intrusiveness into state processes by national judicial officials might weaken American federalism, which in turn might weaken the kind of democracy that Madison set out as the goal of his "compound republic," did not cause Brennan to pause in his defense of individual rights and interests. It is as if electoral and political processes and institutions had become sufficiently suspect by the mid-1960s, and the good that was achievable through the courts so well established, that any sacrifice of rights to the preservation of those processes and institutions made no sense to Brennan. If all that seems to count is the present moment, and if you hold to a generally unidimensional rights-oriented view of society and to the belief that democratic orders are highly resilient, then the willingness to protect political or electoral procedures at any cost to individual liberties is likely to be small.

In keeping with the thrust of the *Dombrowski* reasoning, Brennan again overturned a lower court decision in 1974 that he felt reflected an unacceptably narrow conception of federal judicial oversight powers. The question was whether people could gain declaratory relief when state criminal prosecutions threaten the exercise of fundamental rights, even if no action was pending. Brennan's majority opinion in *Steffel* v. *Thompson* affirmed the power of federal courts to provide relief in the absence of any pending state prosecution if parties "[demonstrate] a genuine threat of enforcement of a disputed state criminal statute."[25] The petitioners in this case had ceased distributing antiwar material at a shopping center because of the threat of prosecution for criminal trespass. The merits of preemptive action were considerable in his opinion since federal authorities would be well positioned to clarify constitutional issues so as to reduce state confinements of rights to a minimum. Although references to federalism-related issues can be found in Brennan's opinion, the possibility that the federal system might be weakened by opening up state action to increased oversight by national officials is not seriously entertained. Sensitivity to federalism or other political forms is clearly secondary to his interest in providing the maximum protection for the exercise of fundamental liberties such as freedom of expression.

If to err is human, then to choose to err on the side of overemphasizing protection for rights in cases such as *Steffel* is for Brennan to move decidedly in the direction of the divine. Results clearly are critical for Brennan, as is context. His failure to dwell on the arguments of Madison and other leading Founders that a healthy federal system would be a valuable safeguard for rights might be attributed, at least in part, to the conviction that practice had not lived up to theory. Practice needed reform, and the insertion of the judiciary as an overseer that would be sensitive to rights concerns and not be tempted to defer to political interests was an important part of Brennan's reform agenda. If anywhere, efficacious government action in his opinion was likely to come from the judiciary rather than the legislative or executive branches or the bureaucracy. Political rule, even the New Deal variety, had shown itself to be flawed. For Brennan, the goals of liberalism could best be safeguarded by a judiciary that is in principle, but not in fact, above politics. The cover that this provides for judicial activism serves Brennan's ends well. Not only is the judiciary in his view less tainted than other political institutions, but the documented failings of the electoral system and government officials provide convenient justifications for judicial involvement in affairs that are decidedly political in nature.

From the examples cited above it should be apparent that making the case for breaking down structural barriers to the judicial forum was of critical importance to Brennan; writing the majority opinion for the Court was secondary. If he could not write forcefully for the entire Court in jurisdiction and justiciability cases, he wrote vigorous dissents. When the Burger Court was unwilling to liberalize rules of standing in two 1974 cases, Brennan unapologetically charged his colleagues with sidestepping their constitutional duties. In *Schlesinger* v. *Reservists Committee to Stop the War*[26] and *United States* v. *Richardson*,[27] Chief Justice Warren Burger refused to open the judicial forum to parties wishing to challenge both the reserve membership of members of Congress under the incompatibility clause of the Constitution and the refusal of Congress to provide a public accounting of the budget of the Central Intelligence Agency under the statement and account clause. For Burger, the original petitioners in both cases were seeking to use the courts to air generalized grievances, an activity more properly belonging in his estimation to the political process. In words reminiscent of the arguments of Frankfurter and Harlan in *Baker*, Burger observed that the Constitution does not provide a judicial remedy for all grievances. That the political process may be "slow, cumbersome, and unresponsive" was not sufficient to justify judicial intervention for the Chief Justice.[28] The obvious message was that representative government is not without costs. Powell, writing a vigorous concurrence, was equally unimpressed with the attempt of the petitioners to make an end run around established democratic processes: "Relaxation of standing requirements is directly related to the expansion of judicial power. It seems to me inescapable that allowing unrestricted taxpayer or citizen standing would significantly alter the allocation of power at the national level, with a shift away from a democratic form of government."[29] Preserving the integrity of traditional democratic processes of government is assigned more than enough constitutional weight by Powell to offset the possible sacrifices that might be required of individual parties. In an important sense, Powell was merely calling on colleagues such as Brennan to protect the political institutions and structures that for Holmes were crucial to the formulation of democratic social and economic policies. But Brennan saw the judiciary as having a more "paternalistic" obligation than did Holmes, that is, a responsibility to advance right policies and not merely right processes.

In a dissent in *Reservists* that also applied to *Richardson*, Brennan let it be known that he would not be silent when the Court closed its doors to petitioners such as the ones who sought relief in these two cases. He argued that it should be sufficient that the petitioners made "good-faith allegation[s]" that the practices in question resulted in constitutional injuries.[30] In short, allegations of injury, as compared to evidence of injury in fact, ought to be enough to trigger judicial intervention. He added that the coordinate branches need not feel unduly threatened by the risk of judicial review since the substantive claims would still need to be shown to be meritorious. If the charges were valid, however, then forcing the executive and legislative branches to alter their practices would be a perfect form of judicial action for Brennan. Unlike Burger and Powell, Brennan attended less to the demands and costs of maintaining democratic processes of governance and more to the importance of minimizing curtailments of rights or checks on individual autonomy. A detailed examination of the impact on democratic processes of granting standing in these cases was unnecessary because the whole controversy was taken to be unproblematical. There was no doubt in his mind that the parties deserved a hearing.

For Brennan, not only is representative government in no danger of losing its vitality or legitimacy when citizens are permitted to use the courts to challenge governmental action, but by reviewing such challenges the judiciary is positioned to add to the credibility of the political system. The courts can confer legitimacy by upholding challenged actions or can restore it when necessary by forcing reforms of deficient practices. But more decisive than the political gain is Brennan's belief that the availability of judicial oversight is constitutionally required. He didn't need to be reminded by Powell that to concede to the demands of the petitioner in *Richardson* would enlarge the power of the judiciary, for Brennan's very objective was to expand the judiciary's ability to assist new classes of claimants who allege that their rights have been violated. Judicial deafness to such allegations is only tolerable if constitutionally required and this, for him, is rarely the case. This theme reappeared eight years later in Brennan's reply to William H. Rehnquist's unwillingness to grant standing to taxpayers who sought to challenge the transfer of federal property to a religious organization on the grounds that this action violated the establishment clause.[31] Rehnquist did not find the requisite personal injury in *Valley Forge Christian College* v. *Americans United for Separation of Church and State, Inc.* to satisfy the Article III requirements for a case or controversy. In his view, Americans United were attempting to use the courts as "publicly funded forums for the ventilation of public grievances."[32] According to Rehnquist, to go to the merits in this case would be for the Court to leave its proper place in the constitutional system. By contrast, for Brennan the proper role of the Court is to do whatever it can to see that rights are perfectly protected. His rebuke of Rehnquist is instructive: "*not one word is said about the Establishment Clause right that the plaintiff seeks to enforce.*"[33] His decision to accentuate through the use of italics the asserted failure of the majority to pay attention to the rights dimension of the suit reveals much about Brennan's view of technical rules of justiciability such as standing when the Court is asked to step in to guarantee rights. The separation of powers defense of such rules, and of judicial self-restraint, was subordinated to the substantive rights claims that the petitioners sought to advance. Institutional considerations shrank almost from view as weighty constitutional interests, just as federalism was diminished as a barrier to justiciability in *Baker* v. *Carr.* The contrast with Publius's handling of institutional concerns in *The Federalist Papers* could not be more dramatic.

Navigating the Administrative State

For persons who are uncomfortable with extensive judicial oversight of public and private action, William Brennan offered a justification for an activist judiciary based on the special dangers associated with the modern administrative state that New Deal liberals contributed so much to establish. A classic expression of this theme appears in his opinion in *Simon* v. *Eastern Kentucky Welfare Rights Organization*, a 1976 standing case:

> In our modern-day society, dominated by complex legislative pro-
> grams and large-scale governmental involvement in the everyday lives
> of all of us, judicial review of administrative action is essential both for
> protection of individuals illegally harmed by that action and to ensure
> that the attainment of congressionally mandated goals is not frustrated
> by illegal action. . . .[34]

Judicial oversight turns out to be necessary to render the modern administrative state defensible as well as tolerable. Where Powell, who wrote
for the majority, believed the Court should make it tough for parties to
receive standing in order to keep the judiciary in its proper domain and
protect the integrity of the judicial branch in our democratic system,
Brennan believed the Court should be prepared to relax rules of justiciability for the same reasons. The liberal state is only really complete,
according to Brennan, when the people can enjoy all of what it promises
with no fears, and this necessitates the constant possibility of invoking
aggressive judicial oversight of government action.

The dangers posed by modern government were never far from
Brennan's thoughts. In a dissent written toward the end of his tenure on
the Court, he observed that "the very pervasiveness of modern government . . . creates an unparalleled opportunity for intrusion on personal
life."[35] This remark appeared in *Bowen, Secretary of HHS* v. *Gilliard*, a case
involving a federal regulation that restricted access to public assistance by
mothers who had a child living in the household who also received
support from a father. In order to continue public assistance for other
members of the household, the child receiving paternal support seemingly had to decide either to leave the care of the mother or forego
support from the father. Here was an example for Brennan of the special
threats that coincide with the administrative state. *Bowen*-type dilemmas
were quintessential administrative state tragedies for Brennan and confirmed his belief that access to a judiciary that is sensitive to the interests
of all people ought to be wide-open. This is another example of the
way in which Brennan's jurisprudence both complements and seeks to
complete the work of the political and judicial liberals who preceded
him. While the Brownlow Report of 1937 spoke of reigning in the
"Fourth Branch" of the government by increasing the executive's control of the bureaucracy, Brennan's jurisprudence is grounded in the conviction that this is insufficient and that the oversight of the judicial
branch is needed to assure administrative responsibility.[36] Hence the im-

portance he assigned not only to expanding standing but to creating procedural guarantees enforceable by the courts such as the right to a pretermination hearing for people receiving public benefits and services.[37]

Not surprisingly, appeals to administrative convenience elicited little sympathy from Brennan. His concerns were overwhelmingly rights-based and focused on freeing people from constraints on their ability to pursue a preferred way of life. Protecting personal rights against forces that can easily become "Draconian" is a theme that marked his defense of the exclusionary rule and of broad use of the habeas corpus and contempt powers of the courts.[38] Brennan had no problem defending a vigorous use of all the weapons in the judicial arsenal not only when he sensed that public officials were derelict in protecting rights or brazenly violating them, but as measures intended to keep officials honest. In a spirited dissent in *Spallone* v. *United States*, a much publicized case arising out of a District Court ruling against members of the Yonkers City Council for refusing to comply with an order to desegregate public housing, Brennan roundly criticized the majority for taking what he characterized as an excessively cautious approach to the use of the contempt power to protect constitutional rights. Where Rehnquist found the District Court's contempt charges against the councilmen to be too sweeping and took the opportunity to admonish lower court judges not to be too eager to regulate legislative conduct, Brennan found it to be entirely appropriate for the judiciary to "[decide] to err on the side of being safe rather than sorry."[39] For good measure, and in keeping with the view that judicial involvement in public affairs is critical to the achievement of a defensible republic of rights, he noted that "a court's valid command to obey constitutional dictates is not subject to override by any countervailing preferences of the polity, no matter how widely and ardently shared."[40] On first blush this may not appear to be a radical observation, but what separates it from the arguments of a Chief Justice John Marshall or even Oliver Wendell Holmes is the broad reading given by Brennan to the matters that fall within the scope of legitimate judicial review. Once rules of justiciability such as standing and the political questions doctrine have been narrowed and the contempt and habeas corpus powers of the courts have been expanded, the range of issues and questions subject to judicial consideration becomes almost limitless. In contrast to Holmes who urged vigorous judicial defense of rights that are indispensable to a healthy democratic political process such as freedom of speech and press but showed considerable deference to legislative handling of policy issues touching not only the economy but personal freedoms such as reproduction, Brennan insisted that the Court reserve the authority to review virtually any decision, public or private, that might not comport with the principle of libertarian dignity.[41] The insistence that the Court must carefully guard its authority to scrutinize a broad range of policy matters explains the ease with which Brennan rebuffed the calls issued by colleagues such as Burger, Powell, and Rehnquist to retain significant barriers to standing or to limit use of the habeas corpus or contempt powers when their employment might weaken the federal system or democratic political processes. If Holmes's decision to uphold state sterilization in *Buck* v. *Bell* is an example of what results from such counsel, then this approach represents not the height of prudence but a form of judicial callousness that for Brennan is offensive to the Constitution.

Brennan repeatedly observed that one inescapable part of the special trust reposed in the judiciary with the appearance of the modern administrative state is a duty to interpret the "majestic generalities" of the Constitution to suit the times.[42] His calls for zealous attention to administrative processes, for example, reflected the belief that the Constitution must be kept equal to new dangers and new aspirations. While the legislative and executive departments are invited by him to participate in this process, it is clear that he viewed the courts as having a special responsibility for seeing that this occurs. Although he often insisted that the "original intent" of the Founders was to design a flexible Constitution that was open to continuous interpretation, his principal concern had to do less with deciphering, or adhering to, the intent of the Framers and more with eradicating barriers that constrain freedom of expression and choice of lifestyles by the people who make up the republic at any moment. Liberation from prior interpretations of the Constitution turns out to be the right of each generation: "What the constitutional fundamentals meant to the wisdom of other times cannot be their measure to the vision of our time. Similarly, what those fundamentals mean to us, our descendants will learn, cannot be the measure to the vision of their time."[43] Redefining the language of the Constitution not only is a means of allowing society to accommodate changing preferences, but also permits the people to gain greater control of their way of life, one of Brennan's tests of whether the "dignity" of a person is being protected. As with the Progressives who preceded him, Brennan expected new interpretations of the Constitution to expand and not contract protected rights and interests.

A classic example of Brennan's vision of how the judiciary must be vigilant to ensure that constitutional principles are construed to meet constantly changing circumstances appears in his dissent in *Lopez* v. *United States*, a 1963 case involving the use of wiretapping to gain evidence.[44] While Justice Harlan and the majority accepted the government's position that wiretapping is not strictly covered by the Fourth Amendment ban against illegal searches and seizures, Brennan vigorously asserted that the Court could reach its conclusion only by elevating constitutional form over substance and by entrapping the Constitution in nineteenth-century thinking. He saw no difficulty in extrapolating a limitation on wiretapping from the principles of the Fourth Amendment. To do otherwise, indeed, was to "[contribute] to a climate of official lawlessness" and run the risk that "as a people we may become hagridden and furtive."[45] As this quotation reveals, Brennan reacted critically to processes and practices at odds with his vision of a society that protects self-expression, and individual self-determination, to the fullest degree. His dissent in *Lopez* represents only one of many occasions when he urged his colleagues to interpret the Constitution to fit the times, which in this case meant keeping up with scientific innovations.[46] And in this regard, appeals to history, popular preferences, and precedent are necessarily of limited value, if not even dangerous. As he declared in *Abington School District* v. *Schempp*, an early 1960s establishment clause case, "an awareness of history and an appreciation of the aims of the Founding Fathers do not always resolve concrete problems."[47] Glancing all the way back to the founding period, Brennan used the occasion of another establishment clause case in 1983 to identify a multiplicity of reasons for the Court to be especially skeptical about legislative judgments on constitutional issues: "Legislators, influenced by the passions and exigencies of the moment, the pressure of constituents and colleagues, and the press of business, do not always pass sober constitutional judgment on every piece of legislation they enact, and this must be assumed to be as true of the Members of the First Congress as any other."[48] This observation can cover Madison, who served in the First Congress, as well as those legislators who voted for the Flag Protection Act of 1989 that Brennan declared unconstitutional a year later. As is evident from his remarks in *Abington School District*, the "task" of "translating" the terms of the Constitution to fit contemporary situations turns out for Brennan to necessitate a liberation from historical norms and majoritarian preferences.[49] The role of the judge in helping to shape and reshape the American way of life could hardly be described in more elevated terms. This is in contrast with Alexander Hamilton's *Federalist* 78 defense of a judiciary that would use its great powers to preserve rather than help reform the way of life of the American people. It barely needs repeating that Brennan was optimistic about the results of wedding his version of judicial activism with the aim of earlier reformers who wished to use government to correct the remaining "bitter wrong[s]" that were sources of fear, insecurity, and inequality. Whether the judiciary was designed to address all such wrongs, including those traceable to cultural factors, or is capable of doing so, are issues that cannot be separated from a serious evaluation of Brennan's jurisprudence and to which we shall have to return. To anticipate another issue that arises in the next two chapters, it is not clear in his jurisprudence why the interpretive flexibility that he labored so hard to defend could not be turned against either his own ends or for that matter his means, that is, an imperfectly democratic judicial institution prepared to challenge electoral majorities.

High-Toning the Judicial Oath

Lurking behind Brennan's defense of judicial superintendence of the constitutional system is the special interpretation that he gave to the oath taken by justices and to what he characterized as the "sublime mission" of his profession in a 1957 address.[50] References to his own oath to uphold the Constitution and his duties as a member of the legal profession appear repeatedly in his opinions. The judicial oath in particular is cast as a sacred obligation to defend his view of the goals of the constitutional order, specifically the achievement of a society committed to the principle of "libertarian dignity."[51] The judicial oath carries a moral quality not merely because it is cast as an "oath" but because of the high responsibilities that accompany it. In an address at New York University presented shortly after his elevation to the Court, and no doubt with himself in mind, Brennan stressed that the sublime mission of the legal profession required that he and his colleagues in the legal field "not rest until we have done everything within our power" to ensure that the judicial system does not contribute to the denial of rights or perpetuate suffering due to unredressed injuries.[52] The emphasis given by him to this obligation explains his impatience with actions that do not accord with his interpretation of the Constitution as well as his insistence on pressing forward with personal views even when they have been repeatedly rejected by a majority of his colleagues, perhaps best represented by his tenacious proclamations of the incompatibility of capital punishment with the Eighth Amendment's ban on cruel and unusual punishments.[53] The high moral cast that Brennan assigns the judicial oath both permits and invites justices to stand above appeals to separation of powers or to prevailing opinions about such practices as capital punishment.

It is noteworthy that Brennan enlisted Madison, the "father" of the American Constitution, to legitimate an expansive view of the responsibilities that are attached to the judicial oath. In a hard-hitting dissent in *United States* v. *Leon*, a Fourth Amendment criminal evidence case, Brennan quoted from an address by Madison to the First Congress on June 8, 1789, where he observed that "independent tribunals of justice will consider themselves in a peculiar manner the guardians of [constitutional] rights . . . ; they will be naturally led to resist every encroachment upon rights expressly stipulated for in the Constitution by the declaration of rights."[54] Brennan invoked this passage frequently during his tenure. For him, these words defined the sacred trust that Madison and the American people have reposed in the judicial branch. Madison's remarks are given a sweeping interpretation that dovetails with Brennan's insistence that the integrity of the constitutional order depends on a judiciary that is faithful to the high charge that he associated with the oath. That Madison likely did not share Brennan's expansive view either of the rights protected by the Constitution or of the power of the courts does not receive even passing notice. While Brennan claimed that "judicial power resides in the authority *to give meaning* to the Constitution," Madison spoke of a judiciary that protected "expressly stipulated" rights. He also observed in the closing weeks of the Constitutional Convention that the Court's power of constitutional review was limited to matters of a judicial nature, a remark later obscured for posterity by Hamilton's and Marshall's defense of a broad power of review in *Federalist* 78 and *Marbury* v. *Madison*.[55]

Brennan's construction of Madison's thoughts on the judiciary was the equivalent of placing a gloss on a law in order to render it useful and defensible. That Brennan likely never doubted the accuracy of his reading of Madison's remarks can be assumed. But overriding any disinterested concern with Madison's original intentions was a desire to legitimate judicial action that accommodated a highly egalitarian and rights-oriented state. When Brennan reflected on the meaning of due process of law in his Cardozo lecture of 1987, for example, the emphasis was squarely on ensuring that "individual dignity has been honored, . . . [and] the worth of . . . individual[s] has been acknowledged."[56] To fit his standards, judgments must be based on a proper "sensitiv[ity] to the balance of reason and passion that mark a given age. . . ."[57] Acknowledging that judges as human beings cannot, and indeed should not, escape the *effect* of "passion" on their deliberations, he added that due process was guaranteed only when judges *give expression* to the "reason and passion" of the times. By his own admission, however, mere subscription to the sentiments of the day cannot be sufficient, but only adherence to those sentiments that affirm "individual dignity." Simple majoritarianism finds no home in Brennan's jurisprudence. Nevertheless, the unstated assumption is that the people have reached a stage of enlightenment that makes it likely that "the balance of reason and passion" reflected in contemporary public opinion will result in the advancement of human dignity. The duty of the courts is to curb and redress any lapses that might occur. It is noteworthy that Brennan worried more about lapses traceable to government action than to those arising from the conduct of private parties. Thus he took special care to remind public officials "to treat citizens not as subjects but as fellow human beings."[58] Here is the source of Brennan's most enthusiastic defense of governmental forms or, in more common terms, procedures and institutions. In contrast to Alexis de Tocqueville's call for promoting respect for formalities as a way of civilizing democracy by promoting correct "mores" (habits and opinions) in the people, Brennan approached procedural safeguards for defendants in criminal proceedings and for recipients of public benefits and privileges as one-dimensional devices for protecting individual rights. His treatment of legal and constitutional forms abstracted from any public interest-related concern for Tocquevillean "mores" or for competent and economical government. Protecting the possibility for individual definition through the exercise of private rights, not making people into the kind of rational participants in self-government envisioned by Publius in *The Federalist Papers*, is the dominant theme of Brennan's opinions. Publius's "rational" citizen recognizes that decent and competent republicanism requires that behavior be formalized in a manner that puts private interests to work for the advancement of justice and the common good. Here is the rationale behind the decision to allow presidents to seek reelection to an indefinite number of terms and to provide senators with reasonably lengthy terms of office that will permit them to transcend the momentary demands of the people. Where Madison in *Federalist* 51 argued that the delegates to the Constitutional Convention first had to figure out how to "enable the government to control the governed," and only after that could they confidently devise ways to "oblige it to control itself," Brennan was preoccupied with ensuring that governmental institutions not get out of control and left little instruction about the need to protect the capacity of those institutions to "control the governed." As already noted, his overriding concern was that each person's freedom to pursue a preferred way of life be encumbered by as few barriers as possible. It is in this spirit that Brennan led the way in weakening the sovereign immunity doctrine that shielded many government agencies and their personnel from liability claims.[59] Exposing government personnel and entities to liability claims translated into greater protection for personal liberties. Caution and even timidity frequently emerged as preferable qualities for government action than vigor or efficiency, except on those occasions when he sought government intervention to protect private rights, whether on behalf of the victims of school segregation or of general social neglect.

Whether Brennan's interpretation of the due process principle comports with the original intentions of the Founders, however, is doubtful. Instead of the image of "fellow human beings" presented by Brennan, many of the leading Founders would no doubt have argued that it is best to view those who are governed as the fellow citizens of those persons who govern them.[60] It was the violation of the responsibilities of democratic citizenship that George Washington believed justified his harsh response to the Whiskey Rebellion, the 1794 insurrection in western Pennsylvania provoked by the imposition of U.S. taxes on distilled spirits and stills. The principal duties of rational citizenship take the form of the sacrifices and self-discipline needed to prevent the modern republic of rights from degenerating into anarchy or leading to tyranny. Citizenship of this sort is rational for the very reason that it permits self-government to be viable. In this connection, Founders such as Washington clearly understood that due process protection for property, as with safeguards for other rights, would occasionally entail costs for even decent and innocent parties. Preserving the larger republic of rights that provides benefits to the people generally is not without costs. In line with William Shakespeare's message in *King Lear*, where Cordelia's adherence to the dictates of nature shakes the entire realm, the Founders viewed idealistic attempts to purge the tragic side of political life as doomed to fail, often with devastating consequences for the community. By contrast, Brennan was not convinced that it is necessary to make peace with any practices that impose injuries or curtail full enjoyment of personal liberties. If you assume that the relationship of the people to the government in the modern liberal state is not fundamentally problematical, then the sacrifices that result from procedures based on distrust or suspicion of the governed are indefensible in principle. By associating the legal profession in general and judges in particular with the pursuit of a nontragic state of existence, Brennan indirectly linked his judicial project with the ultimate goal of modernity, that is, the subjugation of nature to the achievement of dependable human happiness.

The conviction that the members of the judicial profession are bound by oath to insist on protection for all rights and redress for all grievances allowed Brennan to distinguish his brand of activism from that of his "conservative" colleagues.[61] He did not consider it to be either unseemly or unprofessional to criticize Burger and Rehnquist Court majorities harshly and openly when he believed that fundamental rights were being eroded, even to the point of publicly inviting federal and state judges to limit the alleged damage being done by the Supreme Court. Indeed, the high sin of the Burger and Rehnquist Courts in Brennan's estimation was that they were making that institution "increasingly irrelevant in the protection of individual rights." Here was a "shocking" situation for him.[62] In the eyes of his critics, however, Brennan was guilty of the sin of arrogance for wanting to move the judiciary to center stage in virtually all matters touching the way of life of the people. Related charges included allegations by colleagues that his "alarmist" rhetoric and "distor[tions]" of majority rulings threatened to undermine public confidence in the Court.[63] That charges of misdirected and alarmist activism were easily disregarded by Brennan can be accounted for in terms of the end-oriented cast that he gave to the judicial oath. He saw no contradiction between his warnings that his brethren were acting like Platonic Guardians when he objected to their reasoning and his own defense of the unilateral construction of judicial remedies, even in "policy" areas historically left to legislative management.[64] The test of acceptable judicial activism for Brennan took the form of consistency with the principles of his jurisprudence of libertarian dignity and of the comprehensive constitution doctrine that holds that all rights deserve protection and that no injuries should go unredressed. Thus he declared that unacceptable judicial action "turn[s] a blind eye to social progress and eschew[s] adaptation of overarching principles to changes of social circumstances."[65] Judicial action that lacked apparent sensitivity to the historical moment received his most damning condemnation. Action of this kind is deemed to be at "war" with the Constitution and merits being folded into all other government action that endangers liberty interests.[66] Seen in its broadest terms, a judiciary that is faithful to Brennan's construction of the oath will ensure that governmental conduct, to include court action, imposes minimal restrictions on the ability of people to pursue a lifestyle or way of life of their choosing. It is in this connection that he issued repeated warnings about the dangers of "overreaching officialdom" and of a government that might easily "grow remote, insensitive, and finally acquisitive of those attributes of sovereignty not delegated by the Constitution."[67]

The heightened valuation assigned rights by Brennan is really a reflection of the central position that personal "will" and "values" came to occupy in his fully developed legal thought. It is significant, for example, that in the first major right to die case Brennan could find nothing to trump Nancy Cruzan's wish never to be left suspended by medical technology in a permanent vegetative state.[68] Missouri officials had but one duty in his eyes, that is, to determine what Cruzan wanted done with her body. Missouri's insistence that it be permitted to develop a policy that favors life over death failed to elicit any sympathy from Brennan. When the Court several years earlier had sustained a Connecticut law that excluded medically unnecessary abortions from a Medicaid-funded program, he had protested that indigent women would be forced "to bear children they would not otherwise *choose to have*. . . ."[69] He found the results in *Maher* v. *Roe* to be at odds with *Roe* v. *Wade,* which he interpreted as establishing the "fundamental right of pregnant women *to be free to decide* whether to have an abortion."[70] The existence of such burdens on the ability of individuals to shape a way of life for themselves could not be reconciled by Brennan with the principle of libertarian dignity. The fact that the state was not directly prohibiting abortions in the case of indigent women was unpersuasive. In a revealing remark, Brennan pointedly added that "infringements of fundamental rights are not limited to outright denials of those rights."[71] This was a theme to which he would recur, but again without success, in a Fourteenth Amendment due process case that turned on the tragic consequences of child abuse. In *DeShaney* v. *Winnebago County Department of Social Services,* Chief Justice Rehnquist refused to hold that due process guarantees were violated by Wisconsin officials who failed to remove a child from an abusive father.[72] The Fourteenth Amendment, according to Rehnquist, does not impose an affirmative obligation on states to eradicate all practices that might constitute interferences with the exercise of personal liberties or freedoms. For his part, Brennan insisted that county officials were adequately warned of the dangers of leaving the child with the parent and hence were guilty of committing a constitutional sin through inaction. Clearly, he was not prepared to absolve sins of omission any less lightly than sins of commission.

In the context of Brennan's jurisprudence, *Cruzan, Maher,* and *DeShaney,* like *Baker* long before them, are prime examples of the deficiencies that continued to characterize democratic politics during the post–New Deal period. These cases provided useful support for his defense of a vigilant and liberally activist judiciary. If the interventionist posture was generally desirable in his estimation, cases such as *Maher* confirmed his belief that it was especially crucial that the Court be prepared to intervene to respond to defects in political decision making in cases

involving the "politically powerless," a class that for him included immigrant children, minorities, the poor, the mentally disabled, and minors.[73]
No stretch of the Constitution or judicial power was needed for him to
declare in *Plyler* v. *Doe* that Texas could not prevent local schools from
using state funds to educate children who had not been legally admitted
to the country. In a spirited critique of the law, he declared that the
action taken by the state threatened to "impose a lifetime hardship on a
discrete class of children not accountable for their disabling status." Such
action, for him, ran afoul not only of the Constitution's equal protection
clause, but any reasonable construction of congressional desires.[74]

If you believe with all your heart that history has conclusively demonstrated the unparalleled advantages of liberal democratic societies over
all rivals, then it may seem reasonable to exhibit impatience with governmental practices rooted in appeals to self-defense or self-preservation
that entail confinements of individual and group rights. There should be
no need to demand sacrifices, especially of fundamental liberties, if the
victory has been won by your side, which for Brennan was the case with
the modern, rights-oriented, democratic state. In *Cruzan* and *DeShaney*,
Rehnquist had concluded that it would not be unreasonable for a state
such as Missouri to decide to favor life over death or for a state such as
Wisconsin to direct its officials to err on the side of keeping families
intact. States might associate such stances with preserving healthy democratic communities or the traditional American way of life. These are
arguments based on a broad conception of self-defense or self-preservation. By comparison, Brennan's opinions narrow the realm of legitimate
action in the name of self-defense while expanding the opportunity for
individuals to express themselves via a way of life that is chosen freely
and subject to minimal constraints. The most legitimate form of governmental action in this framework is the type he defended in *DeShaney*,
that is, action taken to ensure that people enjoy full freedom to shape a
way of life for themselves.

Intrusive and insensitive governmental action is a threat not only to
the active enjoyment of rights but to the diversity that Brennan expected
when self-expression and general self-determination is a reality for the
people. Pressured conformity to preeminent opinions and norms was at
least as great an evil for him as, say, threats to due process posed by
ineffective representation by counsel in criminal proceedings or by reliance on illegally seized material to gain convictions. A judiciary that fails
to check both types of dangers violates its sacred "trust." Indeed, unabat-
ing judicial vigilance in the service of mitigating all such dangers is for
Brennan the only acceptable posture consistent with the judicial oath. A

judiciary that is faithful to its oath will not be neutral in the face of majoritarian preferences and practices that impose disabilities on the members of the community and especially the "politically powerless" or expose them needlessly to public or private actions that threaten their liberty interests. Witness his accusation in *Maher* that the Court had shown a "distressing insensitivity to the plight of impoverished women" and his insistence in establishment clause cases that government officials must stay clear of endorsing the religious convictions of the dominant groups in society.[75] His message is unambiguous: for courts to respond favorably to calls for self-restraint that would mean tolerating inequality or turning a blind eye to situations that leave people feeling uncomfortable would be tantamount to abdicating constitutionally imposed responsibilities and would consign the country to the status of an incomplete or imperfect democratic society.

Brennan's Oath in Political Context

The objective of this chapter has not been to suggest that Brennan believed that government intends to do evil or that all political institutions are defective. What is evident in his legal writing, however, is the conviction that the procedures associated with even "rational" governance too often end up sacrificing private rights and individual autonomy.[76] Even if not usually intentional, any sacrifice of rights or substantial personal interests as a result of government action still constitutes a harm that is incompatible with Brennan's objective of libertarian dignity. And at least for him it is this principle and not the requisites of efficient or "rational" governance that must direct judicial decision making if the modern liberal state is going to live up to its high promise of respecting the equality and dignity of each member of society. Insofar as the pre-*Baker* version of the political questions doctrine could end up protecting "political" interests at the expense of personal rights, then narrowing the terms of this doctrine was seen by Brennan as an appropriate, and really necessary, exercise for judicial officials. The same logic is evident in his defense of ratcheting up the contempt and habeas powers of the federal courts even at some cost to separation of powers and federalism. If Madison relied heavily on separation of powers and federalistic arrangements to get competent and non-tyrannical government, Brennan was prepared to make extensive use of rights-based claims initiated by private parties to check government action.

For Wilsonian liberals, the major task left for America was to devise political and administrative structures that would give effective expression to the popular will. By comparison, for Brennan the principal task that remained was to employ judicial means to ensure that maximizing the opportunity for self-expression and self-determination for all people, and not adherence to majoritarian preferences or efficiency calculations, constituted the driving force behind all political and administrative processes. Within the context of his opinions, a democracy that respects the personal worth and equality of all its members and that diligently works to eradicate sources of unhappiness and impediments to individual autonomy in the pursuit of a preferred way of life constitutes the true last stage of historical development. And this is best done by harnessing reason, nature, tradition, and the dominant mores of society while unleashing the human "will" in a particularistic and not collectivist form. Placed in the framework of old natural law thinking, this vision of the perfected democratic order is for Brennan the product of "right reason." He could happily defend the American Constitution as "higher law" because he was convinced that it was designed to promote just this kind of democratic order or at least could be construed in a way that lends support to the achievement of such an order. The Constitution satisfies his test of right reason. Needless to add, his own objectives are immeasurably advanced by being associated with a higher law that is said to be derived from right reason and that is subject to judicial enforcement.

If McDonald's-style fast food is emblematic of the modern egalitarian-leaning bourgeois state, Brennan's aim was to see that the judiciary serves as a convenient drive-up facility that permits the members of society who labor under real or perceived constraints to get what they want, in the form they want it, with minimal discomfort or inconvenience. Demythifying the Constitution and political institutions, reducing standing barriers, and expanding the contempt and habeas corpus powers of the courts all contribute to bringing this about, as does accommodating nontraditional tastes. The principle of the sovereignty of the citizen body that informed the work of the Founders gives way to the virtual sovereignty of each individual over his or her own way of life. The result sought is a society where recognition of the essential dignity of each person means tolerating an almost infinite range of personal preferences. To this end, spiritedness must be disarmed and reason must make its peace with the passions or desires. For the modern administrative state to be tamed, governing rules as well as institutional arrangements must accommodate the expression of personal tastes and preferences; indeed, the merest subordination of the informal by the formal begins to look like tyranny. The elevation of the passions and desires relative to reason rivals the idyllic image of lions consenting to lie peacefully at the side of lambs. In both instances, the ideal cannot be realized without nature being tamed or overcome. Brennan's jurisprudence accurately reflects the fact that the nontragic existence to which Progressive and New Deal thought pointed depends not only on a profound reconceptualization of established processes but on mounting a challenge to nature itself. Nothing less than this was behind the assault that Brennan mounted against gender distinctions.

There is nothing in Brennan's legal writings to suggest that the society he desired should not seek to relieve its members of all the cares of living, to paraphrase Tocqueville, as it seeks to relieve them of all the fears of living. A century and a half after its appearance, Tocqueville's *Democracy in America* is still identified by many scholars as the definitive study of the modern democratic state. While Tocqueville himself had observed even before the *Dred Scott* v. *Sandford* decision that political questions tend to become judicial questions in America, he did not suggest that it is beneficial to the health of democratic states for national courts to make themselves ready devices for the vindication of all rights and resolution of all conflicts. He understood that it was good for a democratic citizenry to toil at governance. His call for an active citizenry and even personal assertiveness would provoke no protest from Brennan. The rub is in the accompanying recognition by Tocqueville that a democratic citizenry must reconcile itself to forms and procedures that allow government to constrain choices or impose sacrifices. Nor did he believe that it was desirable to strip the institutions and rules of society of whatever mystique may have accrued to them over time. He understood that the way established procedures play out in practice can dramatically influence each person's interests, which, in turn, supplies a powerful incentive for participation in public affairs. Permitting people to endure not only the pain of their own mistakes but the failures of their fellow citizens was for Tocqueville essential to having a democracy with liberty rather than a "barbaric" form of democracy.[77] Frankfurter's handling of the malapportionment challenge in *Colegrove*, for example, invited citizens to accept the costs and challenges of Tocquevillean-style politics. In contrast to the position of his former law professor and eventual colleague on the Court, Brennan challenged both the desirability and the necessity of such a compromise with the ideal of a nontragic and demystified democratic state. Compromise can be seen as capitulation when the objective being pursued is believed to be both compelling and attainable. And as we have seen, the objective is nothing less than realizing the Enlightenment promise of greater freedom and the attainment of comfortable preservation but without the stultifying effects of science or of economic rationality that have come to be associated with modern "rational" action. Allowing cost–benefit analysis to dictate policy, for example, can have a formidable restraining effect on freedom of action. In this sense, Brennan's jurisprudence also reflects the desire to escape the tyranny of "reason" that is evident in the modern scientific tradition. There was nothing accidental in Brennan's repeated attacks on Rehnquist for relying on rational basis analysis when determining whether government action is constitutional. But when traditional "rational" defenses of government action are rendered suspect for being imperfect or incomplete or for confining freedom, a charge that might be laid at the doorstep of all human action and inventions, then nothing may remain to prevent claims to govern from being made in the name of mere prejudices or, for that matter, the will of the strongest.

The above reservations notwithstanding, by the vision contained in his opinions of what remains for the American republic to be completed, as well as his labors on behalf of this project, it is not unreasonable to place William Brennan alongside Woodrow Wilson, Oliver Wendell Holmes, and Franklin Roosevelt as a major liberal figure of the twentieth century. This status is deserved both for the view of the completed constitutional system that Brennan articulated and for the influence his opinions have exerted on the way of life of the people during much of the second half of the century. His opinions add up to a concerted and well-intentioned effort to cultivate, and not merely protect, the largest possible degree of self-expression and self-determination for the members of the society. The construction he gave to his oath of office permitted nothing less. But more than the special obligation he associated with his oath, it was the conviction that protecting robust and uninhibited expression would indeed produce a better world that accounts for the spiritedness that was so characteristic of Brennan's legal writings. Significantly, Madison's fear that excessive emphasis on personal liberties might make effective democratic governance impossible in practice led him to take a cautious position on the addition of a separate "Bill of Rights" to the Constitution. Washington, for his part, fully recognized the value of fostering a prejudice in favor of beneficial institutions and practices. Whether Brennan asked too much of the people and the judiciary in particular, and of the constitutional system in general, are subjects to which this study will return. To address such issues effectively, and to appreciate fully his vision of a perfected democratic community, it will be necessary first to examine his interpretation of the First and Fourteenth Amendments.

Notes

1. 438 U.S. 265 (1978).
2. 480 U.S. 616 (1987).
3. 491 U.S. 397 (1989).
4. 380 U.S. 51 (1965).
5. 497 U.S. 261 (1990).
6. See, for example, *Dombrowski* v. *Pfister*, 380 U.S. 479 (1965); also see his dissent in *Schlesinger* v. *Reservists Committee to Stop the War*, 418 U.S. 208 (1974) and *Public Citizen* v. *United States*, 491 U.S. 440, 450–51 (1989).
7. In *Great Atlantic and Pacific Tea Co.* v. *Cottrell*, a case involving the permissibility of retaliatory economic sanctions imposed by Mississippi on the sale of Louisiana milk, Brennan argued for the Supreme Court that the states should come to the courts for assistance when confronted by protectionist barriers that may violate the principle of a national economic system, rather than engage in self-help (424 U.S. 366, 380 [1976]). The same message is addressed repeatedly to individual parties claiming to be aggrieved as a result of government action. For instances when Brennan counseled reliance on judicial redress, see *Laird* v. *Tatum*, 408 U.S. 1, 40 (1972); *Bishop* v. *Wood*, 426 U.S. 341, 354 (1976); and *Rusk* v. *Cort*, 469 U.S. 367, 383 (1962).
8. 369 U.S. 186 (1962).
9. Earl Warren, "Mr. Justice Brennan," 80 *Harvard Law Review* I, 2 (1966).
10. See *Shaw* v. *Reno* (509 U.S. 630 [1993]), a case having to do with whether some citizens of North Carolina raised a judicially cognizable claim when protesting the state's creation of a majority-black congressional district, and *Miller* v. *Johnson* (519 U.S. _____ [1995]), a case arising out of a challenge to a similar district created in Georgia.
11. 328 U.S. 549 (1946).
12. Ibid. at 556.
13. 1 Cranch 137 (1803).
14. 369 U.S. at 211.
15. Ibid. at 226.
16. Ibid. at 217.
17. Ibid.
18. The Court's deferential approach to legislative use of the commerce power can be seen in the majority opinions by Justice Tom Clark in the two major civil rights cases of 1964, *Katzenbach* v. *McClung* (379 U.S. 294) and *Heart of Atlanta Motel, Inc.* v. *United States* (379 U.S. 241), and in *Maryland* v. *Wirtz* (392 U.S. 183 [1968]), a case sustaining the extension of the federal Fair Labor Standards Act to certain classes of state employees.
19. Ibid. at 269–70.
20. Ibid. at 339–340.
21. 380 U.S. 479 (1965). A year after *Dombrowski*, Brennan again defended a generous view of judicial power to hear cases and provide remedies in his opinion for the Court in *United Mine Workers of America* v. *Gibbs*, 383 U.S. 715 (1966).
22. 380 U.S. at 492.
23. Ibid. at 498.

24. See Powell's dissent in *Elrod* v. *Burns* (427 U.S. 347 [1976]) and Scalia's dissent in *Rutan* v. *Republican Party of Illinois* (497 U.S. 62 [1990]).

25. 416 U.S. 452 (1974). A decade and a half after *Steffel*, Brennan ruled in *City of Lakewood* v. *Plain Dealer Publishing Co.* that a newspaper did not have to wait until it had been denied a permit to bring a facial challenge to an ordinance that gave the mayor broad discretion over the placement of newspaper racks on public property. 486 U.S. 750 (1988).

26. 418 U.S. 208 (1974).

27. 418 U.S. 166 (1974).

28. Ibid. at 179.

29. Ibid. at 188.

30. 418 U.S. 208, 235.

31. *Valley Forge Christian College* v. *Americans United for Separation of Church and State, Inc.* 454 U.S. 464 (1982).

32. Ibid. at 473. Rehnquist repeatedly observed that the Court should avoid confrontations with the coordinate branches of the national government whenever possible and use its power to declare constitutional rights and "measure the authority of governments" as a last resort. Ibid. at 471.

33. Ibid. at 491.

34. 426 U.S. 26, 65 (1976). Writing for the Court in *Simon*, Powell refused to grant standing to several indigents, and organizations representing the interests of the poor, who sought to challenge an IRS ruling that allowed nonprofit hospitals to seek favorable tax status while limiting indigents to emergency room care. Powell ruled that the petitioners had not demonstrated that the action of the IRS had resulted in true injuries to them. More importantly for Brennan who ended up concurring on the grounds that the controversy was not yet ripe, Powell noted that there are some essential standing requirements that even Congress is powerless to eliminate. Brennan bristled at this suggestion, which he saw as limiting the ability of Congress to arm people to challenge administrative action. Believing that the modern administrative state was responsible for numerous and varied threats to many individual freedoms, Brennan welcomed legislative efforts that expanded the means, including recourse to the courts, available to persons whose rights were threatened by bureaucratic action or inaction. For further reflections on this general theme see his majority opinion in *Marcus* v. *Search Warrant* (367 U.S. 717, 729 [1961]) and his dissents in *Nollan* v. *California Coastal Commission* (483 U.S. 825, 864 [1987]) and *DeShaney* v. *Winnebago County Department of Social Service* (489 U.S. 189 [1989]). Just prior to *Simon*, Brennan had squared off against Powell in another standing case where a variety of petitioners sought to challenge the zoning ordinance of Penfield, New York, on the grounds that it effectively excluded people of low and moderate income. Writing in dissent, Brennan accused Powell of using a divide-and-conquer strategy to avoid granting standing to any of the plaintiffs. *Warth* v. *Seldin*, 422 U.S. 490 (1975).

35. *Bowen, Secretary of HHS* v. *Gilliard*, 483 U.S. 587, 610 (1987). Further attention to this theme can be found in *Labor Board* v. *Brown*, 380 U.S. 278 (1965); also see both his Georgetown Address, 19–20, and "The Bill of Rights and the States," 31.

36. Brownlow Report, 53.

37. A forceful defense of pretermination hearings appears in Brennan's majority opinion in *Goldberg v. Kelly*, 397 U.S. 254, 264–65 (1970). Gerald Gunther, a leading legal scholar of the period, described *Goldberg* as "the major case launching the procedural due process revolution of the early 1970s." Gerald Gunther, *Cases and Materials in Constitutional Law* (Mineola, N.Y.: Foundation Press, 1980), 10th ed., 647. Brennan's view of the importance of judicially enforceable hearings can also be found in his majority opinion in *A Quantity of Book v. Kansas* (378 U.S. 205 [1964]) and his dissent in *Mathews v. Eldridge* (424 U.S. 319 [1976]).

38. Reference to a "Draconian" order appears in *Sable Communications of California v. FCC*, 492 U.S. 115, 135 (1989). For references to the value of the exclusionary rule and a permissive use of the habeas corpus power by federal judges see his opinions in *United States v. Calandra* (414 U.S. 338, 357–60 [1974] {Brennan dissenting}) and *Dombrowski v. Pfister* (380 U.S. 479 [1965] {majority opinion}).

39. *Spallone v. United States*, 493 U.S. 265 (1990) [Brennan's dissent at 281].

40. Ibid. at 284. Brennan rebuked Congress for targeting people in need of aid in his majority opinion in *U.S. Department of Agriculture v. Moreno,* which overturned legislative action designed to limit access to food stamps by so-called "hippies." 413 U.S. 528, 538 (1973).

41. Brennan, for example, would be hard-pressed to justify Holmes's decision in *Buck v. Bell,* which sustained a Virginia law that permitted the sterilization of a person deemed to be mentally incompetent. Particularly offensive, and embarrassing, to Brennan would have been Holmes's declaration that "three generations of imbeciles are enough." 274 U.S. 200 (1927).

42. Georgetown Address, 11.

43. Ibid., 17. A related observation appears in *Marsh v. Chambers,* an establishment clause case: "[T]he Constitution is not a static document whose meaning on every detail is fixed for all time by the life experience of the Framers." 463 U.S. 783, 816 (1983).

44. 373 U.S. 427 (1963). In another 1963 case, *Wong Sun v. United States,* Brennan used a strict view of probable cause when overturning a drug conviction. Writing in dissent in this 5–4 case, Justice Clark charged Brennan with making the work of police officers too difficult. 371 U.S. 471, 499.

45. 373 U.S. at 470–71. Brennan urged the Court to be attentive to the problems posed by "zealous officers" right up to his retirement. For example, see *Horton v. California* (496 U.S. 128 [1990] {Brennan dissenting}) and *Michigan Department of State Police v. Sitz* (496 U.S. 444 [1990] {Brennan dissenting}).

46. See Brennan's dissent in *Marsh v. Chambers*, at 816.

47. 374 U.S. 203, 234 (1963).

48. *Marsh v. Chambers*, at 814–15.

49. 374 U.S. at 236–37. An appeal to "contemporary community standards" as the appropriate standard for resolving controversies appears in *Roth v. United States,* the earliest of numerous majority opinions that he authored in major First Amendment cases (354 U.S. 476 [1957]). While Brennan assigned prevailing community preferences or standards great weight in *Roth*, it did not take him long to add that adherence to majoritarian preferences had to be measured

against the judge's personal sense of what best promotes justice in any given case.

50. William J. Brennan Jr., *Modernizing the Courts*. (New York: Institute of Judicial Administration, 1957), 4–5. This was an address presented before the New York University Law Alumni Association.

51. Very early in his tenure Brennan reflected on the high and delicate task of protecting rights, especially against governmental threats, that fell to members of the Court. *Uphaus* v. *Wyman*, 360 U.S. 72, 84 (1959) [Brennan dissenting].

52. Brennan, *Modernizing the Courts,* 4–5 (1957). His preoccupation with the responsibilities of the legal profession and courts can also be seen in "How Goes the Supreme Court?" 36 *Mercer Law Review* 781–94 (1985), and "Color-Blind, Creed-Blind, Status-Blind, Sex-Blind," 14 *Human Rights* 1, 30–37 (Winter 1987).

53. Brennan's views on capital punishment are spread over many volumes of the *Supreme Court Reports*, including his opinions in *Furman* v. *Georgia* (408 U.S. 238, 290, 305 [1972]) and *Walton* v. *Arizona* (497 U.S. 639, 675 [1990] {Brennan dissenting}). Brennan's dissent in *Walton* also applied to *Lewis* v. *Jeffers*, 497 U.S. 764 (1990). In many respects, capital punishment represented for Brennan the highest form of the denial of libertarian dignity.

54. 468 U.S. 897, 930 (1984). Also see his opinions in *United States* v. *Calandra* (414 U.S. 338, 356–57) and *Bishop* v. *Wood* (426 U.S. 341, 354).

55. Brennan's remark appears in his Georgetown Address, 14 (emphasis added). Madison's observation that the delegates to the Constitutional Convention endorsed only a limited power of what we call "judicial review" came on August 27, 1787. See Max Farrand, ed., *The Records of the Federal Convention of 1787* (New Haven: Yale University Press, 1966), II: 430.

56. William J. Brennan Jr., "Reason, Passion, and 'The Progress of the Law,' " 10 *Cardozo Law Review* 3, 16 (1988).

57. Ibid.

58. Ibid., 15.

59. See *Bivens* v. *Six Unknown Named Narcotics Agents*, 403 U.S. 388 (1971). Eleven years earlier, Brennan asserted in another government employee immunity case that "the courts should be wary of any argument based on the fear that subjecting government officers to the nuisance of litigation and the uncertainties of its outcome may put an undue burden on the conduct of the public business." *Barr* v. *Matteo*, 360 U.S. 564, 589 (1959) [Brennan dissenting].

60. An excellent examination of Washington's views on what would be required for the American experiment in democratic government to work can be found in Lorraine and Thomas Pangle, *The Learning of Liberty* (Lawrence: University of Kansas Press, 1993). The authors provide useful insights into the explanation for Washington's handling of the Whiskey Rebellion in Pennsylvania and his stern commitment to law-abidingness.

61. In this connection, compare Brennan's reasoning supporting the Court's decision in *Furman* v. *Georgia* (408 U.S. 238, 269), the 1972 capital punishment case that compelled virtually all the states to revisit the procedures they used when considering imposition of the death sentence, with his criticism of Rehnquist's majority opinion in *National League of Cities* v. *Usery*, 426 U.S. 833, 875 (1976).

62. See *Oregon* v. *Elstad*, 470 U.S. 298, 359, 363 (1985) [Brennan dissenting]. A particularly harsh attack on the Burger Court for allowing a "frightening" situation to arise by its alleged failure to adequately protect persons against "arbitrary" uses of authority by police officers appears in his dissent in *Paul* v. *Davis*, 424 U.S. 693, 721, n. 9 (1976). Brennan appealed directly to the states in his dissent in *Michigan* v. *Long* to guarantee rights more completely than was being done by the Burger Court; see 423 U.S. 96, 120–21 (1975).

63. Justice Powell criticized Brennan in *United States* v. *Calandra* (414 U.S. 338, 355–56, n. 11) for the use of "alarmist" language, while Justice Sandra Day O'Connor chided him for not giving a fair characterization of the opinion of the Court in *Oregon* v. *Elstad* (470 U.S. 298, 318, n. 5).

64. See, for example, Brennan's opinions in *Bishop* v. *Wood*, 426 U.S. 341, 354, 355; *Bivens* v. *Six Unknown Named Narcotics Agents*, 403 U.S. 388, 396, 397; and *Richmond Newspapers* v. *Virginia*, 448 U.S. 555, 595, n. 20. In his concurrence and dissent in *Regents of the University of California, Davis* v. *Bakke*, he insisted that relief should often be afforded parties even in the absence of specific evidence of victimization. 438 U.S. 265, 378.

65. Georgetown Address at 15. Also see Brennan's critique of Powell's majority opinion in *Simon* v. *Eastern Kentucky Welfare Rights Organization*, 426 U.S. 26.

66. *Dombrowski* v. *Pfister*, 380 U.S. 479, 492; also his opinion in *Bowen* v. *Gilliard*, 483 U.S. 587, 632–33.

67. Also see Brennan's opinions in *United States* v. *Leon* (468 U.S. 897, 960 [1984]), *Time, Inc.* v. *Firestone* (424 U.S. 448, 478 [1976]), and *Marsh* v. *Chambers* (463 U.S. 783, 816–17 [1983]). A warning about the dangers of "oppression" from state administrative action appears in his dissent in *DeShaney* v. *Winnebago County Department of Social Services*, 489 U.S. 189, 212.

68. Emphasizing the centrality of Nancy's interests in the *Cruzan* case, Brennan faults Missouri for failing to respect "her will" and "her values." 497 U.S. 261, 330.

69. 432 U.S. 464, 483 (1977) [emphasis added].

70. Ibid. at 484 [emphasis added]. On the importance of not disabling people when it comes to the management of government benefits and services, see Brennan's opinion in *Goldberg* v. *Kelly*, 397 U.S. 254, 264–65.

71. 432 U.S. at 487. It is impossible to read Brennan's dissent in *Maher* without being struck by the weight he assigned to eliminating state interference with the exercise of fundamental rights. Ibid. at 488.

72. 489 U.S. 189 (1989).

73. *Harris* v. *McRae*, 448 U.S. 297, 332. Judicial vigilance in the protection of the rights of the mentally ill is the major theme of his dissent in *Colorado* v. *Connelly*, 479 U.S. 157 (1986).

74. *Plyler* v. *Doe*, 457 U.S. 202, 223, 226 (1982).

75. For the quote from *Maher* see 432 U.S. at 483. On Brennan's position on the dangers posed by government endorsements of religious views see his opinion in *Marsh* v. *Chambers*, 463 U.S. 783.

76. Brennan dwelt at length on the dangers posed by Weberian-style bureaucratic organizations that "[aspire] ultimately to banish passion from government altogether, and to establish a state where only reason will reign," in his Cardozo

lecture of 1988. William J. Brennan Jr., "Reason, Passion, and 'The Progress of the Law,' " 10 *Cardozo Law Review* 18, 19.

77. For Tocqueville's defense of active citizen involvement in public affairs through participation in associations and service on juries, see *Democracy in America,* J. P. Mayer, ed. (New York: Anchor Books, 1969), 262–76.

Chapter Three

ROBUST, UNINHIBITED, AND WIDE-OPEN: THE FIRST AMENDMENT AND THE IDEA OF THE SELF-CONSTITUTING SELF

> Those who won our independence believed that freedom to think as you will and to speak as you think are means indispensable to the discovery and spread of political truth; that without free speech and assembly, discussion would be futile; that with them, discussion affords ordinarily adequate protection against the dissemination of noxious doctrine; that the greatest menace to freedom is an inert people; that public discussion is a political duty; and that this should be a fundamental principle of the American government. . . .
> —Oliver Wendell Holmes, *Whitney v. California*, 274 U.S. 357, 375 (1927)

> The constitutional vision of human dignity rejects the possibility of political orthodoxy imposed from above; it respects the right of each individual to form and to express political judgments, however far they may deviate from the mainstream and however unsettling they might be to the powerful or the elite. Recognition of these rights of expression and conscience also frees up the private space for both intellectual and spiritual development free of government dominance, either blatant or subtle.
> —William J. Brennan, Jr., Georgetown Address (1986)

If the beginning of the twentieth century witnessed attacks on prevailing political and economic practices first by Progressives and later by New Deal reformers in the name of democratic freedoms, the century ended with business interests themselves taking a leading role in pushing a "do your own thing, let it all hang out" philosophy that conservatives attacked as destructive of the elements of a decent and stable social order. The prevalence in the mid-1990s of ads for everything from jeans to alcoholic beverages that unabashedly endorsed individual spontaneity, sexual freedom, and even adolescent rebelliousness is evidence of the

57

completeness of the victory of the rights movement that came to matur-
ity by the middle of the century. By the 1960s, jurists had fashioned a
body of law that required more guarantees for rights at the same time
that it provided fewer protections for governmental interests. More was
being asked of political institutions and less was being given in terms of
constitutional support for efficient and effective government. For example, challenges to loyalty tests for government employees and to the
privilege doctrine that permitted government officials wide latitude in
managing the public workforce, as well as government benefits, received
increasingly favorable responses from courts during this period. That
there might be a problematical side to the defense of personal freedom,
something that Jean-Jacques Rousseau and other major figures associated
with the defense of natural freedom had long conceded, was hardly anywhere to be seen.[1]

William Brennan quickly associated himself with the movement
to enlarge individual freedoms and redefine the constitutional basis of
legitimate governmental action. The process of freeing self-expression
from significant political constraints had been initiated before Brennan
joined the Supreme Court. What came of age with his assistance was a
defense of self-expression that was not tied to the attainment of some
political good or to the superiority of self-awareness or personal enlightenment over self-destruction. By the mid-1960s the traditional distinction between expression that serves the ends of what is naturally or
conventionally good or useful and expression that is destructive of social
or personal interests came to be viewed with suspicion as an easy vehicle
for justifying either self- or governmental censorship. Once tainted for
being an easy conduit to censorship, this distinction could easily be sacrificed to the alleged benefits of increased, and freer, expression.

It was the political domain that bore the brunt of the cost involved
in expanding protection for personal freedoms or liberties. Political and
governmental interests suffered both in terms of the direct actions that
were taken to narrow the constitutional weighting of those interests and
by the fallout from the idealism of the rights movement. Not even the
best of democratic republics is going to be able to satisfy the demand
that all rights are always and everywhere to be protected and that all
injuries should be redressed. When added to the contemporaneous claim
that the meaning of founding documents such as the Constitution and
Bill of Rights is indecipherable or that these documents have consis-
tently been misinterpreted until the present, the cumulative effect of
the entire movement was to challenge general deference to established
practices and societal norms. At the least, this thinking invites people to

believe that support for government actions may properly vary with the issue or activity being scrutinized. While Brennan's contribution to this development began modestly with his majority opinion in the *Roth*[2] pornography regulation case in 1957, certainly by 1962 with his majority opinion in *New York Times* v. *Sullivan*[3] he was making the case for a perceptible sublimation of political interests to the demands of free expression, that is, freedom from institutions and norms that restrain expression and individual autonomy.

Jnited States, Brennan the
le carefully distinguishing
convicted under a federal
and advertising. The lib-
of his endorsement of an
ommunity standards" and
"average person" would
terial appeals to "prurient
n Rule that allowed mate-
ect of isolated segments on
h test opened the door to
the obscenity field, the full
the government's victory
ne historical foundations of
st on absolute precision in
ferential appearance to his
of prosecutors marginally
would soon become much
al deference to regulations
ect was quickly coming to

ing and end of the develop-
ression area would become
clear not only from the opinions that followed in the 1960s but from his own rejection of the Roth test sixteen years later in *Paris Adult Theatre I* v. *Slaton* (1973). In the end, *Roth* just did not provide sufficient scope for self-definition through self-expression to satisfy Brennan. And this after all was what he came to see as the critical core of First Amendment freedoms. A classic example of the "matured" Brennanesque reading of

the First Amendment appeared in *CBS* v. *Democratic National Committee*, a case arising out of a commercial network's refusal to air political ads.[4] Although his dissenting opinion repeatedly linked this amendment with the advancement of truth, democracy, and self-fulfillment, it is evident that the last consideration eclipsed the first two in importance: "The First Amendment values of individual self-fulfillment through expression and individual participation in public debate are central to our concept of liberty."[5] As is plainly evident from this remark, self-fulfillment is the high goal for which self-expression and participatory democracy become the means. Improved democratic government takes the form of a significant side benefit, but still effectively a side benefit. Self-fulfillment is equated with self-construction, which in its ideal form for Brennan necessitates virtually free access to all forms of expression by others.

Bluntly stated, expression for Brennan deserves special protection against being "cabin'd, cribb'd, and confin'd," to paraphrase William Shakespeare's Macbeth, for the reason that it serves the end of control over one's destiny. The connection between freedom of expression and personal development was forcefully articulated by Brennan in a mid-1980s address at Georgetown University:

> The constitutional vision of human dignity rejects the possibility of political orthodoxy imposed from above; it respects the right of each individual to form and to express political judgments, however far they may deviate from the mainstream and however unsettling they might be to the powerful or the elite. Recognition of these rights of expression and conscience also frees up the private space for both intellectual and spiritual development free of government dominance, either blatant or subtle.[6]

An early version of this defense of expression freed of governmentally constructed obstacles is visible in Brennan's 1964 decision in *New York Times* v. *Sullivan*.[7] Here, more than in earlier cases such as *Roth*, can be found concrete evidence of his willingness to devaluate traditional governmental interests in order to free up space for personal expression.

The *Sullivan* case came to the Supreme Court against the backdrop of the civil rights movement and the *Brown* v. *Board of Education* decision of 1954. L. B. Sullivan, commissioner of public affairs in Montgomery, Alabama, had brought a libel action against the *New York Times* for printing a full-page advertisement that charged Montgomery officials with harassing black students and Dr. Martin Luther King Jr. Relying on several inaccuracies in the allegations contained in the ad, a state court awarded Sullivan general damages of $500,000. Alabama law did not require proof of pecuniary injury or loss, nor did it require a showing of malicious intent, in order to gain general damages. It was sufficient that the allegations were false. The principal question before the U.S. Supreme Court was whether the Alabama law could be reconciled with First Amendment protection for speech and press. Brennan's answer was a blunt no! After observing in *Roth* that libel, like obscenity, "was outside the protection intended for speech and press," he now declared in equally definitive fashion in *Sullivan* that even libelous expression "must be measured by standards that satisfy the First Amendment." Brennan anticipated the conclusion he would reach by noting that the case had to be considered "against the background of a profound national commitment to the principle that debate on public issues should be uninhibited, robust and wide-open. . . ."[8] That some of the statements were erroneous and that Sullivan's reputation might have been damaged were discounted as acceptable costs of "uninhibited" and "wide-open" debate. Rather than embrace an "absolutist" position on freedom of speech and press, however, Brennan instead developed the "malice rule" for which the *Sullivan* case has become famous. As will become increasingly evident, the emphasis that he gave to the effects of decisions and to maintaining flexibility in constitutional interpretation meant that he typically endorsed the practical results desired by First Amendment absolutists, but without explicitly embracing their philosophical position. Given Brennan's aims, avoiding the absolutist straitjacket made more sense than embracing it.

To recover damages for defamatory expression related to the performance of the official duties, Brennan declared in *Sullivan* that a public official must prove that the offensive statements were made with " 'actual malice'—that is, with knowledge that [they were] false or with reckless disregard of whether [they were] false or not. . . ."[9] The effect of this standard was to make it almost impossible for public officials to win libel cases and, thus, to free the print and video media to publicize allegations with minimal concern for their accuracy or impact on the confidence of the people in government. It is, of course, the latter concern that supplied the best principled defense of laws such as Alabama's that provided generous support for the reputation of public officials. After all, officials whose reputations have been tarnished are likely to be less effective in promoting law-abidingness than persons believed to be morally and civilly upright. Since suspicion of governmental power already had deep roots in modern natural rights principles, it is not surprising that Alabama's asserted interest in protecting state officials from caustic attacks that might detract from their ability to govern effectively would be challenged in a republic based on those principles. Alabama was on a collision course with justices who looked upon natural rights principles as requiring suspicion of governmental power as well as the continuous enlargement of the sphere of private decision making. The fact that it took so long to weaken statutory protection for the reputation of public servants is evidence of the continuing vitality into the twentieth century of the belief that even a democratic populace must be habituated to respect governmental institutions and the law.

Until the rights revolution in the 1960s there was a shared understanding that it was in the common interest of the people to protect the conditions that make for effective democratic government, even if not all those conditions were set out in the Constitution. Hence, for example, legislative and executive authorities were permitted to impose a variety of rights-constraining requirements on people who were in the government's employ, from limits on their freedom to engage in collective bargaining and strikes to restrictions on their ability to participate in partisan political activities. Insofar as such restraints were intended to serve the ends of effectiveness in government or to encourage public confidence in the fairness and respectability of government, they are consistent with the concerns of the Founders who believed that the success of the American republic would depend on the capacity of the political order to act decently and competently and on the perception by the people that it acted this way. The Founders also understood the importance of masking the true powers of the government in a community based on natural rights thinking that holds political power to be suspect as always capable of giving birth to tyranny.[10] If people who are anxious about governmental authority see the real power of the government, then they might be more inclined to impose debilitating checks on that power. James Madison, for example, worried that a successful effort by the Anti-Federalists to add a bill of rights to the Constitution might directly or indirectly weaken the government.[11] In fact, prominent political figures well into the twentieth century recognized that the government needed room to protect the interests of the whole community even at the cost of some confinement of personal liberties. Abraham Lincoln's suspension of the privilege of the writ of habeas corpus is one example of this thinking, Oliver Wendell Holmes's willingness while on the Massachusetts Supreme Court to limit the freedom of speech of public employees is another, and Congress's passage in 1939 of the Hatch Act with its limitations on the types of partisan activities that members of the federal civil service might engage in is still another.[12]

The federal government continued to win some significant cases involving restraints imposed on subversive activities and organizations as late as the beginning of the 1960s, or just prior to the *Sullivan* decision. Felix Frankfurter and John Marshall Harlan, for example, wrote opinions in two 1961 cases that sustained registration and reporting requirements imposed on the Communist Party. Brennan, however, submitted dissents in both *Communist Party* v. *Subversive Activities Control Board*[13] and *Scales* v. *United States*[14] that found the government's arguments insufficient to overcome constitutional requirements of due process. Insofar as Brennan began with the assumption that the government's appeal to security interests was inadequate to justify judicial deference since it carried uncertain constitutional weight, these dissents anticipate the approach that would define his opinion in *Sullivan.* By 1965, one year after he had announced that public officials must go about their work with what amounted to fig-leaf protection against defamatory allegations, Brennan was assigned the task of vindicating the position of the dissenters in the earlier Communist Party registration and reporting cases. The question in *Albertson* v. *Subversive Activities Control Board* was whether the Fifth Amendment shielded members of the Communist Party from registration requirements, and Brennan's answer was in the affirmative.[15] The threat of prosecution presented by "mere association" with this party was sufficient to support a claim of privilege.[16] Brennan had come to believe by the mid-1960s that only the courts could be trusted to be alert to the dangers of government restraint on expression and association. In what would quickly become a much cited majority opinion, he announced in matter-of-fact language in *Freedman* v. *Maryland*, a 1965 case involving a challenge to that state's motion-picture censorship statute, that "only a judicial determination in an adversary proceeding ensures the necessary sensitivity to freedom of expression."[17] In the area of expression, trust in political officials and bureaucrats, whether state or federal, and political parties was officially out of favor.

If Brennan seemed to depreciate the practical and constitutional weight of governmental interests in *Sullivan* and the Communist Party registration cases, his message would be unmistakable by the time he authored his majority opinion in *Texas* v. *Johnson,* the controversial flag-burning case of 1989, as he was closing out his career. The road to his vindication of Gregory Lee Johnson's action was paved with opinions attacking the centuries-old sovereign immunity doctrine and traditional patronage practices as well as the government's ability to counter subversive activity by compelling members of the Communist Party to comply with registration requirements.

Fiddling with the Scales:
Ratcheting Rights Up and Driving Government Interests Down

The end of the Warren Court in 1969 did not bring an end to judicial aggressiveness in the advancement of personal and group liberties. In fact, 1971 stands out as one of the most significant years in expansive First and Fourteenth Amendment jurisprudence. That year saw the Burger Court uphold court-ordered busing in *Swann* v. *Charlotte-Mecklenburg Board of Education*,[18] defeat a Nixon Administration attempt to suppress the publication of sensitive Defense Department documents on the Vietnam War in *New York Times* v. *United States*,[19] rebuff an effort by Los Angeles officials to punish an anti-war protester for offensive expression-related conduct in a courthouse in *Cohen* v. *California*,[20] extend the limits on state aid to church-affiliated schools in *Lemon* v. *Kurtzman*,[21] and assist affirmative action programs with its decision in *Griggs* v. *Duke Power Co.*[22] that rendered most applicant screening tests suspect. This was also the year of *Bivens* v. *Six Unknown Named Federal Narcotics Agents*, a case involving a damage action brought under the Fourth Amendment.[23] Brennan wrote for the majority in *Bivens* and created a new judicial remedy for people seeking damages against government employees charged with abuse of authority. Justice Harry Blackmun accused Brennan of engaging in "judicial legislation" since Congress had not decided to amend the sovereign immunity doctrine to provide for remedies in cases where federal agents violate Fourth Amendment rights in the course of performing their duties.[24] For Brennan, however, both the principle that all injuries should be subject to redress and the "[great] capacity for harm" enjoyed by government agents warranted the unilateral action taken by the Court on Bivens's behalf.

The same concern for the harms that might be inflicted by the government or its agents was also visible in Brennan's development of an almost impossible standard that would have to be satisfied to restrain publication of even classified material (*New York Times* v. *United States*, the 1971 Pentagon Papers case).[25] While avoiding a direct endorsement of Justice Hugo Black's absolutist position, Brennan did the next closest thing by declaring that "only governmental allegation and proof that publication must inevitably, directly and immediately cause the occurrence of an event kindred to imperiling the safety of a transport already at sea can support even the issuance of an interim restraining order."[26] Here is a standard that is about as close as one can get to taking an absolutist position with regard to government restraint of the press without publicly embracing absolutism. The demands made of the government by Brennan virtually guarantee in practice the same results that follow from Black's absolutist reading of the First Amendment.

The assertiveness of the *Bivens* decision and the almost impossible hurdle that Brennan erected in the Pentagon Papers case are mirrored in a number of significant opinions penned in 1970s First Amendment cases. Still avoiding an explicit endorsement of the absolutist position of Black, Brennan argued for an increasingly pure rights-oriented social order. An excellent example of his movement to a purer position on First Amendment freedoms can be found in his dissent in *Paris Adult Theatre I* v. *Slaton*.[27] Writing for the Court, Chief Justice Warren Burger upheld the imposition of a civil injunction preventing the showing of allegedly obscene films at two "adult" theaters in the Atlanta area. In language that was obviously directed at 1960s decisions such as *Stanley* v. *Georgia* that left in limbo state regulations that were based on an asserted interest in the morality of the people, Burger proclaimed that the states have a legitimate interest in regulating the commercial distribution of obscene material and the exhibition of such material in public places. He traced this interest to the authority that resides in the states to check threats to public safety and to decency in society. The fact that the theaters limited access to consenting adults did not save them from the injunction. Burger's reasoning and conclusion found no ally in Brennan.

Two important statements appear relatively early in Brennan's dissent in *Paris*. First, he announced his abandonment of the approach he had set out in *Roth*. That approach, whether in its original form or as refined subsequently, was declared by Brennan to be deficient on both First (freedom of expression) and Fifth Amendment (due process) grounds. After a sixteen-year trial period, he was now convinced that the *Roth* approach did not sufficiently shield protected expression from the chilling effect of obscenity regulations at the same time that vagueness problems exposed people to possible entrapment. The disagreements between federal and state judicial officials sparked by the existence of ambiguous standards also convinced Brennan that the time had come for a new course to be charted in the obscenity area. Clearly, however, the major difficulty had to do with what he termed the failure of the *Roth* approach to protect First Amendment "values." Here is the second important observation that comes early in his dissent. The significance of his use of the word "values" can hardly be exaggerated. In ordinary speech, values are conventionally contrived weightings that typically trace their origins to human preferences. The common tendency is not to speak of the natural value of a thing or the value conferred by nature, but rather of the value assigned by human beings who have more or less of a preference for the object in question. Looked at in this context, Brennan's reference to First Amendment values opens the door wide to constitutional relativism. It certainly fit with his belief that each generation should be permitted to determine what the Constitution means for their time. By contrast, the view that legitimate government should defend freedom of speech did not represent merely a "value" judgment for leading Founders such as Madison.

For the founding generation, the rights to freely assemble and to share ideas through speech or in print were traceable to the naturally free condition of human beings. Influential figures from the founding period such as Madison believed that individual liberties such as freedom of speech and assembly were independently validated by the modern theory of natural rights. It is also important to remember that a conception of human excellence, even if modest by Aristotelian standards, lay behind the Founders' defense of free speech, press, and assembly. This is what is revealed by Madison in his *Federalist* 10 remark that the "first object of government" is the protection of "the faculties of men" or, more to the point, the exercise of these faculties.[28] That he believed some exercises of human faculties are more defensible than others is evidenced by the distinction he drew in the same essay between unacceptable "factious" activities and activities that are not "factious in nature."[29] The word "values" conceptually diminishes the innate status of such freedoms while permitting in practice greater variability than modern natural rights theory originally allowed. The variability permitted by the use of the term "values" in *Paris* served Brennan's ends quite well. The weight of First Amendment freedoms, for example, can more easily be inflated when the emphasis is on "values" rather than on fixed principles. The flip side of this inflation of personal freedoms appears in the practice of treating government restrictions on First Amendment freedoms as inherently suspect because of their tendency to devalue, or depress the value, of these freedoms.

The beginning of Brennan's dissent in *Paris* anticipated his conclusion. Unlike Burger, Brennan concluded that he could find no state interest that would justify efforts to bar the "distribution even of unprotected material to consenting adults."[30] Although he repeatedly referred to the damage done to the Court's reputation and to its relationship to state courts by all prior and current approaches to obscenity regulation, it is clear that his principal concern was with the effect of such regulations on the First Amendment. As the following declaration makes clear, that a state's intentions are laudable and its actions carefully devised become virtually irrelevant when First Amendment freedoms are at risk: "Even a legitimate, sharply focused state concern for the morality of the community cannot, in other words, justify an assault on the protections of the First Amendment."[31] To be fair, Brennan acknowledged that the police powers embrace the regulation of activities affecting the morals of the people and he repeatedly affirmed that special weight attaches to the interest of the states in protecting children and unconsenting adults from obscene material. This said, he left little room for justifying such regulations as evidenced by his admission in a footnote late in the opinion that it would be "erroneous" to conclude from his dissent that he would concede considerable authority to the states to limit exposure of unconsenting adults and juveniles to unprotected obscene material.[32] The permissibility of such regulatory action was very much an open question in his mind.

Also indicative of the difficulties Brennan associated with legitimating obscenity regulations is his declaration in *Paris* that "unprovable, although strongly held, assumptions about human behavior" provide insufficient grounds for supporting a statute that threatens First Amendment freedoms.[33] But it is just such assumptions, as Lincoln so well reminded his contemporaries in the Gettysburg Address, that define us as a separate community. Thomas Jefferson's self-evident truth of the equality of all people was for Lincoln a "proposition" endorsed by "our fathers." "Strongly held" propositions and assumptions are the basis for virtually all legislation, as are shared "value" judgments.[34] If the desirability of autonomous individualism is the irreducible starting point of your reasoning, however, then you might conclude like Brennan that access even to ideas of little social worth should not be confined by regulations based on unproven assumptions.[35] It is this reasoning that emerges from his *Paris* dissent. Holding in reserve his views on distribution to minors and unconsenting adults, Brennan concluded that the Constitution must be interpreted to prohibit all levels of government from attempting "wholly to suppress sexually oriented materials on the basis of their allegedly 'obscene' contents."[36] The state's interest in the morality of the community effectively is subordinated to self-expression and this, in turn, is seen to be dependent on a liberal construction of First Amendment rights. The last nail in the coffin comes with an argument based on the consequences of permitting such regulatory legislation: "For if a State, in an effort to maintain or create a particular moral tone, may prescribe what its citizens cannot read or cannot see, then it would seem to follow that in pursuit of that same objective a State could decree that its citizens must read certain books or must view certain films."[37] While

Madison might argue that common sense should be sufficient to illumi-
nate the difference between restricting access to some literature and
mandating exposure to other literature, Brennan's exaggeration of the
dangers in the form of a "slippery slope" argument reveals both the
degree to which he distrusted governmental regulation of personal liberties and the immense weight that he assigned to maximizing individual
autonomy. It is the latter goal that he had in mind when he referred to
the "well-being of our free society."[38]

Any doubt that individual autonomy is integral to Brennan's interpretation of First Amendment rights can be dispelled by even a cursory
reading of his 1973 dissent in *CBS v. Democratic National Committee*,[39] a
1973 case that involved a network's refusal to air political ads.[39] On the
matter of whether CBS's refusal to air political ads ought to be treated
principally as public or private, Brennan pointed to government licensing of the broadcast media along with the distinctive power exercised
by broadcasters over the dissemination of material as evidence that the
activities of the networks partake more of the quality of public than
private action. Building on this claim, he then asserted that the purpose
of the First Amendment, the preservation of "an uninhibited marketplace of ideas," requires that people have access to "forums of communi-
cation" that will permit the widest possible dissemination of their
views.[40] By implication, access to the electronic media and effective
speech or expression are inseparable. To appreciate the full significance
of this linkage it is necessary to understand that the First Amendment for
Brennan does not stop at protecting mere speech; it also covers the
conditions for effective speech. As noted earlier, although his opinion in
CBS repeatedly linked the First Amendment with the advancement of
truth, democracy, and self-fulfillment, the last consideration clearly
eclipses the first two when all interests are weighed.[41] According to
Brennan, "The First Amendment values of individual self-fulfillment
through expression and individual participation in public debate are central to our concept of liberty."[42] Self-fulfillment really is the high goal for
which self-expression and participatory democracy become the means.
Improved democratic government is not overlooked, but it is relegated
to the status of a secondary benefit. In this same vein, adherence to
democratic proceduralism takes a backseat to the accommodation of
"individual dignity" advanced through self-expression.

What *CBS* highlights is Brennan's belief that each person be positioned to make his or her own statement on matters of personal interest.
To cite from a footnote in *CBS*: "For the individual's interest in express-
ing his own views in a manner of his own choosing is an inherently
personal one, and it can never be satisfied by the expression of 'similar'

views by a surrogate spokesman.''[43] The difference in the law between "interests" and "rights" does not seem to matter when the "interest" that is at stake has to do with self-expression. Direct personal expression alone for Brennan will permit people to gain "some measure of control over their own destinies."[44] Needless to say, the implications of this argument for representative government are enormous. The fact that Brennan had become increasingly worried about the problem of government stultification of personal expression during his first decade and a half on the Court only added to the urgency he now ascribed to freeing up access to the broadcast media. That "chilling" public action by CBS or government bureaucrats might be well intentioned and not vindictive or discriminatory counted far less in his scheme of things than the effects.[45] The attention to effects would also be writ large in his Fourteenth Amendment jurisprudence.

The cultivation of vigilance and wariness when it comes to judging the actions of public entities is reminiscent of Jefferson's insistence that decent republicanism can exist only in a society whose members understand the primacy of natural rights and have been educated to recognize and thwart threats to those rights, especially by ambitious people with access to governmental authority. Hence Jefferson's observation that should he have to chose to "have a government without newspapers, or newspapers without a government, [he] should not hesitate a moment to prefer the latter."[46] This view of healthy republicanism tolerated much more questioning of the rules and norms of society than Madison, for example, thought desirable.[47] As Jefferson assigned less weight than Madison to continuity and stability as qualities that lend strength to laws in order to maximize protection for natural rights, so Brennan likewise discounted the weight assigned to regulations or practices designed to promote security or moral decency so as to create the widest possible opening for self-defining expression or, more to the point, personal autonomy. If Brennan was at one with Jefferson when it came to cultivating vigilance and even suspicion of government officialdom, however, he was not as inclined as Jefferson to single out a specific way of life (e.g., one defined by the agrarian virtues and by a civic education that teaches the necessity of self-discipline and public vigilance) as necessary to decent republicanism.

Significantly, there is nothing in Brennan's reasoning to indicate that desirable forms of self-fulfillment, insofar as any judgments can be made about personal preferences, necessitate the capacity to exercise self-control. In this connection it bears noting that one of his concerns in *CBS* was that network executives, sensitive to the dangers posed by the airing of controversial material, may well opt for broadcasting "only established—or at least moderated—views."[48] The possibility that the very "dominance of the electronic media as the most effective means of reaching the public," which for Brennan is a reason to facilitate full public use of this technology, should in fact produce special caution or "moderation" on the part of broadcasters merits no serious attention in the dissent. To give serious attention to this possibility would risk legitimating restraint in a way that would threaten the wide-open society that has all the marks of an absolute good in Brennan's jurisprudence. The result is that moderation takes on the appearance of a vice rather than being treated as a defining quality of responsible broadcasting.

For their part, Founders such as George Washington and James Madison believed that quality democracy, as with meaningful freedom, can exist only where the passions are subject to control, or moderated, by reason or reasonable public policies. Hence Washington's tough response to the Pennsylvania insurrection of 1794 and Madison's preoccupation with checking factious interests. Besides raising a possible threat to decent democracy, self-fulfillment that is rooted merely in the historical action of expression can supply no legitimacy for personal or governmental action that cannot be challenged as simply arbitrary. If the appropriateness of expression or its validity is not based on consistency with standards that transcend discrete historical acts, all that is left is the subjective value ascribed to actions by actors based on personal or individual desires. Assuming that self-fulfillment is associated with the attainment of human excellence for Brennan, then what emerges is a formalistic view of excellence that elevates action itself over the substance or content of any action. Excellence comes to be associated with abstract action, not with a particular understanding of the desirability of some actions and not others. In effect, Brennan constructs the equivalent of a two-edged sword that can be employed in the service of anarchy as easily as it might serve the ends of civilized existence.

The same sensitivity to any restrictions on First Amendment rights that drives Brennan's dissents in *Paris* and *CBS* also was the moving force behind the plurality opinion that he authored three years later in *Elrod* v. *Burns*, a patronage case out of Illinois.[49] The question before the Court was whether patronage practices in the case of persons holding nonpolicy positions impose an unacceptable burden on protected rights. The rights Brennan had in mind were the so-called construed freedoms of belief and association, not explicit First Amendment liberties. By 1976, these construed rights, along with privacy and expression, had already been elevated to the same status as such explicit rights as freedom of speech and of the press. Unlike his colleague Black who questioned the discovery by the Court of new personal freedoms like privacy, Brennan found nothing problematical in accepting the existence of these construed rights.

Although reference is made in Brennan's opinion in *Elrod* to the "free functioning of the electoral process" and the "proper functioning" of democratic government, he left little doubt that his dominant concern was that "political belief and association" are left as unfettered as possible.[50] Citing from *New York Times* v. *United States*, the 1971 Pentagon Papers case, Brennan reminded his audience that "The loss of First Amendment freedoms, for even minimal periods of time, unquestionably constitutes irreparable injury."[51] From a 1943 flag salute case, *Board of Education* v. *Barnette*, he borrowed language that could produce only one result in *Elrod*, that is, the dismissal of the challenged practices for imposing too great a cost on constitutionally protected freedoms: "[if] there is any fixed star in our constitutional constellation, it is that no official, high or petty, can prescribe what shall be orthodox in politics, nationalism, religion, or other matters of opinion or force citizens to confess by word or act their faith therein."[52] No more damning indictment could be offered by Brennan of patronage practices in a democratic society. The utility of patronage to a vibrant two-party system or to healthy democratic government was hardly treated as a matter worthy of serious attention. As the Court after the 1960s had difficulty in assigning constitutional weight to any asserted governmental interest in protecting morality, now the healthy functioning of a competitive two-party system was relegated to the category of ambiguous government interests. In *Elrod*, as in his concurrence in the Pentagon Papers case five years earlier, Brennan presented himself as a balancer and not an absolutist, but his treatment of practical matters of governance left little room for traditionally protected governmental interests to emerge victorious when competing with individual rights claims.

In all fairness, it must be admitted that Brennan could draw on ample precedents by 1976 that also abstracted from the practical side of governance. This still does not diminish the leadership role he happily assumed in this movement. Significantly, it was precisely a concern about such practical day-to-day issues as lawlessness in the form of vigilantism and related activities that led a young Abraham Lincoln in 1838 to propose the promulgation of a "political religion" that would require that "every American . . . swear by the blood of the Revolution, never to violate in the least particular, the laws of the country; and never to tolerate their violation by others." Lincoln comes close to counseling

the use of indoctrination to reinforce law-abidingness. "Let reverence
for the laws," he added in his address, "be breathed by every American
mother, to the lisping babe, that prattles on her lap—let it be taught in
schools, in seminaries, and in colleges;—let it be written in Primmers,
spelling books, and in Almanacs;—let it be preached from the pulpit,
proclaimed in legislative halls, and enforced in courts of justice."[53] Here
was advice based on a belief that decent democratic societies are fragile
things needing careful nourishment and protection. By contrast, for
Brennan democratic orders prove their worth by surviving unending
tests of fire. There is the presumption that true democracies are sufficiently resilient to withstand such tests. This confidence is characteristic
of Wilsonian-style "end of history" reasoning, and specifically the belief
that the modern democratic state has triumphed over all rivals.

    If Lincoln worried in 1838 that lawlessness and lack of respect for
government would undermine our free society, Brennan saw government confinement of personal liberty interests as the principal threat to
be checked in the 1970s. This theme surfaced in his dissent in *Paul* v.
Davis, another 1976 case that arose out of a challenge brought by the
respondent against police officials who included his photo in a flyer
of active shoplifters.[54] He claimed damages following the dismissal of
shoplifting charges. Writing for the majority, William H. Rehnquist dismissed the claim for relief under federal statutes. Citing John Marshall's
opinion in *Marbury*, Brennan accused the majority of abdicating on the
Court's "role" as a "bulwark against governmental violation of the . . .
legitimate expectations of every person to innate human dignity and
sense of worth."[55] He saw no need to give the government the benefit
of the doubt and feared the consequences of such deference. By the
mid-1970s, appeals to the Court's role as the principal examiner of government action and to the primacy of human dignity in the constellation
of things protected by the Constitution were fixtures of his jurisprudence. By the end of the decade Brennan was a dependable critic of
any hint of judicial deference to governmental regulation in the First
Amendment area. This was amply evident in an especially revealing
1978 dissent in a case involving action taken by the Federal Communications Commission against a radio station that aired vulgar language
during afternoon hours.

    FCC v. *Pacifica Foundation* arose out of a complaint that followed
the airing of a George Carlin "Filthy Words" monologue by a New
York radio station.[56] The FCC notified the station that material such as
Carlin's monologue should be broadcast during late evening hours when
it would be less likely to be heard by children. A record of the FCC

warning was placed in the station's file. The station charged the government agency with exercising a form of censorship since the issuance even of a warning might affect a station's ability to gain recertification of its license. Justice John Paul Stevens, writing for the Court, sustained the FCC's action as a reasonable time and place regulation of expression. He took pains to note that broadcast media are easily accessible to children and that injuries can quickly occur within one's private domain from unexpected transmissions before any action can be taken by the listener. Considering the unique problems posed by the transmission of offensive language over the airways, Stevens found the action taken by the FCC to be reconcilable with the First Amendment. He was careful to stress that the decision in no way sanctioned outright censorship. In short, Stevens's tone and ruling were moderate by almost any standards. But not by Brennan's.

The fury of Brennan's dissent is testimony to the depth of both his commitment to individual autonomy and his suspicion of governmental regulatory action that constrains personal liberties. Based on an isolated reading of his dissent it would be easy to conclude that Stevens had authorized the government to engage in the kind of limitations on speech and expressive action associated with the Star Chamber or with the Alien and Sedition Acts of 1798. Stevens's restrained acceptance of the FCC's time and place order became for Brennan "another in the dominant culture's inevitable efforts to force those groups who do not share its mores to conform to its way of thinking, acting, and speaking."[57] This observation had been preceded by another in which he asserted that the majority was guilty of "acute ethnocentric myopia."[58] By the standards of the street, this may be tepid rhetoric, but in learned circles in the late 1970s, Brennan's charges were damning in nature. To accuse a person of acute ethnocentric myopia was harsh criticism at a time when the failure to endorse ethnic diversity and multiculturalism was generally associated with racism and other forms of social and political extremism. For Brennan, the regime of the First Amendment must not only permit, but really invite, people to "flout majoritarian conventions" and to "[use] words that may be regarded as offensive by those from different socio-economic backgrounds."[59] It is up to the people to decide whether they wish to engage in such communications or hear such expression from others. Without doubt, his ideal was a "marketplace unsullied by the censor's hand."[60]

While Holmes had defended the "marketplace of ideas" concept much earlier in the century, he left room for regulation of speech and press when circumstances warranted. Brennan's formula now left little room for government regulation. In point of fact, all he was doing was taking Holmes's reasoning to its next level, but this in itself is not insignificant. Where Holmes left a real opening for public policies that restrict lifestyle choices so long as they emerge from a free and democratic marketplace of ideas, Brennan's response in *Pacifica Foundation* was that the upbringing of children is the responsibility of parents with little if any opening for government involvement. He added that some parents may wish to make the offensive language of Carlin's monologue part of the education received by their children. There is no discernible room for the government to second-guess the decisions that parents might make in these matters, even if the government is reflecting majority preferences that have been shaped by exchanges within an unfettered marketplace of ideas. Indeed, it is precisely for deferring to such majoritarian policies that Stevens comes under withering attack.

Based on his opinions in cases such as *Pacifica Foundation* and *Paris Adult Theatre*, the signal being sent by Brennan at the end of the 1970s was that danger lurked everywhere. The actions of political officials, especially on the state level, bureaucrats, political parties, and majority coalitions were all suspect. What is not suspect is a judiciary populated by jurists who are disposed to use their authority to advance the ideal of libertarian dignity. Here is Brennan's own version of a defensible form of spiritedness employed in the service of a society whose highest goal is to promote individual autonomy and self-determination through robust, uninhibited, and wide-open expression. The clear emphasis is on protecting expression as a form of action, not thought. Any effort to make *thoughtfulness* relevant to decisions about what expressions to protect would threaten the openness Brennan believed crucial to true self-determination and "dignified" existence. Admittedly, the argument that protecting free expression is good for democracy never disappears from sight. It is revealing, however, that he was not uncomfortable in authoring his opinion in *Elrod* without carefully scrutinizing the possibility that patronage practices might be good for democratic government. The final litmus test is not whether democratic processes of governance permit majority coalitions to emerge victorious in both electoral and policy battles, or that governmental institutions attain a higher degree of competence and efficiency, but whether individuals are generally free to define their own way of life, especially through expressive activity.

While it would be difficult to be bolder than he was in *Pacifica Foundation*, Brennan's uncompromising insistence on judicial preservation of the maximum of individual autonomy continued to be writ large in the opinions he submitted in First Amendment cases until his retire-

ment in 1990. He saw himself advancing just this objective when he led
the Court in limiting the power of school boards to remove books from
middle school and high school libraries in *Board of Education, Island Trees
Union Free School District* v. *Pico.*[61] For Brennan, these libraries are best
seen as places of individual enrichment and self-education. Free access
to ideas in school libraries is a prerequisite in his mind to "active and
effective participation in the pluralistic, often contentious society in
which [students] will soon be adult members."[62] What Brennan saw in
such school board action was an obvious attempt to suppress unwanted
ideas. Interestingly, he sidestepped the fact that ideas also can be weeded
out in the process of making decisions about what material to add to a
school library. But while he observed that his decision did not "affect in
any way the discretion of a local school board to choose books to *add* to
the libraries of their schools," he had to be hoping that the message he
was sending would affect decisions having to do with both the removal
and the addition of library material. As in *Pacifica Foundation*, evidence
that public officials might be attempting to determine what should be
"orthodox" or acceptable in society brought a stern warning from Brennan. Certainly by the time of *Pico* in 1982, the authority that Founders
such as Washington and statesmen such as Lincoln would have entrusted
to the government to give some shape to public opinions and conduct
was rendered entirely suspect by Brennan's jurisprudence. With rights
expanded to serve something approximating autonomous individualism,
any government action that smacked of promoting conformity, or even
a preference for particular values, took on the appearance of being tyrannical. This is not insignificant. When sensitivity to governmental constraints is heightened to the point where any exercise of authority can
be construed as potential or actual tyrannical action, then instilling a
habit of law-abidingness in the citizen body may prove to be an impossible task for public officials.. That such effects might follow from his reasoning serves to dramatize why it is necessary to study the political
consequences of judicial decision making.

Making Certain the "First" Does Not Come Last

The First Amendment themes that resounded with ever-increasing
vibrancy in Brennan's writings from *Sullivan* to *Pacifica Foundation* received their final uncompromising articulation by him in several controversial majority opinions he authored during his last two years on the
Court. At least as far as the First Amendment is concerned, Brennan

retired as the intensity of his arguments was reaching the crescendo stage. The decisions that he handed down in *Texas* v. *Johnson* (flag burning— 1989) and *Rutan* v. *Republican Party of Illinois* (patronage-based restrictions on association and belief—1990) represented major victories for his expansive view of the liberties covered by the First Amendment. His success came at the expense of Justices such as Rehnquist and Antonin Scalia whose defense of judicial self-restraint and a literalist interpretation of the Constitution failed to command sufficient support to protect asserted governmental and political interests against individual rights claims. If we could assume that Brennan had the ability to predict in 1956 how his career would end in 1990, then here might be an explanation for the report carried in the *New York Times* that he seemed "immensely pleased" at the news conference announcing his appointment to the Court. In the minds of scholars and others who value self-determination through broad freedom of expression and association, *Texas* v. *Johnson* and *Rutan* allowed Brennan, like so many romanticized "old western" heroes, to retire in a blaze of glory.

The Court agreed to hear *Texas* v. *Johnson*, a highly controversial and much publicized flag desecration case, at the end of Ronald Reagan's second term.[63] Even many of Reagan's critics conceded that he had done the country a favor by successfully reawakening a spirit of patriotism in the people. He worked hard to etch the image of America as a shining city upon a hill into the consciousness of the people. His efforts were supported by the work of prominent religious leaders such as Jerry Falwell and Pat Robertson who counseled respect for old-fashioned American values, which for them were largely derivative from the Judeo-Christian tradition. The combination of these developments meant that while the situation that existed when the Court heard *Texas* v. *Johnson* was not identical to what it faced in *Brown* v. *Board of Education* or *Roe* v. *Wade*, the *Johnson* case came very close to matching the political volatility of *Brown* and *Roe*.

Gregory Lee Johnson was one of a number of demonstrators who gathered in Dallas in 1984 to protest the policies of the Reagan Administration while the Republican Party was holding its national convention. The demonstrators marched through parts of Dallas while chanting political slogans that were critical of the Republicans and several Dallas-based corporations. As the demonstration drew to a conclusion in front of the city hall building, Johnson doused a flag that had been handed him by a fellow protester with kerosene and set it on fire. Johnson was later arrested and prosecuted for desecrating a "venerated object." Although initially convicted and sentenced to one year in prison and fined

$2,000, the Texas Court of Criminal Appeals found for Johnson on the grounds that the First Amendment protected his expressive activity. In his opinion for the Supreme Court, Brennan affirmed the ruling of the Court of Criminal Appeals.

It is clear from the outset of Brennan's opinion that he believed the doctrinal foundation for a ruling in favor of Johnson was already solidly rooted in existing First Amendment law. By targeting expression for confinement in order to protect governmental interests, Texas subjected itself in his view to the highest form of judicial scrutiny. In defense of their position, Texas officials claimed that Johnson could be prosecuted for engaging in actions that threatened breaches of the peace and that the state possessed authority to preserve the flag "as a symbol of *nationhood* and *national unity*."[64]

For Brennan, "no reasonable onlooker" could have interpreted Johnson's action as a "direct personal insult or an invitation to exchange fisticuffs."[65] The assumption that "reasonable onlookers" understand the importance of toleration and of preserving a climate hospitable to the exchange of ideas is critical to the conclusion that little if any room should exist for the regulation of expression on breach of the peace grounds. By definition, Brennan's "reasonable onlookers" would tolerate a limitless variety of expressions in order to have a healthy democratic society.

What Brennan's argument does not account for is the presence in society of unreasonable as well as reasonable people. One of the principal purposes of legislation is to control and direct the conduct of unreasonable persons. While Brennan's argument might make considerable sense in a republic that values freedom of expression and is composed entirely of reasonable people, his approach has a potentially disabling effect in a social order made up of both reasonable and unreasonable persons. This point is significant not only in terms of the requirements that might be set for a "fighting words" prosecution, but with regard to Texas's claim to be able to preserve the flag as an object of veneration and "nationhood." Political orders rely on a combination of compulsion and instinctual obedience to govern unreasonable people. As for a choice between reliance on force and right habituation, most people would say that the second approach better suits a democracy than the first. Waving the flag while playing the national anthem, for example, can be an effective way of getting some people to cooperate with essential public policies that are otherwise unintelligible to them. The ideal, of course, is to have a republic made up entirely of persons with whom it is possible to enter into reasoned discourse about what is proper, right, or just. No nation state, however, has ever been so fortunate as to have had only such citizens. Brennan could not allow the presence of unreasonable types to justify restraints of the sort imposed by Texas for the same reason that he objected to Burger's appeal to morality in *Paris Adult Theatre* and to tradition in *Lynch* v. *Donnelly*, an establishment clause case involving the display of a nativity scene on public property. In each instance, the argument used to defend the challenged action leaves the door open to government constraints on the ability of people to pursue a preferred way of life. The alternative approach reflected in Brennan's opinions is to presume that the actions of someone like Johnson are unproblematical or should be unproblematical. Providing constitutional cover for flag burning was the equivalent for Brennan of declaring that "right reason" favored toleration of Johnson's conduct.

In short order, then, Brennan reduced Texas's case to the claim that a state may protect the flag as an important symbol. The response that he crafted to this claim was clever and revealing. After asserting that the action taken by Texas was content-based or designed to regulate the message being communicated, he reminded state officials that they are powerless to drive out ideas merely because society finds them to be "offensive or disagreeable." Brennan added that he saw no neutral or objective way of discriminating between symbols that are "sufficiently special" to warrant unusual protection and others that lack such status. In his words, "To conclude that the government may permit designated symbols to be used to communicate only a limited set of messages would be to enter territory having no discernible or defensible boundaries."[66] The absence of a bright line or clear principle that would allow "special" symbols to be easily identified and protected leaves the states and the country in his estimation with no alternative but to group the flag with all other unprotected governmental symbols. The response that common sense might provide some guidance in making such distinctions does not figure into his "constitutional" calculations.

Brennan's opinion ends with the disarming observation that the state's interest in promoting respect for the flag and the country will best be advanced by protecting Johnson's actions. In effect, Texas officials are told that they will get more of what they really want by protecting Johnson than by convicting him. The unmistakable message is that toleration of Johnson's actions will be construed as a sign of the country's strength and commitment to individual liberty. Brennan added in closing that the way to "preserve the flag's special role is not to punish those who feel differently about these matters. It is to persuade them that they are wrong."[67] Johnson's critics are invited to fly their own flags and to "counter a flag-burner's message . . . by saluting the flag that burns. . . ."[68] The argument that the proper response to bad speech is toleration and good speech was hardly Brennan's invention, it can be traced at least as far back in American constitutional law to the opinions of Holmes and Louis Brandeis in *Gitlow* v. *New York* and *Whitney* v. *California* in the 1920s. The Court, however, had not bought into these arguments in *Gitlow* and *Whitney*. Justice Edward Sanford wrote opinions for the Court in both cases that reflected traditional thinking about what governments are permitted to do in the name of self-defense or self-preservation to protect the way of life of the people. By 1989, however, Brennan was able to put together a majority that went along with the claim that government may not protect special symbols from abuse as a way of impressing "unreasonable" persons with the importance of law-abidingness or as a form of self-defense. Gone from view is the effect of actions such as Johnson's on "[un]reasonable onlookers" who may interpret the state's inability to protect the flag, or outright toleration of flag burning, as a sign of weakness. It might easily be argued, for example, that the state's interest in preserving the integrity of symbols or emblems of the country such as the flag is great precisely due to the special difficulties involved in governing unreasonable, not reasonable, people. For those citizens who are deaf to the appeals of reason, the state must govern through force or appeals to passion or emotion. In democratic societies, moving people to behave by appeals to passion is much more desirable than ruling persons through the exercise of force or authority. Brennan's reasoning in *Johnson,* however, may have the ironic effect of leaving political officials with having to rely more on force to govern people if they are not to settle for a situation where responsible behavior is merely a product of chance or good luck.

While Brennan was successful in forging a coalition to support his position in *Johnson,* he did not escape unattacked. Rehnquist submitted an emotional dissent that opened with a review of the special place that the American flag has occupied in the country's history. His account included numerous references to the "mystical reverence" shown the flag by Americans in general, and especially by troops in wartime. With this appeal to patriotism as a kind of preface, Rehnquist developed a legal argument with a twofold thrust. On the one side, he set out to devalue Johnson's activity by observing that the public burning of the flag is "no essential part of any exposition of ideas." This argument played on the Court's declaration in *Chaplinsky* v. *New Hampshire,* a 1942 case involving the use of "fighting words" directed at a policeman by a Jehovah's Witness, that some forms of expression "are no essential

part of any exposition of ideas, and are of such slight social value as a
step to truth that any benefit that may be derived from them is clearly
outweighed by the social interest in order and morality."[69] Once having
reduced the constitutional value of Johnson's action to his satisfaction,
Rehnquist then sought to add to the weight of the state's claim by noting
that there was good reason to believe that the controversial effect of flag
burning might incite a breach of the peace. In the context of the weights
he finally assigned to the competing interests, the burden on Texas was
simply to establish the reasonableness of its action. The state did this to
Rehnquist's satisfaction. In a passage that harkens back to earlier views
of what the government may do in the name of self-defense or self-
preservation, Rehnquist reminded Brennan that "[surely] one of the
high purposes of a democratic society is to legislate against conduct that
is regarded as evil and profoundly offensive to the majority of
people. . . ."[70] He then added that the Court's decision to protect flag
burning "risks the frustration of the very purpose for which organized
governments are instituted."[71] Implicit in this reasoning was an attack on
much of the thrust of First Amendment law since Brennan's appointment to the Court.

Arguments such as those offered by Rehnquist, however, could
only have had the effect of leading Brennan to redouble his resolve to
protect activities such as Johnson's. The completed or fully consummated democratic state for Brennan cannot coexist with the suppression
of expression by any majority on grounds of offensiveness, nor can it
exist in the presence of the belief that governments should be permitted
to confine the expressive activities of some persons because others in
the community may not be "reasonable onlookers." If anything, the
argument that some people may be governable only when symbols of
the nation are protected against desecration, and when majoritarian preferences on matters such as flag burning are enforceable against dissenters,
could only provoke Brennan to further solidify his views on the importance of judicial aggressiveness in protecting self-defining expression.
The decision in *Johnson* was an unmistakable shot across the bow of
Reaganite Republicans and the religious right in America. Lincoln's call
for the cultivating of law-abidingness became all but a moot issue in
liberal jurisprudence by 1989. In terms of the realities of governance,
however, Brennan's expansive reading of First Amendment liberties was
far from unproblematical.

If Brennan put both national and state officials on notice that they
must make their peace with expression that offends national pride or
patriotism in *Johnson*, he reminded party officials that they may not use

political power to chill forms of association or belief with which they disagree in *Rutan* v. *Republican Party of Illinois* one year later. The issue in *Rutan* was the constitutionality of basing promotion or transfer decisions in the case of public employees on party affiliation or support. In *Elrod*, Brennan had written an opinion for the Court that found patronage dismissals in the case of persons in nonpolicy making positions to be in violation of the First Amendment. Now the Court was being asked to extend the proscription to promotions, transfers, recalls from layoffs, and related personnel decisions.

Brennan had no difficulty in dismissing the argument that the petitioners in *Rutan* were disabled from appealing to the First Amendment since they had no right to transfers or promotions. While the Court has not held that people can claim to possess a public office as a matter of right, by 1990 it had been well established that public benefits could not be made available on terms that infringe constitutionally protected interests. The old privilege doctrine that permitted governments great latitude in imposing conditions on the holding of public offices had been discredited by the end of the 1960s with decisions such as *Pickering* v. *Board of Education*, a case that overturned disciplinary action against a teacher who had written a letter to a local newspaper in which he criticized the school board for its handling of budgetary matters.[72] To the claim that the challenged personnel practices were not punitive, Brennan responded that political loyalty tests place some employees in the position of having to compromise their political views and affiliations or suffer adverse employment-related consequences. He could find no gain in terms of increased governmental efficiency or greater vitality for the political parties that might justify the damage done to First Amendment rights.

As in the Pentagon Papers case and elsewhere, Brennan refused to embrace an absolutist position at the same time that he made it difficult if not impossible for the government or political officials to produce sufficient evidence to offset the weight of First Amendment freedoms. Where Scalia in dissent in *Rutan* assigned considerable weight to tradition and the contribution of patronage practices to producing healthy political parties, Brennan demanded a demonstrable connection between political affiliation and effectiveness in carrying out assigned duties. Only if patronage practices pass a version of strict scrutiny would Brennan accede to them. The practices challenged in *Rutan* obviously failed this test.

Scalia responded with a "balancing" approach that only required evidence that patronage practices provide support for the two-party system and, by extension, American democracy. The connection between patronage and party discipline as well as the utility of patronage in fostering the integration of immigrants and minorities into society and the political process supplied all the proof that he believed was needed to sustain the challenged practices. As for the charge of coercion in the realm of association and expression, Scalia saw this as an exaggeration of the situation faced by someone who occupies a patronage position. He just did not see that anyone was being coerced into breaking a law or violating the Constitution. It was his position that people were merely being asked to go along with a reasonable, but admittedly not the only, way of organizing a public personnel system. It should be sufficient in his view that the demand that government employees give allegiance to the dominant political party be shown to be one useful way of protecting the health and vitality of the two-party system and democratic political processes. Needless to add, these arguments are convincing only if you both depreciate the First Amendment problem created by patronage practices and elevate the significance of the governmental or political interests that the practices are designed to promote. By 1990, and after rejecting similar arguments from Rehnquist in *Texas* v. *Johnson*, Brennan's refusal to go along with both sides of Scalia's equation was predictable.

A Whole Greater than the Parts

If appeals to rights even as recently as during the New Deal period were couched in the language of traditional social, economic, and political institutions such as free markets and coalitional politics, Brennan labored hard during his thirty-four terms to separate rights-based claims from such potentially confining contexts. This was clearly apparent in his opinion for the Court in *Eisenstadt* v. *Baird*, the 1972 Massachusetts case having to do with the distribution of contraceptives to minors by nonlicensed people.[73] Where seven years earlier in *Griswold* v. *Connecticut* the Court had overturned a state law that restricted access to contraceptives on the grounds of interference with intimacies that lie at the core of the marriage relationship, Brennan eagerly observed in *Eisenstadt* that the right to privacy protects the freedom of "individuals," whether married or not, to decide if they wish to beget a child.[74] Venturing into what Burger in dissent called the "uncircumscribed area of personal predilections," Brennan pierced through established social and political forms and institutions to protect individual decision making.[75] This is also what he was doing in First Amendment cases such as *Paris Adult Theatre* and *Texas* v. *Johnson*.

Brennan's project represented a well-intentioned effort to consummate what earlier twentieth-century liberals had initiated. The goal was to have a social order that permitted people the maximum degree of self-expression and self-determination. For Brennan, human beings affirm their humanness and gain dignity through the different forms of expression that are equated with control over their own life. On one level, this willingness to see history and prevailing social norms weakened as potential obstacles to self-direction fits with the view, often associated with the nineteenth-century philosopher of liberalism John Stuart Mill, that critical questioning constitutes a far more enlightened basis for decision making than tradition. But at a deeper level, Brennan's purpose can only be achieved if the devaluation of history and tradition is not tied to a defense of enlightened action. It is noteworthy, for example, that he did not dwell on the fact that freedom of expression does not equate to reasoned speech or that the defense of expression in apolitical terms can end up legitimating antipolitical, or at least politically undesirable, results. Nor do we find him reflecting on the difficulties presented by the fact that not all human beings adhere to his standards of reasonable action. What is commonly found in his legal writings is the expectation that people will act reasonably, usually meaning with toleration, when they encounter someone in the process of burning an American flag or that they can be made to understand why the death penalty amounts to cruel and unusual punishment even in the case of a person convicted of the most heinous of crimes. As he was prepared to trust people to be understanding (not withstanding his skeptical approach to majoritarian perspectives), so he believed that democratic institutions are largely self-sustaining.

Where Plato, or even a modern theorist like Jean-Jacques Rousseau, believed that decent political orders are fragile and require censorship of some forms of expression, whether it be Homer's observations on the warring tendencies of the gods or the dangers of the theater to the republican virtues of the people of Geneva, Brennan saw the absence of censorship as a mark of a society that is confident of its resilience and that values the fullest expression of human freedom. Censorship represented for Plato and Rousseau a form of action designed for self-defense in the highest sense, that is, preserving the way of life of a civilized people. In the context of this historical defense of censorship, expression that endangers prevailing moral norms can be confined as legitimately as speech or publications that threaten national security. Although they were operating fully within the modern natural rights tradition, there was still something of the traditional understanding of what is required to preserve a decent society reflected in the thinking of Madison and other leading Founders who worked on the Constitution and Bill of Rights. While Madison clearly understood the importance of First Amendment freedoms, he recognized that some confinement of even fundamental liberties was essential to the advancement of comfortable preservation for the people as a whole. Hence his expressed fear that the emphasis on the preservation of personal freedoms desired by some Anti-Federalists might undermine the strength of the new national government established by the Constitution. It is too often forgotten that when Madison identified in *Federalist* 51 the principal objectives that had to inform the work of the Constitutional Convention he first singled out the importance of seeing that the government would be capable of "control[ling] the governed."[76] Only as a second task did he identify the importance of ensuring that the government was arranged to "control itself." The constitutional protection for speech, press, and assembly sought by Madison was linked to this understanding of what is required to have a competent and effective democratic order. These freedoms were understood to be essential to healthy or beneficial political discourse. The Madisonian view of the First Amendment also comprehended protection for the proper exercise of the "faculties" of the people, to paraphrase *Federalist* 10. What is too often forgotten is that this protection for political speech or the exercise of personal "faculties" in the acquisition of property represented ways of limiting as well as liberating human action. Madison was seeking to protect a specific way of life and left a real opening for restricting forms of expressive action that might not promote that way of life. He saw the utility and necessity, in other words, of fostering a prejudice in favor of beneficial institutions and practices.

By contrast with the historical defense of censorship, Brennan assumed the resilience of modern democratic orders and the desirability of enlarging the sphere of autonomous individual action. Thus he inflated the "value" of First Amendment freedoms and assigned less weight to preserving the requisites of competent and effective government than did Madison. By abstracting from the specific concerns and fears that lie behind *Federalist* 10 or Rousseau's critique of the presence of the theater in Geneva, Brennan freed himself to challenge both the necessity and the desirability of any confinement of expressive action.

Brennan believed that it was not unrealistic to call for liberation from established practices and opinions in order to advance personal dignity because he was confident that persons could be made to see their common rights and overlapping interests. In short, the relativism with regard to the opinions and preferences of all people that Brennan posited as essential to the affirmation of the dignity of all persons is rooted in his optimism about the possibility of universal reasonableness, for example, the reasonableness presumed of the people who viewed Johnson's act of flag burning. In this same vein, the reduction of speech to mere expression, as well as the reference to First Amendment "values" and the attention to the effects of judicial interpretation rather than the discovery of original intentions, accommodates the egalitarianism of Brennan's First Amendment jurisprudence as well as his belief in the desirability of the continuous shaping and reshaping of lives in the name of "dignified" existence.

What is sacrificed, however, in the name of openness to all forms of expression, and in the cause of universal self-determination, is the possibility for distinguishing between speech that serves the ends of justice or the common good, or that which is beautiful, and that which is not. In the context of Brennan's jurisprudence there really can be no larger truth than individual opinions or preferences. In this sense the real must always be individual. But the process of reducing personal opinions to mere preferences whose ultimate worth cannot be tested or known in any definitive way necessarily trivializes those opinions or, worse yet, reduces them to the status of prejudices. This is true whether the aim is to have a society whose members engage in easygoing and nonjudgmental conversations or in the spirited exchange of radical opinions and ideas. Insofar as the making and remaking of ourselves through expression becomes the decisive human action, then we become mere historical beings whose lives are abstracted from standards that permit judgments to be made about what is just or good which are not merely subjective judgments or the product of power politics. There is nothing here to prevent people from seeking to give meaning to their existence through Nietzschean-like exertions of will, even if only on the scale of a flag burner. Nor is it possible within this framework to claim with any persuasiveness that prejudices that favor established institutions are better than prejudices that do not support these institutions. An alternative to this view is to argue that reasonable action necessitates the separation of reason from unreason and the advancement of the one and the discouragement of the other.

It seems not unfair to conclude that life in a society that effectively places the actions of unreasonable people on a plane with reasoned actions could be quite unpleasant, especially for reasonable people. Surely this could be a dispiriting experience for any reasonable person. Moreover, the effect of detaching or severing First Amendment law from some of the deepest convictions and prejudices of the people could be quite unsettling for any community. Radically unselfconscious people, especially if they are blind to their own mortality, may lead free and distinctive lives, but they are also likely to be prone to unpredictable behavior. The reply to these reservations, of course, is that Brennan's ideal is to have a society of reasonable people. Until this occurs, people who are "enlightened"—as defined by his standards—will understand the case for affording everyone the opportunity to affirm his or her dignity through robust and uninhibited expression. At the same time, people who are unwilling to abide unorthodox or unpleasant expression may have to be subjected to greater control than either Neo-Nazis who insist on engaging in public demonstrations or persons who wish to burn the American flag.

Where some naturalists undermine personal responsibility and accountability by treating all action as derivative from genes or environment, Brennan's jurisprudence carries the danger of undermining personal accountability by freeing people from constraints based on the prevailing norms and traditions of society. If the position staked out by many naturalists makes it impossible for persons to claim real authorship of anything, Brennan unleashes individuals to claim an almost infinite right to extend personal authorship to all things. Why the unleashing of human action that may be entirely self-regarding should not lead in practice to anarchy or barbarism rather than civilization is not clear in his jurisprudence, especially as long as the problems posed by the presence of unreasonable persons have not disappeared. According to Alexis de Tocqueville, the task of political leadership in democratic times is to contain the problems arising from individualism that threaten civilized existence. These problems take the form of mediocrity and soft despotism, or the appearance of a government that "provides for [the people's] security, foresees and supplies their necessities, facilitates their pleasures, manages their principal concerns, directs their industry, makes rules for their testaments, and divides their inheritances."[77] Tocqueville's proposal for dealing with mediocrity and soft despotism was to so arrange society as to encourage the cultivation of proper mores, or customs, habits, and opinions, in the people. He did not hesitate to distinguish between mores that are productive of a decent democracy and those that are not. Respect for formalities and appropriate traditions, administrative decentralization, and the restraining effect of religion on materialism are among the lessons set out in *Democracy in America*.

Tocqueville's fears regarding the ill effects that might arise from the unleashing of democratic impulses had been anticipated by Madison during the founding period. An important part of Madison's response to what he took to be the characteristic problem of modern democracies, factiousness, was to create a government that could "control the governed." It was his keen awareness of the ease with which people give in to factious impulses that explains his reluctance to assign too much prominence to a bill of rights and to encourage the investment of personal energy in economic or commercial more than in narrow philosophical pursuits. It may seem ironic at the end of the twentieth century that the "father" of the Bill of Rights wanted to tame rather than inflame the tendency of the people to use the rhetoric of rights to challenge governmental action. The explanation is that Madison understood that it is possible to appeal too easily and frequently to one's rights; that is, that it is possible to have too much of a good thing. If it might accurately be argued that in Brennan's ideal society the affairs of the people would all but take care of themselves, Madison believed that public affairs must be carefully managed by persons who understand human instincts and impulses as well as the limits of what can be achieved in political life.

While Brennan avoided embracing First Amendment absolutism in the fashion of Justice Black and never abandoned his healthy reservations about the threats posed by a national bureaucratic state, what is not highlighted in Brennan's jurisprudence that is prominent in Tocqueville's and Madison's political thought is the recognition that civilized democracy comprises a specific way of life that necessitates the careful channeling of individual impulses.[78] Tocqueville, for example, recommended that special efforts be made in democratic states to entice people to join associations and become active in local government. These were for him devices that work to moderate individualism and preserve in the people a capacity to maintain democracy with liberty. As for Madison, he urged that people be encouraged to invest themselves in pursuits that are likely to moderate rather than inflame factious tendencies and impulses. Hence his preference for an attachment to economic or commercial activities that require compromise or negotiation for them to be successful. In short, there would seem to be a greater role for the prudent shaping of expression and association for Tocqueville and Madison, for a special kind of democratic statesmanship in the area of First Amendment freedoms, than is acknowledged by Brennan.

If Brennan is right about the resilience of the American democratic order and the connection between human dignity and the ability of people to make and remake themselves virtually at will, then every moment's toleration of restrictions based on an attachment to a fixed way of life tied to traditional values does violence to the rights of the members of the community. On the other hand, if Brennan's thinking prevails but his assumptions are faulty, then there is good reason to fear that the democratic republic that Madison labored so hard to construct will be in serious peril. To say this is not to question the depth or sincerity of Brennan's commitment to advance the best interests of the people. What can and must be questioned is whether their interests will finally be advanced if his views prevail. In the case of persons like Brennan who actively seek to exercise influence or power, the desire to do good is an insufficient shield against criticism when the effects of their actions harm national interests. Shakespeare reminded his readers in *King Lear* that even the noblest of people can shake social orders to their foundations by demanding that they accommodate demands that exceed their limits. This is one of the overarching issues that also arises in connection with Brennan interpretation of the Fourteenth Amendment, a subject to which we now turn.

Notes

1. That censorship might be a necessary mechanism for the promotion of decent republicanism is the major theme of Rousseau's famous letter to D'Alembert on the theater. Rousseau worried about the effect of both comedies and tragedies on community spirit and on the qualities of character that he believed would be required for modern republics to sustain true human liberty. See Allan Bloom, trans., *Politics and the Arts* (Ithaca: Cornell University Press, 1960).

2. 354 U.S. 476 (1957).

3. 376 U.S. 254 (1962).

4. 412 U.S. 94 (1973).

5. Ibid. at 201. Brennan worried about government action that might provoke self-censorship no less than regulations that amounted to direct censorship. In this connection, see his dissent in *City of Lakewood* v. *Plain Dealer Publishing Co.*, 486 U.S. 750 (1988).

6. Brennan, "Address to the Text and Teaching Symposium," in *The Great Debate: Interpreting Our Written Constitution* (Washington: Federalist Society, 1986), 22–23.

7. 376 U.S. 254 (1964). The importance of facilitating "public scrutiny" of government operations is a theme addressed by Brennan in his concurrence in *Richmond Newspapers, Inc.* v. *Virginia*, 448 U.S. 555, 592 (1980).

8. 376 U.S. at 270. Several footnote references to John Stuart Mill's *On Liberty* appear in Brennan's opinion. See ibid. at 272, n. 13, and 279, n. 19. Brennan's arguments in *Sullivan* represented an enlargement on the theme of his opinion in *Speiser* v. *Randall* in which he rejected a state restriction on extending a veterans' tax exemption to people who advocated the violent overthrow of

the government: "The man who knows that he must bring forth proof and persuade another of the lawfulness of his conduct necessarily must steer far wider of the unlawful zone than if the State must bear these burdens." 347 U.S. 442, 526 (1958). Brennan also anticipated later attacks on the privilege doctrine with his declaration in *Speiser* that the states may not infringe free speech on the grounds that the benefit that would be lost was merely a privilege and not a right.

9. 376 U.S. at 280. Seven years after *Sullivan*, Brennan extended the malice rule to a civil libel action based on a radio broadcast about a person's involvement in an event of public interest. The "public interest" principle significantly expanded the reach of the malice rule beyond public officials to the chagrin of Justice White, who accused Brennan of "displac[ing] more state libel law than [was] necessary to decide the case." *Rosenbloom v. Metromedia*, 403 U.S. 29, 41, 59 (1971).

10. An excellent account of how modern liberal states must hide political power to preserve it is found in Harvey C. Mansfield Jr., *Taming the Prince: The Ambivalence of Modern Executive Power* (New York: Free Press, 1989).

11. A provocative treatment of Anti-Federalist fears regarding the creation of a strong national government and a large commercial republic appears in Herbert J. Storing, *What the Anti-Federalists Were For* (Chicago: University of Chicago Press, 1981).

12. Holmes's declaration that people in the government's employ might be required to limit their speech appeared in *McAuliffe v. Mayor of New Bedford*, 155 Mass. 216 (1892).

13. 367 U.S. 1 (1961).

14. 367 U.S. 203 (1961). Harlan and Brennan also found themselves on opposite sides in several controversial criminal due process cases in the 1960s. Where Brennan went along with extending the right to counsel to the accusatory stage in *Escobedo v. Illinois* (378 U.S. 478 [1964]) and to virtually any police interrogation in *Miranda v. Arizona* (384 U.S. 436 [1966]), Harlan authored stinging dissents that attacked the majority for undermining law enforcement in America (see 378 U.S. at 493). Brennan persisted in his efforts to ensure maximum protection against "coercive" police practices during the 1970s in several forceful dissents (see *Harris v. New York*, 401 U.S. 222 [1971] and *Michigan v. Mosley*, 423 U.S. 96 [1975]).

15. 382 U.S. 70 (1965).

16. Ibid. at 77.

17. 380 U.S. 51, 58 (1965).

18. 402 U.S. 1 (1971).

19. 403 U.S. 713 (1971).

20. 403 U.S. 15 (1971).

21. 403 U.S. 602 (1971).

22. 401 U.S. 424 (1971).

23. 403 U.S. 388 (1971).

24. Ibid. at 430. Brennan applied the argument found in *Bivens* to municipalities in his majority opinion in *Owen v. City of Independence*, 445 U.S. 622 (1980). Among other points, Brennan ruled in *Owen* that mere assertions that local officials acted in "good faith" will not shield municipalities from liability actions brought against them. He added that the Court had to presume that Congress

intended to extend liability to municipalities in the absence of direct evidence
to the contrary. This interpretation was required by the principle that the Constitution and the nation's laws are designed to ensure that all rights are protected
and all injuries are redressed. To quote from the opinion: "How 'uniquely amiss'
it would be, therefore, if the government itself—'the social organ to which all
in our society look for the promotion of liberty, justice, fair and equal treatment,
and the setting of worthy norms and goals for social conduct'—were permitted
to disavow liability for the injury it has begotten." Ibid. at 651. It made sense to
Brennan that the "whole people" should bear the cost of repairing any damage
done to individual parties by municipal action. This argument is in contrast with
the more traditional position that a reasonable case can be made for protecting
the "whole people" from the costs of official actions gone awry by not requiring
that the community cover such costs for all victims. Writing in dissent in this
5–4 case, Lewis Powell suggested that Brennan's decision would "hamper local
governments unnecessarily." Ibid. at 658.

    25. 403 U.S. 713 (1971).

    26. Ibid. at 726–727.

    27. 413 U.S. 49 (1973). Brennan authored a number of opinions for the
Court in the obscenity area between *Roth* and *Paris Adult Theatre*. In *Ginzburg*
v. *United States*, one of several obscenity cases heard by the Court in 1966,
Brennan upheld a conviction on the grounds that there was evidence that the
petitioner had been guilty of pandering (383 U.S. 463, 471, 474–75; see also his
opinion upholding a conviction over Black's dissent in *Mishkin* v. *New York*, 383
U.S. 502 [1966]). In the much publicized Fanny Hill case of 1966 (*Memoirs* v.
Massachusetts), however, Brennan made it tougher on prosecutors by declaring
that material is obscene only if it is shown to be *"utterly* without redeeming
social value" (383 U. S. 413, 419). It is this requirement that Burger directly
rejects in *Paris Adult Theatre*.

    28. *Federalist* 10, 78.

    29. The distinction between factious and nonfactious activity is often lost in
commentaries on *Federalist* 10, hence the tendency to characterize all interest
group activity as "factious" in nature. In fact, Madison is clear about the distinction between activities that are factious and those that are not. Critical to the
distinction is the effect of activities on rights and the common good: "By a
faction I understand a number of citizens, whether amounting to a majority or
minority of the whole, who are united and actuated by some common impulse
of passion, or of interest, adverse to the rights of other citizens, or to the permanent and aggregate interests of the community. Ibid., 78.

    30. 413 U.S. at 113.

    31. Ibid. at 112.

    32. Ibid. at 114, n. 29.

    33. Ibid. at 109–110.

    34. By the mid-1980s, the Supreme Court was caught up in a debate over
the sufficiency under the Constitution of basing laws on what Justice Byron
White in *Bowers* v. *Hardwick*, the 1986 Georgia homosexual sodomy case, referred to variously as "notions of morality" and "moral choices." With Brennan
in dissent, the Court refused to declare in *Bowers* that such "notions" or
"choices" are an "inadequate rationale" for supporting a restriction on homo-

sexual sodomy (478 U.S. 186). Several years after *Bowers*, however, the Court could muster only a plurality that went along with a "morality" defense of an Indiana nude dancing regulation. In his concurrence, Justice David Souter agreed with the outcome but preferred to uphold the statute as a device for preventing prostitution, sexual assaults, and related criminal activity. See *Barnes* v. *Glen Theatre*, 501 U.S. 560 (1991).

35. See 413 U.S. at 86, n. 9.

36. Ibid. at 113.

37. Ibid. at 110.

38. Ibid. at 88.

39. 412 U.S. 94.

40. Ibid. at 184.

41. Ibid. at 94.

42. Ibid. at 201.

43. Ibid. at 196, n. 38.

44. Ibid. at 193. Brennan was insistent that if the United States is to be a shining city upon a hill, then people must be given "private space" to develop themselves free of encumbrances. Brennan, "The Constitution of the United States: Contemporary Ratification," 27 *South Texas Law Review* 443, 445 (1986).

45. The principal burden for Brennan is always on those who would regulate speech or expression through the print or broadcast media. See *Richmond Newspapers, Inc.* v. *Virginia* (448 U.S. 555, 585 [1980]) and *San Francisco Arts and Athletics* v. *United States Olympic Committee* (483 U.S. 522, 571 [1987]). The "chilling effects" of government intrusiveness in the lives of the people is a theme of Brennan's majority opinion in *Eisenstadt* v. *Baird*, a case that resulted in the Court overturning the respondent's conviction for distributing contraceptives to an unmarried woman (405 U.S. 438 [1972]).

46. Jefferson to Edward Carrington, January 16, 1787. Cited in Lorraine and Thomas Pangle, *The Learning of Liberty* (Lawrence: University of Kansas Press, 1993), 111.

47. Madison responded directly to Jefferson's defense of involving the people in regular reviews of the laws and Constitution in *Federalist* 49, 314: "frequent appeals would, in great measure, deprive the government of that veneration which time bestows on everything, and without which perhaps the wisest and freest government would not possess the requisite stability."

48. 412 U.S. at 187–88. In this connection see Brennan's affirmation of the importance of ensuring that "all points of view" have an "equal opportunity to be heard" in *New York Times* v. *Sullivan* (376 U.S. at 95–96) and *Carey* v. *Brown* (447 U.S. 455, 463 [1980]).

49. 427 U.S. 347 (1976).

50. Ibid. at 356, 372, 356.

51. Ibid. at 373. Brennan's willingness to inject the Court into intraoffice disputes to afford protection for free expression on the part of people working for the government also appears in his dissent in *Connick* v. *Myers*, a 1983 case that arose out of the dismissal of the respondent, an assistant district attorney in New Orleans. Justice White, writing for the Court, argued against "constitutionaliz[ing]" the employee's grievance and for according deference to the judgment of the "employer." By contrast, Brennan called on the Court to make its

own appraisal of the conflict and faulted White for "narrowing the class of subjects on which public employees can speak without fear of retaliation" (461 U.S. 138, 168, 158). For Brennan, Myers could be seen as performing an important service by sharing information with the people on such subjects as "morale in public offices" (ibid. at 165). Brennan complained about both the degree of deference afforded public employers by White and the "deterrent" effect of the decision (ibid. at 170). The argument Brennan offered for diminishing the range of actions that are not matters of public interest is fully consistent with the generous view of the Court's powers discussed in chapter two and his commitment to the fullest possible degree of freedom of expression and access to information.

52. 427 U.S. at 356; also note *Barnette* at 319 U.S. 624, 642 (1943).

53. Roy P. Basler, ed., *The Collected Works of Abraham Lincoln* (New Brunswick: Rutgers University Press, 1953), I:112.

54. 424 U.S. 693 (1976).

55. Ibid. at 734–35.

56. 438 U.S. 726 (1978).

57. Ibid. at 777.

58. Ibid. at 775.

59. Ibid. at 776.

60. Ibid. at 772. Brennan never wavered in his insistence that the Court give no ground in freedom of expression cases. Thus, for example, while the majority of his colleagues found appeals to privacy, tranquillity in the home, and the moral and civic well-being of the people of Puerto Rico to be sufficient grounds to uphold government regulations on neighborhood picketing and commercial advertising in two 1980s cases, Brennan was unpersuaded. See his dissents in *Frisby* v. *Schultz* (487 U.S. 474 [1988]) and *Posadas de Puerto Rico Associates* v. *Tourism Co. of Puerto Rico* (478 U.S. 328 [1986]).

61. *Board of Education, Island Trees Union Free School District No. 26* v. *Pico*, 457 U.S. 853 (1982). In an earlier public school case, Brennan dissented from a ruling by the Court that paddling students did not constitute cruel and unusual punishment in violation of the Eighth Amendment. *Ingraham* v. *Wright*, 430 U.S. 651 (1977).

62. 457 U.S. at 868. Six years after *Pico*, Brennan found himself dissenting in another school censorship case. In *Hazelwood School District* v. *Kuhlmeier* (484 U.S. 260 [1988]), the Court agreed to review a challenge to the actions of a principal who excised several articles from the school newspaper that was produced by a journalism class. Where Justice White found the action to be sustainable under the First Amendment, Brennan had no difficulty in finding the principal guilty of "insidious" conduct at odds with "the cherished democratic liberties that our Constitution guarantees." In familiar Brennanesque style, he declared that "such unthinking contempt for individual rights is intolerable from any state official." Ibid. at 290. The description of the conduct of the school official as "insidious" mirrors the harshness of Brennan's condemnation of Justice Stevens in *Pacifica Foundation*. Immoderation in the condemnation of government confinement of First Amendment rights takes on all the qualities of virtuous conduct.

63. 491 U.S. 397 (1989). Congress responded to the Court's decision to protect flag burning in *Texas* v. *Johnson* with the Flag Protection Act of 1989. The

Supreme Court, with Brennan again writing the majority opinion, struck down the law in a 5–4 decision. He declared the federal law to be an unacceptable effort to suppress expression. Returning to themes from *Texas* v. *Johnson* and *Pacifica Foundation*, he asserted that the government cannot target expression for punishment simply because society finds the ideas being expressed to be offensive or disagreeable. *United States* v. *Eichman*, 496 U.S. 310 (1990).

64. 491 U.S. at 413. Texas officials understood that they would have to overcome the rulings and arguments found in several flag cases decided in the late 1960s and early 1970s. See especially *Street* v. *New York* (394 U.S. 576 [1969]), *Spence* v. *Washington* (418 U.S. 405 [1974]), and *Smith* v. *Goguen* (415 U. S. 566 [1974]). Needless to add, these precedents strengthened Brennan's position and made Rehnquist's task that much more difficult.

65. 491 U.S. at 409. The "fighting words" principle had already been narrowed by the time of *Texas* v. *Johnson*. Brennan, for example, could draw support for a strict interpretation of "fighting words" from Harlan's opinion for the Court in *Cohen* v. *California* (403 U.S. 15 [1971]).

66. 491 U.S. at 417.

67. Ibid. at 419.

68. Ibid. at 420.

69. 315 U.S. 568, 572 (1942) [Justice Frank Murphy's opinion for the Court].

70. 491 U.S. at 435.

71. Ibid.

72. 391 U.S. 563 (1968). In *Pickering*, Justice Thurgood Marshall found that government employees, in this case a school teacher, are protected by the First Amendment against arbitrary dismissal for speaking out on public issues in a manner that may embarrass their employer. An important precedent for the claim that public benefits cannot be made contingent on the sacrifice of constitutionally protected interests was established by Brennan as early as 1963 in his opinion for the Court in *Sherbert* v. *Verner* (374 U.S. 398 [1963]).

73. 405 U.S. 438 (1972).

74. Ibid. at 453.

75. Burger's remark appears in *Eisenstadt*, 405 U.S. 438, 472.

76. *Federalist* 51, 322.

77. Alexis de Tocqueville, *Democracy in America*, ed. J. P. Mayer. (Garden City, N.Y.: Doubleday and Co., 1969), 692.

78. Over the dissents of William O. Douglas and Abe Fortas, Brennan gave Mississippi a victory in a case arising from a challenge brought by black civil rights activists against the state's anti-picketing law (*Cameron* v. *Johnson*, 390 U.S. 611 [1968]). Such a break with Douglas in a First Amendment case, however, was quite rare.

Chapter Four

RECASTING THE REPUBLIC: AN EMANCIPATIONIST VIEW OF THE FOURTEENTH AMENDMENT

If the constitutional amendments [13th and 14th] be enforced,
according to the intent with which, as I conceive, they were
adopted, there cannot be, in this republic, any class of human beings
in practical subjection to another class, with power in the latter to
dole out to the former just such privileges as they may choose to
grant.

   —John Marshall Harlan, *Civil Rights Cases* (1883)

[C]onstruing the Fourteenth Amendment to offer shelter only
to those interests specifically protected by historical practice . . .
ignores the kind of society in which our Constitution exists. We
are not an assimilative, homogeneous society, but a facilitative,
pluralistic one, in which we must be willing to abide someone else's
unfamiliar or even repellent practice because the same tolerant
impulse protects our own idiosyncrasies. . . . In a community such
as ours, "liberty" must include the freedom not to conform.

   —William J. Brennan, Jr., *Michael H.* v. *Gerald D.* (1989)

*I*n the consolidated *Slaughterhouse Cases* of 1873, the first major decision by the Supreme Court on the Fourteenth Amendment, Justice Joseph P. Bradley submitted a dissent in which he urged his colleagues to
worry less about the practical implications of their interpretation of the
amendment than about uncovering its intended goals.[1] Like Bradley,
William Brennan's Fourteenth Amendment jurisprudence was not
driven by a concern to ensure that the Court's workload remained manageable; but unlike Bradley, Brennan was less preoccupied with identifying original intentions than in determining how the amendment might
be employed to secure rights by variously checking or legitimating government action. There is little doubt that he used the due process and

equal protection language of the Fourteenth Amendment as skillfully as any justice to bring about an expansion in the sphere of individual rights and liberties.

When Brennan joined the Court in 1956, Justices Hugo Black and Felix Frankfurter were already involved in a decade-old debate on the meaning of the due process clause of the Fourteenth Amendment. For Black, the drafters of the Fourteenth had intended to bring the states under the requirements of the Bill of Rights. This is the so-called total incorporation position. By contrast, Frankfurter saw the due process language of the amendment as requiring that all state action satisfy a fundamental fairness test.[2] Black accused Frankfurter of empowering the justices to impose their subjective views on the states, thereby endangering both fundamental rights and the federal system, while Frankfurter believed that Black was placing the states in straitjackets in defiance of both the history and the language of the Fourteenth. For his part, Brennan joined Black in incorporation cases such as *Mapp* v. *Ohio* (exclusionary rule),[3] *Gideon* v. *Wainwright* (right to counsel),[4] and *Duncan* v. *Louisiana* (jury trial).[5] Frankfurter dissented in *Mapp*, as did his ally John Marshall Harlan who went on to dissent in *Duncan* after Frankfurter had left the Court. Brennan did not write for the Court in any of these cases. His significant opinions in the Fourteenth Amendment area did not typically come in these first-order incorporation cases but in the next tier of cases that went beyond questions having to do with whether specific Bill of Rights guarantees apply to state action. An example is his defense of pretermination hearings in welfare or disability benefits cases such as *Goldberg* v. *Kelly*[6] and *Mathews* v. *Eldridge*.[7] In like fashion, he did not author separate opinions in major substantive due process cases such as *Griswold* v. *Connecticut*[8] and *Roe* v. *Wade*,[9] but he actively lobbied for extending the principles of *Griswold* and *Roe* in cases such as *Eisenstadt* v. *Baird*,[10] *Cruzan* v. *Missouri Department of Health*,[11] and *DeShaney* v. *Winnebago County Department of Social Services*.[12] But notwithstanding the attention that his opinions in procedural and substantive due process cases have received, it is Brennan's authorship of major opinions dealing with the use of racial and gender classifications in equal protection clause cases that is principally responsible for the significant reputation that he enjoys in Fourteenth Amendment law. It is just this part of the Fourteenth as well that carries the greatest potential for altering the character of the American republic. The principle of equality in democratic times has the power to dramatically confine liberty interests. Witness the clash of these powerful interests in reverse discrimination suits (for example, *Regents of the University of California, Davis* v. *Bakke*[13] or *Johnson* v. *Transpor-*

tation Agency, Santa Clara County[14]) and in cases having to do either with the application of open housing requirements to the transfer of personal property or with access to services in private establishments covered by the Civil Rights Act of 1964.[15] Brennan both understood the potential of the equal protection principle for changing America and became an early activist for employing the full power of this principle to advance the cause of libertarian dignity.

Checking and Prodding Government: Due Process in the New Age of Rights

A preoccupation with government adherence to proper procedures, whether connected with the common law tradition or legislative action, can be traced in the United States all the way back to the colonial period. Thomas Jefferson could declare King George to be a tyrant, and therefore no longer worthy of the allegiance of the American people, as a result of his arbitrary actions that were endangering fundamental rights. But if the leading Founders understood that due process requirements must be adhered to for government to be legitimate, there was a limit to how far they pushed such requirements. As has already been noted, the creation of a political order that was capable of governing the people was for James Madison the first task of the delegates at the Constitutional Convention. The political system that they developed left broad authority to the states in the form of their police powers. Brennan joined the Supreme Court at a time when it was increasingly limiting how the states could employ these powers. As noted in chapter three, this was a time when all governments, national, state and local, found their authority to act under the principle of self-defense being limited.

It was clear from Brennan's first years on the Court that he would champion strict obedience to the due process requirements of the Bill of Rights. In *Raley* v. *Ohio*, a 1959 subversive activities case, he wrote an opinion that overturned convictions based on the refusal to answer questions before the state Un-American Activities Commission.[16] Brennan declared that the original defendants had effectively been "entrapped" in violation of the constitutional privilege against self-incrimination since each was led to believe that he could invoke the privilege. While Brennan could gain support to save only three of the four defendants, he left no doubt as to his conclusion that all the convictions were constitutionally infirm. Two years later, he found himself

dissenting in cases that sustained the reporting and registration requirements imposed on the Communist Party. In both *Communist Party* v.
Subversive Activities Control Board and *Scales* v. *United States*, Brennan
found that the government's appeal to security interests did not warrant
any relaxation of due process guarantees.[17] The actions of the government in all these cases, as in the racial segregation area, confirmed his
view that a vigilant judiciary holding government officials to strict adherence to due process requirements was essential to the preservation of
liberty. It was in this spirit that he declared in his much cited majority
opinion in *Freedman* v. *Maryland*, a case arising out of a challenge to the
state's motion-picture censorship statute, that "because only a judicial
determination in an adversary proceeding ensures the necessary sensitivity to freedom of expression, only a procedure requiring a judicial determination suffices to impose a valid final restraint."[18] Judicial processes,
here in the form of access to adversary proceedings, become the model
for all government action that bears on the rights or substantial interests
of the people. This reasoning places the judiciary itself squarely at center
stage when it comes to managing the modern democratic state. Brennan's insistence on the soundness of his position only intensified during
the 1970s and 1980s.

Brennan's majority opinion in *Goldberg* v. *Kelly*,[19] a 1970 AFDC
(Aid to Families with Dependent Children) case, provides an excellent
example of how far he was prepared to push the position he had taken
in *Freedman*. Indeed, he went far enough to provoke Justice Black to
charge him with engaging in judicial legislation.[20] What occasioned this
criticism was Brennan's insistence on treating welfare entitlements as a
form of "property" deserving of judicial protection against potentially
abusive administrative action. Hence his declaration that a pretermination hearing must be provided prior to the cessation of welfare benefits.
His elevation of the status of AFDC-type assistance was grounded in
the same reading of the Constitution that supports his jurisprudence
of libertarian dignity. For Brennan, the nation is fulfilling its pledge to
"promote the general Welfare, and secure the Blessings of Liberty to
ourselves and our Posterity" when it provides dependable public assistance to people who, for whatever reason, may lack the means to provide for their basic needs.[21] The linkage with the founding is significant,
for it permits Brennan to find legitimacy for government assistance outside of statutory action or majoritarian preferences. And Brennan left no
doubt as to his interpretation of the fundamental mission of this country:
"From its founding the Nation's basic commitment has been to foster
the dignity and well-being of all persons within its borders."[22] Here is

language typical of his jurisprudence. It can be assumed that he understood the practical significance of casting public assistance in obligatory and not merely discretionary terms. This constitutional elevation of welfare entitlements was buttressed with a "victimization" argument: "We have come to recognize that forces not within the control of the poor contribute to their poverty."[23] If there is a general obligation to promote the "well-being of all persons," this responsibility becomes especially acute for him in the case of those individuals and groups who are at the mercy of "forces" beyond their control. The practical effect of his appeal to the "Nation's basic commitment . . . to foster the dignity and well-being of all persons" was to position people to make demands of the government without embarrassment or sense of guilt. They would be asking for no more than what they are due. At least in terms of the situation presented in *Goldberg*, an important device for ensuring government accountability is the availability of pretermination hearings. Evidence that the welfare bureaucracy had "difficulties in reaching correct decisions on eligibility" only provided added support for the conclusion he reached, but was not essential once the analogy had been established between welfare entitlements and property rights.[24]

It is important to recognize that Brennan's characterization of the government's responsibilities in essentially moral terms is not what sets him apart from the leading Founders. Madison, for example, had something more than some simple formalistic principle in mind, say that all equals be treated equally, when he spoke of "justice" being the end of government in *Federalist* 51. He made it clear that among other things a just government would not provide cover for "factious" groups. What separates the reasoning of *Goldberg* from Madison's political thought is the explicit invitation extended by Brennan for claims to be brought against all forms of government activity or even inactivity. The argument that government *must do* whatever it *can do*, when wedded to the belief that individual self-expression and the maximum of personal autonomy are the highest goals of the liberal state, creates the possibility for a continuous inflation of government responsibilities and almost infinite challenges to governmental institutions at all levels.

With the addition of Justices Lewis Powell and William H. Rehnquist, the Burger Court was poised by 1972–73 to retrench from the liberalism of the Warren era. Brennan found himself fighting hard to preserve the position staked out in *Goldberg*, and with increasing frequency the results could not have been gratifying. He dissented from a succession of early and mid-1970s rulings that left government owing less to citizens claimants than seemed to be required by precedents such as *Goldberg*. In *Richardson* v. *Wright*, a 1972 case in which the Court refused to hold that persons have a right to an oral presentation when decisions are being made regarding the suspension of Social Security disability benefits, Brennan accused the majority of "abdicating [their] responsibilities."[25] Appealing directly to his 1970 opinion in *Goldberg*, he protested that "reasons of added expense" should never be sufficient to limit the demands of due process. In an important observation that fit with the view of the Constitution and the founding that he had set out in 1970, Brennan noted that the state's interest in seeing that payments are not erroneously terminated outweighs the state's concerns about fiscal and administrative burdens.[26] Ensuring that individual parties are not harmed trumps appeals based on interests, such as the financial state of taxpayers, that are only indirectly related to the rights of claimants. Brennan's position is good evidence of the fact that additional protection for individual parties in cases such as *Richardson* can be advanced by abstracting from the connection between fiscal and administrative burdens and the effective protection of the rights and interests of the people. It was the Court's unwillingness to abstract from these considerations that produced more dissents from him in *Weinberger* v. *Salfi* (1975) and *Mathews* v. *Eldridge* (1976).[27]

In *Weinberger*, the question was whether people should be permitted on an individual basis to challenge a duration-of-relationship Social Security eligibility requirement for surviving wives of deceased wage earners. The lower court had invalidated the statutory presumption that a spouse married to an insured person for fewer than nine months had entered into the marriage for the purpose of gaining access to survivor's benefits. Mrs. Salfi had demanded a hearing under the due process clause of the Fifth Amendment to present evidence to rebut the presumption. In rejecting her demand, Rehnquist used a rational basis approach in concluding that Congress could reasonably determine that administrative and fiscal considerations are sufficient to offset any "imprecision" that might result from the application of the rule. Brennan submitted a dissent in which he objected to the Court's denial of individualized hearings. He singled out for special criticism the impression that administrative efficiency could justify denying persons an opportunity to gain a hearing at which they might plead their case.[28]

A year later in *Mathews*, Brennan complained about the majority's increasingly minimalist approach to due process guarantees. This time it was Justice Powell who held that there was no constitutional right to an oral hearing prior to the termination of disability benefits under the Social Security program. Powell essentially agreed with Solicitor General Robert Bork's argument that the posttermination procedures available to aggrieved claimants were sufficient to satisfy due process requirements. Bork's second task had been to persuade the Court that pretermination hearings would impose prohibitive administrative and financial burdens on the agency. Appealing to the principle of judicial self-restraint, and adopting a balancing formula that weighed administrative costs alongside protection for personal interests, Powell accepted the cost-benefit analysis presented by Bork. In words that were reminiscent of Frankfurter's counsel of restraint in *Baker* v. *Carr*, Powell noted that "[in] assessing what process is due, substantial weight must be given to the good-faith judgments of the individuals charged by Congress with the administration of the social welfare system that the procedures they have provided assure fair consideration of the entitlement claims of individuals."[29] This declaration was in sharp contrast to Brennan's rebuttal argument on behalf of judicial vigilance and assertiveness. As already noted in chapter two, the special threats posed by the bureaucratic state were for him an independent justification for judicial activism.

In *Mathews*, as in the *Richardson* and *Weinberger* cases, Brennan rejected the government's appeal to costs and the sufficiency of existing pretermination and posttermination procedures. The Constitution demanded more than the existing modest procedures for him because the country was capable of doing more. When he asserted that it was "no argument" that George Eldridge could seek other forms of public assistance during the posttermination period, the point was both that the Constitution required an evidentiary type of hearing prior to termination of benefits and that the federal government could afford to extend such hearings to aggrieved parties.[30] Government practices could, and therefore should, meet the demands of constitutional theory construed in light of the ideal of libertarian dignity.

The way in which Brennan interwove what the Constitution demands in principle with what the country is capable of providing in practice carried over from the procedural to the substantive due process area of constitutional law. Excellent examples of the pervasiveness of this reasoning can be found in several Fourteenth Amendment cases that came at the very end of his judicial career, most notably *DeShaney, Michael H.* v. *Gerald D.*, and *Cruzan*.

Alongside his majority opinions in *Texas* v. *Johnson* and *Metro Broadcasting* v. *FCC* (a 1990 racial preference case), Brennan's dissents in *DeShaney, Michael H.*, and *Cruzan* reveal just how much he had come to expect by the time of his retirement. The "liberty" interests protected by the due process clauses of the Fifth and Fourteenth Amendments are both multidimensional for Brennan and almost infinitely expansive. In *DeShaney*, the issue was state culpability for failure to protect a young child who had been victimized by an abusive parent. Joshua DeShaney's mother sought compensation from the state after the child was left with severe brain damage following an attack by the father, who had been assigned custody of the child when the parents divorced. Several incidents preceding the final tragic beating had alerted authorities to the possibility that abuse might be occurring, but the policy of Winnebago County was to err on the side of holding families together. Chief Justice Rehnquist, speaking for the Court, denounced the conduct of the father but ruled that the failure of state officials to act did not represent a deprivation of liberty in violation of the due process principle of the Fourteenth Amendment. It was his position that the Constitution does not impose an "affirmative" duty on the state to protect individuals against all harms, especially "private violence." While the people through their representatives might prefer a rule of liability that would hold state officials responsible for inaction in cases such as the one before the Court, Rehnquist rejected the claim that liability was required to satisfy the constitutional requirements of due process.

In Brennan's mind, the Court had interpreted the Constitution as being "indifferent" to state "indifference" in cases such as Joshua's. In so doing, he concluded that the majority had turned its back not only on Joshua but on the Constitution itself. The liberty protected by the Constitution, according to Brennan, comprehended protection against destructive state action and inaction. Indeed, he reminded his colleagues that "inaction can be every bit as abusive of power as action."[31] In the context of this reasoning and the facts of the case, the state's ability to protect Joshua produces an obligation to do so. The omission to act is as legitimate a source of guilt as the commission of a sinful act. The bureaucratic state that posed great new threats to rights for Brennan has inescapable obligations connected with the "affirmative" duties of government. When you add this view of governmental obligations to Brennan's rejection of the appeal to administrative and fiscal costs in cases such as *Richardson* v. *Wright*, the inflationary effect of his reasoning on the "liberty" interests covered by the due process clauses of the Constitution is obvious. It might not be too far-fetched to observe that the final limits to the substantive content of "liberty" for him are the boundaries of the human imagination.

Michael H. v. *Gerald D.* is another 1989 case that exposed the full expansiveness of Brennan's understanding of what is covered by the word "liberty" in the due process clauses.[32] The case provides an excellent example of the judicialization of controversies that followed from the regeneration of substantive due process reasoning after the decisions in *Griswold* and *Roe*. Michael H., the natural father of a child born to the wife of Gerald D., brought suit to gain visitation rights. Blood tests supported the claim of Michael H. to be the father of the child. Under California law, however, a child born to a married woman is presumed to be a child of that marriage. The state courts refused to overrule this presumption and dismissed the demand for visitation rights. Justice Antonin Scalia, announcing the judgment of the Supreme Court, appealed to tradition in upholding the state law. He was careful to note the significance that historically has been attached to protecting the unitary family in America. Reliance on tradition is valuable in his view not only for the assistance that history and established customs and norms provide in supplying content to the "liberty" interests protected by the Constitution, but additionally as a check on the power of the unelected judiciary.

In a dissent that in many respects represented the best last statement of his approach to constitutional interpretation, Brennan disputed not only the claim that tradition supplies an "objective" test of what rights or interests are protected by the Constitution, but even the propriety of relying on tradition irrespective of whether it can provide such standards. He refused to allow appeals to the "unitary family" to automatically outweigh claims raised on behalf of the "parental relationship."[33] The refusal to assign as much weight to history or tradition as Scalia emerged from the same view of American society that had been evident in his dissent in *FCC* v. *Pacifica Foundation*. As he had done to Justice John Paul Stevens in *Pacifica Foundation*, Brennan resorted to caustic rhetoric in denouncing Scalia's reasoning as narrow-minded and dangerous:

> In construing the Fourteenth Amendment to offer shelter only to those interests specifically protected by historical practice . . . the plurality ignores the kind of society in which our Constitution exists. We are not an assimilative, homogeneous society, but a facilitative, pluralistic one, in which we must be willing to abide someone else's unfamiliar or even repellent practice because the same tolerant impulse protects our own idiosyncrasies. Even if we can agree, therefore, that "family" and "parenthood" are part of the good life, it is absurd to assume that we can agree on the content of those terms and destructive to pretend that we do. In a community such as ours, "liberty" must include the freedom not to conform. The plurality today squashes this freedom by requiring specific approval from history before protecting anything in the name of liberty.[34]

For Brennan, the plurality in *Michael H.* had done such "violence" to
the Constitution as to have left it unrecognizable. It was no longer a
"living charter," but a "stagnant, archaic, hidebound document steeped
in the prejudices and superstitions of a time long past."[35] His disagree-
ment with Scalia could not have been greater or his unhappiness more
profound.

Where for Scalia the political community brought into being by the
Constitution is an entity with well-defined social, economic, and political characteristics, for Brennan it is defined less in terms of essential
institutions or practices or traditions and more in terms of the facility
it provides for individual expression and self-determination. Hence the
weight that he gives to each person's "freedom not to conform." All we
really know, and all that the Constitution finally rests on for Brennan, is
the desirability of permitting people the maximum of freedom to choose
a way of life for themselves. There are outer boundaries to this freedom,
but they principally have to do with what is required to maximize the
liberty to define oneself by one's actions or to protect the right of others
to do the same. Extraneous encumbrances on personal freedom are inherently suspect as obstacles to the pursuit of a preferred way of life and,
hence, to individual dignity as understood by Brennan. In this context,
California's regulation is susceptible to attack not mainly because it reflects outdated norms, but more importantly because it takes away from
Michael H.'s personal dignity. The stakes for society could not be any
greater for Brennan. In his judgment, it is tantamount to tyranny to insist
that Michael H. sacrifice his desired way of life in order to protect the
nuclear family. This is the point behind Brennan's claim that it would
be "destructive" to act as if we can give content or meaning to the term
"family." In this regard at least, the requisites of civilized existence are
much less complex for him than they were for James Madison or George
Washington or Alexis de Tocqueville. Once freedom to shape a way of
life for oneself becomes the core of dignified existence, all other consideration of a political, economic, or religious nature can only have a
secondary status. More than this, by casting these considerations as potential threats to freedom, it becomes easier to abstract from them when
deciding how to resolve immediate controversies. That Brennan believed that freedom to shape one's way of life was the central issue that
the Court needed to focus on in the new substantive due process cases
was made abundantly clear in one of his last opinions.

If the government can exercise some control over obscene or libel-
ous material in the name of self-defense or self-preservation, can it also
regulate termination of life decisions involving persons in vegetative

states in the name of self-preservation or, more to the point, to the end of preserving a "civilized" order? This was the crux of the issue that came before the Court in *Cruzan* v. *Missouri*, a tragic case having to do with a woman left in a comatose state as a result of an automobile accident.[36] And as in *Michael H.* and *DeShaney*, Brennan dissented from a ruling that he believed was too deferential insofar as it left considerable discretion with state authorities over especially personal matters. Speaking for the Court, Rehnquist applied the rational basis test to Missouri's declaration that in the absence of a living will the state might insist that a comatose person be retained on life support even in the face of a family's testimony that the victim would not have wanted to be kept alive in such fashion. The Chief Justice could not see that it was unreasonable for Missouri to insist that people who had not completed a living will be kept alive as a way of demonstrating the state's commitment to the value of life, especially since persons such as Nancy Cruzan are in a condition that prevents them from making their own preferences known.

Brennan quarreled with Rehnquist's refusal to apply strict scrutiny to the challenged regulation and with the weight that the Chief Justice assigned to the state's independent interest in the preservation of life. For Brennan, only strict scrutiny would suffice.[37] As for the state's interests in this case, they were limited in his view to discovering what Cruzan would want done with her body. Cruzan's right to decide what would be done with her body trumped all conceivable state interests: "the state's general interest in life must accede to Nancy Cruzan's particularized and intense interest in self-determination in her choice of medical treatment."[38] The only thing that should have mattered to the state was deciphering and following her wishes, which Brennan believed could be attested to by her parents. Making direct reference to Aldous Huxley's depiction of the horrors of the fully regimented state, Brennan declared that to allow state interests to supersede Cruzan's desires "would be too brave a new world for me and, I submit, for our Constitution."[39] If the affirmation of human dignity requires that governmental policies permit people to define and express their personalities with a minimum of interference, then the decision to uphold the Missouri regulation flew squarely in the face of a jurisprudence of libertarian dignity. Brennan's defense of what amounts to a right "to be left alone" exaggerates the side of modern natural rights thinking that asserts that the best political orders allow their members to approximate the condition of perfect freedom and perfect equality that marked life in the state of nature.[40] What this "libertarian" position abstracts from is another side of modern natural rights theory that recognizes the importance of competence in government for the protection of rights. That is to say, theorists such as John Locke argued that life, liberty, and property will be safe only if political orders possess the authority to preserve the conditions required for the enjoyment of comfortable self-preservation by the members of the society. Regulations that are designed to get people to value life over death, as with rules governing the dissemination of obscene material, are rooted in this side of natural rights thought. But this side of modern liberalism is vulnerable to rights-based attacks because of the tendency to equate comfortable preservation with the maximum of freedom to pursue one's own desires. The weakening of the belief that nature sets standards regarding what is proper and just has resulted in a corresponding reduction in the weight that was assigned by Locke, and later by the American Founders, to preserving competence in government and respect for public institutions. In many respects, the fixation with addressing immediate needs and preferences in the context of a rights-based jurisprudence that characterizes Brennan's legal writing represents one form of the trumping of institutional and cultural "means" by an appeal to the abstract "ends" of modernity. Needless to add, the post-1960s habit of exposing and decrying the imperfections of political institutions only adds to the attraction of Brennan's efforts to enlarge the sphere of personal autonomy.

The New Fourteenth Amendment Calculus

It is unclear whether most of the supporters of the Fourteenth Amendment in 1866 understood that the principle of equality contained within itself the capacity to produce a radical change in Madison's republic. There is no doubt that Brennan understood the real potential of the equal protection clause of the Fourteenth Amendment and exploited it the fullest. The intensity and boldness that marked his handling of procedural and substantive due process cases from the end of the 1960s to his retirement was replicated in the equal protection area. As already noted in chapter two, Brennan had no difficulty in finding ample federal authority to counter racial discrimination in both the commerce clause and the Fourteenth Amendment. His mid-1960s opinions in *Katzenbach* v. *Morgan* and *Green* v. *County School Board* revealed his impatience with delays in making good on the promise of *Brown* and his willingness to grant Congress considerable leeway in using its powers to attack lingering segregationist practices.[41] These opinions effectively pointed the country in the direction of taking "affirmative action" to bring about the kind of pluralist order that lurked behind Earl Warren's decision in *Brown*.

Brennan was no more moved by federalism-based claims raised on behalf of state prerogatives in voting rights and school desegregation cases than he had been in *Baker* v. *Carr*, the Tennessee reapportionment case, at the beginning of the 1960s. By the time of his majority opinion in *Katzenbach* v. *Morgan*, he was prepared not just to tolerate virtually unfettered congressional action that targeted racial discrimination but to facilitate such action in the most explicit terms. This 1966 Voting Rights Act case took the form of a challenge to federal action designed to override state literacy requirements. These requirements came under attack as a result of evidence that they were being employed in some areas to limit access by minority persons to the ballot box. Brennan found more than adequate support for the law in Congress's power to enforce the terms of the Fourteenth Amendment. He drew an important analogy between Section 5 of the amendment, the enforcement provision, and the "necessary and proper" clause of Article I of the Constitution.[42] The significance of the analogy could not have been lost on anyone familiar with Chief Justice John Marshall's opinion in *McCulloch* v. *Maryland*.[43] With a clear understanding of the relationship between the power of the national legislature and the power of the then new national government, Marshall used the "n and p" clause to protect the American republic against threats of dissolution posed by jealous state officials. It has been said that Marshall defined legislative power in *McCulloch* with a breadth that was unequaled until the mid-twentieth century. For his part, Brennan combined the power of the "n and p" clause with the deference applied in commerce clause cases to unhinge federal action from restrictions associated with such institutional forms as federalism. The deferential posture that he almost nonchalantly endorsed in *Katzenbach* v. *Morgan* was in striking contrast to his calls in procedural and substantive due process cases for judicial vigilance in the face of the modern administrative state. It was sufficient that Congress "might have" concluded that national protection for minorities was needed against abuses of literacy requirements. There was no insistence that evidence be supplied of the undeniable need for federal action: "it is enough that we perceive a basis upon which Congress *might predicate* a judgment that the application of New York's English literacy requirement . . . [violated] . . . the Equal Protection Clause."[44] The aim, advancing equality in the enjoyment of rights, warranted judicial acquiescence. Deference is not capitulation for Brennan when the government's actions advance the cause of libertarian dignity. Importantly, it was not institutional considerations having to do with the principles of representative government or separation of powers that were decisive. Brennan's deference provoked John Marshall Harlan to declare that the Fourteenth Amendment had been transformed into a " 'brooding omnipresence' over all state regulation."[45] His appeal to federalism, however, elicited no more sympathy from Brennan in *Katzenbach* v. *Morgan* than it had in *Baker*.

That the achievement of desired effects or results counted heavily for Brennan was made abundantly clear in his opinion for the Court in *Green* v. *County School Board*, a school segregation case out of New Kent County, Virginia.[46] In *Green*, the Court considered the constitutionality of a "freedom of choice" plan that left the county's schools segregated according to race. Without declaring such plans to be inherently unconstitutional, Brennan left no doubt that the use of such devices to evade the results intended by *Brown* would no longer be tolerated. Mere elimination of state-imposed racial barriers would not be acceptable. Brennan wanted desegregation plans that "promise[d] realistically to work, and promise[d] realistically to work *now*."[47] What counted was the creation of unitary school systems without further delay. This emphasis on judicially mandated results fits well with his inclination to resolve all doubts about the intentions of the Framers of the Fourteenth Amendment in favor of a generous view of legislative and judicial remedial powers. Brennan's opinion certainly seemed reasonable in light of the obvious merits of the goal and the fact that the old restraints on national action that took the form of appeals to federalism (Tenth Amendment) and the police powers had been rendered suspect by the late 1960s with the abuses of "massive resistance" and the "states' rights" movement. But as with the rush to weaken the presidency after Watergate, the enfeeblement of the federal system and the powers of the states looked less problematical than was true either in theory or in practice. There is no doubt that Brennan deserves to be commended for his contribution to freeing up people from the constraints of segregationist practices. His impatience with delays in dismantling school segregation can hardly be faulted. As noted earlier, however, the desire to do good is not always synonymous with the achievement of good, nor do good intentions excuse people from the effects of their actions when they actively seek to influence events. For Harlan, the undesirable effects had to do with the impact of Brennan's reasoning on the American federal system; other justices openly worried about the threat to democratic governance presented by his arguments, especially his aggressive version of judicial activism.

That Brennan would use all openings to obtain the results he desired was made eminently clear in a concurrence and dissent that he collectively authored with Justices Byron White and Thurgood Marshall in *Oregon* v. *Mitchell*.[48] These three justices objected to the Court's rejection of Congress's attempt to extend the franchise to eighteen-year-olds in state and local elections. Writing for the Court, Justice Black found that Congress had exceeded its constitutional powers when it attempted via an amendment to the Voting Rights Act to set the qualifications for participating in state and local elections. Assigning Brennan specific responsibility for the collective opinion that he submitted with White and Marshall, Black accused his colleague of making arguments that when carried to their "logical conclusion" would "blot out all state power" and leave the states "little more than impotent figureheads." What provoked this charge was Brennan's loose construction of the intentions of the Framers of the Fourteenth Amendment that inflated national prerogatives at the expense of the states.

The collective opinion that carried Brennan's name is a treasure trove of information on his approach to constitutional construction. The opinion runs from pages 229 to 281 in the *Supreme Court Reports* and is devoted largely to an examination of the meaning of the Fourteenth Amendment. Acknowledging that it is possible to find statements by some of the principal figures associated with the amendment, such as Representative John Bingham and Senator Jacob Howard, to support the position that state control of suffrage would not be disturbed by passage of the Fourteenth, Brennan, White, and Marshall insisted that there was sufficient ambiguity in the record to justify the challenged amendment to the Voting Rights Act, which for them made good sense in 1970. Several arguments, in fact, are interwoven in an effort to accommodate the action taken by Congress. On the one hand, there was a pure "ambiguity" argument. We are told that the historical record is just "too vague and imprecise to provide us with sure guidance in deciding the pending cases."[49] This observation followed on the declaration that conflicting and ambiguous statements made during the debates and ratification period make it impossible to "know with certainty that its framers intended the Fourteenth Amendment to function as we think they did."[50] They conceded that Bingham, dubbed "father" of the Fourteenth by many scholars, had at one point observed that the franchise would remain "exclusively" under state control.[51] But statements such as this one were not considered dispositive of the issue by Brennan, White, and Marshall either because other less definitive observations were also made by proponents of the amendment or because they concluded that partisan interests probably compelled Republicans to give this reading to the Fourteenth to avoid arousing fears that might result in a resurgence of Democratic representation in Congress. In short, they argued both that Bingham and others offered contradictory interpretations of the Amendment and that they had good reason to mask their true intentions.

While the argument based on ambiguity created an opening for approving governmental action that seemed to fit the times, as it did in *Brown* for Chief Justice Warren, the collaborative opinion did not stop there. After noting the difficulties that attend any attempt to decipher the intended meaning of the Fourteenth with regard to suffrage regulations, Brennan, White, and Marshall somewhat confidently asserted that the amendment very likely was designed to be "interpreted by future generations in accordance with the vision and needs of those generations." According to this reading of the Fourteenth, legislators such as Bingham and Howard not only recognized that they were leaving major issues unresolved or in an ambiguous state but intentionally did so in order to accommodate "future needs." At least, we are told, this construction of the Fourteenth is "plausible."[52] This last position provided much more legitimacy for innovative legislative action than the mere ambiguity argument. It is important to note, however, that nothing in the opinion indicates that Brennan would not have been content to rest his defense of Congress's action on the ambiguity argument alone. By the time the Burger Court was taking full form in the mid-1970s, any opening that might serve to free persons or generations from norms or practices that shackle and restrain their freedom to act was welcomed by him.

At least at one level it is entirely appropriate for the Court to focus on resolving claims associated with current legal or constitutional conflicts. The judiciary is the institution to which we turn when legal controversies arise between adverse parties. An equally compelling argument, however, can be made in a democratic society for insisting that the judiciary carry out its labors without engaging in policy making of the sort that fundamentally alters existing practices and institutions in the absence of a specific political or constitutional directive. Where Justice Black in *Oregon* v. *Mitchell* counseled a cautious reading of legislative intent and refused to use ambiguity to validate transformative governmental action, Brennan exhibited little if any timidity in using vagueness and imprecision in the record as openings for justifying what he believed was right for the times. In *Oregon* v. *Mitchell*, of course, he could get the result he desired without challenging legislative action since Congress had taken the lead in extending the vote to eighteen-year-olds in state and local elections. The significance of Brennan's position in this case, however, is not that he called for deference to the will of Congress, but that he argued for an interpretation of the Fourteenth Amendment that accommodated the satisfaction of current needs and interests. The belief that each generation should be permitted to interpret the Constitution and laws to fit their needs would be highly visible in several opinions he authored in late 1970s and 1980s affirmative action cases. In short, no great leap must be made to get from his position in *Oregon v. Mitchell* to his arguments in affirmative action and racial preference cases such as *Bakke, United Steelworkers v. Weber, Johnson v. Santa Clara County,* or *Metro Broadcasting.* As will become evident later in this chapter, the same desire to keep the Constitution up with the times, in part by attacking traditional practices that encumber freedom of choice, marked his handling of gender discrimination cases.

Brennan's attention to accommodating the Constitution to immediate social concerns is evident in his defense of what came to be called the "benign" use of racial categories in *Regents of the University of California, Davis v. Bakke.*[53] In an unusual 4-1-4 split, the Court in *Bakke* rejected a racial quota program used to aid minority students seeking admission to the medical school at UC-Davis. Powell, writing for himself and joining the conservative bloc of four led by Stevens, declared that racial quota programs such as the one used by Davis must be subjected to the strictest scrutiny. In Powell's opinion, the Davis plan could not survive this scrutiny. He did acknowledge, however, that affirmative action plans that only treat race as a plus along with other things such as musical skills or athletic ability were permissible under the Constitution. While Brennan was pleased to endorse Powell's announcement that race might be used as a plus by admission staffs, the leader of the liberal bloc in *Bakke* urged toleration of far greater use of race than merely as a plus.

Brennan was entirely comfortable with the employment of racial categories when the goal was the advancement of a group. Noting that precedents such as *Swann v. Charlotte-Mecklenburg Board of Education* had already established that the use of racial classifications could be reconciled with the Fourteenth Amendment, he added that race-based remedies should not be made to depend on "specific proof that a person has been victimized by discrimination."[54] A strong probability of victimization should be sufficient. Without directly challenging Powell's insistence on the application of strict scrutiny, Brennan enlarged the opening for the use of racial quotas by lowering the evidence threshold that had to be met by state agencies such as UC-Davis.

Perhaps the best evidence of Brennan's willingness to relax traditional standards of Fourteenth Amendment review in so-called benign racial classification cases appeared in his reflections on whether the Davis program had the effect of stigmatizing individuals as inferior. As for minority applicants, he noted that the purpose of the set-aside program was to offset the effects of societal discrimination, not accentuate them. As far as nonminority applicants such as Allan Bakke are concerned, Brennan saw no evidence of stigmatization in violation of the equal protection clause or any other constitutional or statutory principle. His dismissal of Bakke's complaint was uncompromising: "there is absolutely no basis for concluding that Bakke's rejection as a result of Davis's use of racial preference will affect him throughout his life in the same way as the segregation of the Negro school children in *Brown I* would have affected them."[55] Brennan added that he could find no principled distinction between Powell's acceptance of Harvard's plan that used race as a plus and the quota program employed by Davis. In short, he found the end or goal of the dual admissions program to be justifiable and could discover no fatal defects in the means. Here was a prime example of state action that he believed was consistent with the principle of libertarian dignity. Indeed, in a telling remark by someone who had long touted the need for judicial oversight of the actions of the modern administrative state, Brennan freely noted that the use of remedies such as the type employed by Davis should not have to await judicial adjudication.[56] In the context of this reasoning, Powell's strict and tough approach to using racial categories in *Bakke*, like Scalia's appeal to tradition and history in *Michael H.* v. *Gerald D.*, comes across as just another effort to interfere with the accomplishment of desirable goals. Similarly, arguments based on the social costs that might arise from classifying people according to race were trumped by Davis's efforts to provide immediate redress for injuries derived from decades of discrimination. Brennan's unwillingness to be governed by the kinds of fears summoned up by justices such as Lewis Powell, Sandra Day O'Connor, and Antonin Scalia in affirmative action/quota cases fits with his refusal in cases such as *Elrod* and *Rutan* to be moved by the claims that the two-party system or the electoral process could eventually be harmed by weakening patronage practices. Brennan's gaze in these cases was fixed on the perceived suffering of immediate victims of governmental or societal practices that restrained self-expression and individual autonomy. In many respects, costs that might be borne by the "whole people" in the form of increased taxation or possible damage to the two-party system or to race relations were too abstract or indirect to count for much in his calculations. His opinion in *Bakke* exposes the full extent to which Brennan's cost-benefit calculations were context dependent.

The same sympathy for actions fashioned to improve opportunities for people belonging to groups historically discriminated against that is evident in Brennan's opinion in *Bakke* can be detected in his opinions for the Court in two other affirmative action cases, *United Steelworkers* v. *Weber* and *Johnson* v. *Transportation Agency, Santa Clara County*.[57] In both cases, white males complained that they had been injured by policies or decisions that advanced the cause of minorities or women. Writing for the Court in these cases, Brennan found the ends or goals of the policies to be commendable and the means sustainable.

The *Weber* case came to the Court in the form of a challenge under Title VII of the Civil Rights Act of 1964 that bars employers and unions from discriminating on the basis of race. Brian Weber brought the suit after being passed over for inclusion in a craft training program by minority workers with less seniority. The program was voluntarily entered into by the Kaiser Aluminum Corporation and the United Steelworkers of America. Under the agreement entered into by the corporation and the union, half of the positions in the training program were designated for blacks. The goal was to bring minority representation in crafts positions up the level of black representation in the local labor force. The fact that the agreement was voluntarily entered into by private and not public entities allowed Brennan to distinguish Weber's complaint from Bakke's. The Fourteenth Amendment, he could note, had long been interpreted as directly restaining "state action," not private action. More important than this point, however, was Brennan's assertion that Congress intended to encourage just such efforts to offset the effects of discriminatory practices. Where Rehnquist in dissent pointed out that the language of Title VII plainly forbids discrimination on the basis of race, Brennan stressed what he believed Congress had intended to achieve through its actions. And in this regard, what was not set out in the language of the law loomed large in his interpretation of the legislation. In an argument reminiscent of the opinion Brennan signed in *Oregon* v. *Mitchell*, ambiguity became a vehicle for achieving the end he desired: "Had Congress meant to prohibit all race-conscious affirmative action, as respondent urges, it easily could have answered both objections by providing that Title VII would not *require* or permit racially preferential integration efforts. But Congress did not choose such a course."[58] This argument was much too "Orwellian" for Rehnquist.[59] For Brennan, and in the spirit of the teaching left by Benjamin Cardozo, this was the kind of facilitative reasoning that helped to ensure that the Constitution and laws remained consistent with the times and advanced the "welfare of society." That the assumption that Congress did not wish to impose unusual federal regulations on private businesses was not fully consistent with what the Court had assumed and upheld in other race-related cases such as *Katzenbach* v. *McClung* and *Heart of Atlanta Motel, Inc.* v. *United States* did not cause Brennan to falter in his endorsement of the ends and means of the Kaiser program. Even Justice Harry Blackmun who concurred in the *Weber* case accused Brennan of using a more "suspect" and "controversial" approach than needed.[60] To understand why he may have been unmoved by these charges it is only necessary to recall from chapter two the importance that he attributed to having a legal system that was attuned to the "reason and passion" of the day. Passion is best accommodated by freedom from subservience to history or tradition or strict interpretations of language. Appeals to the "original intentions" of the authors of legislation, for example, can easily end up restraining the pursuit of current desires. Significantly, Brennan's approach to handling ambiguities or gaps in legislation or in the Constitution leaves Congress with having to respond directly to judicial decisions that approximate policy making or accept the consequences of inaction. He reaffirmed his conviction that this was a legitimate way for the Court to proceed in his opinion in *Johnson* v. *Santa Clara County*, where he used Congress's failure to respond to his reasoning in *Weber* as evidence of agreement.

Johnson v. *Santa Clara County* was another affirmative action case, but this time one that involved action by a government agency that favored the candidacy of a woman over that of a white male. Paul Johnson and Diane Joyce were both deemed qualified for an open position for a road dispatcher with the county Transportation Agency. Johnson's overall score, however, was slightly higher than Joyce's and three supervisors recommended that he be appointed to serve in the open position. Santa Clara's Affirmative Action Office intervened at the request of Joyce, and the Transportation Agency ultimately awarded her the position. In a much publicized suit, Johnson charged the county with violating Title VII of the 1964 Civil Rights Act. The District Court agreed, but the Court of Appeals did not. Brennan, writing for the Supreme Court, affirmed the decision of the appellate court.

Unlike the *Weber* case, *Johnson* directly involved the use of racial and gender categories by a government institution. Moreover, since the agency in question was not acting for the federal government, there could be no appeal to the special remedial powers that are conferred on Congress under Section 5 of the Fourteenth Amendment. What the two cases shared that attracted Brennan's attention was a "voluntary" commitment to improving the representation in the workforce of groups that historically had suffered from pernicious forms of discrimination.[61] With the *Bakke* case in mind, he carefully noted that the Santa Clara plan did not set aside places for women or minorities, but only set targets for representation. Crucial to Brennan's conclusion that the Santa Clara program could pass muster was his reliance once more on congressional silence, this time having to do with the *Weber* ruling of 1979. In an argument that elicited a harsh and even sarcastic response from Scalia, Brennan insisted that the interpretation of Title VII that he had set out in *Weber* should be presumed to be correct since it had encountered no subsequent legislative opposition.[62] To quote from a footnote contained in his opinion: "Congress has not amended the statute to reject our construction, nor have any such amendments even been proposed, and we therefore may assume that our interpretation was correct."[63] In a related remark, he pointedly noted that congressional refusal to accept an "invitation" to "dialogue" with the judiciary may be as significant as a decision to respond through new legislation.[64] Besides the fact that this argument passes over the important difference between conscious or deliberate and unconscious or careless silence, the impression left by Brennan that the judiciary enjoys a measure of freedom to try out interpretations of laws in the course of carrying on a "dialogue" with the legislative department is not unproblematical.

While the Constitution set up three separate departments, they were not designed to be equal in power or importance. The legislative department was clearly set up as the preeminent branch of the government. Not only is it the subject of the first and longest article of the Constitution, but Congress alone was given the power to remove the heads of the coordinate branches while also retaining the authority to discipline, to the point of removing, its own members. The Founders understood that to qualify as a democratic republic, the new American nation would have to permit the people to establish their own laws through their elected representatives, and especially legislative officials. Considered in this context, the principal role of the judiciary is to enforce the terms of statutory law and the Constitution. It is in this sense that the judiciary, to recur to Alexander Hamilton's *Federalist* 78, can be said to have no "will" of its own. Brennan's construction of the "dialogue" that can transpire between the judicial and legislative branches at least comes very close to permitting the judiciary to express its "will" with regard to either the ends or the means of public policies. Investing the judiciary with its own "will" fits well with the belief that one of the responsibilities falling to judicial officials is to ensure that the laws conform to the "reason and passion" of the times. What is at least diminished, if not entirely sacrificed, to achieve this objective is a *Federalist* 78 view of the place and role of the Court in the constitutional system. But legitimacy for the exercise of "will" must come from somewhere. For Brennan, as has repeatedly been noted, the source of legitimacy is the goal of maximizing individual autonomy through self-expression.

Dismantling discriminatory practices and multiplying opportunities for diverse forms of expression were twin themes that marked Brennan's last major contribution to constitutional law in the affirmative action and quota areas. His success in putting together a majority in support of a congressionally authorized FCC licensing program that benefited minority persons stands out as one of the more dramatic victories that he enjoyed during his thirty-four terms on the Court. The Rehnquist Court had been particularly hard on liberal causes during 1989. So unhappy was Senator Edward Kennedy at the end of 1989 that he undertook to advance a new civil rights law whose very purpose was to undo the damage that he believed had been done by the Supreme Court. Against this backdrop, Brennan succeeded in gaining support for a ruling in *Metro Broadcasting* v. *FCC* that affirmed the constitutionality of an FCC program that gave distinct advantages in the transfer of some broadcast licenses to minorities without requiring evidence of prior injury due to discrimination.[65] The announced goal was to diversify ownership of stations and, thereby, diversify the content of broadcasts.

After summarizing the goals and procedures associated with the minority preference program, Brennan recurred to Chief Justice Warren Burger's decade-old opinion in *Fullilove* v. *Klutznick* as a precedent for the appropriateness of judicial deference to congressional uses of "benign" racial classifications. The Court had rejected in *Fullilove* a challenge to a congressionally mandated set-aside requirement tied to federally funded public works projects.[66] This precedent allowed Brennan to treat judicial deference in cases such as *Metro Broadcasting* as no longer requiring serious commentary or defense. In short, the application of a more relaxed test than strict scrutiny was taken to be unproblematical. And the new "intermediate" test provided ample room for Congress to award preferences, even if not justified by prior discrimination:

> We hold that benign race-conscious measures mandated by Congress—even if those measures are not "remedial" in the sense of being designed to compensate victims of past governmental or societal discrimination—are constitutionally permissible to the extent that they serve important governmental objectives within the power of Congress and are substantially related to the achievement of those objectives.[67]

Brennan had no problem in finding that both parts of his test were satisfied in *Metro Broadcasting;* that is, the promotion of broadcast diversity fulfilled the first part of the test (an important government objective), and the preference program was found to be an effective means of achieving this end. His endorsement of the stated goal of the preference program took little effort. Government measures designed to free up the expression of "diverse" and even "antagonistic" sources of information and views on subjects of public interest fit well with Brennan's opinions in a host of First Amendment cases.

To give the government a clean victory, however, Brennan understood that it would be necessary to show that the means being employed by the FCC to promote broadcast diversity not only were likely to be effective but did not impose impermissible burdens on nonminorities. Recognizing that he could hardly argue that the complaining parties in cases such as *Metro Broadcasting* had suffered no impairment of property or personal interests, he fell back on the argument frequently made in censorship cases that innocent parties must be prepared to bear the cost or "burden of the remedy." As the Jewish people of Skokie, Illinois were told in the mid-1970s that the emotional suffering that they might endure as a result of the freedom allowed American Nazis to publicize their views through parades was a necessary "cost" of democracy, so the "burden" imposed on nonminorities who lost out under the FCC preference program constituted just another acceptable "cost." Although Brennan spoke of the burdens that innocent parties might be required to bear in order to "remedy" past injustices, he plainly intended to legitimize governmental actions that are not just remedial in nature.[68] The "costs" imposed on nonminority competitors for broadcast licenses or persons such as Allan Bakke or Brian Weber, as with any weakening of federalism or the two-party system that might result from the decisions in *Baker* v. *Carr* or *Elrod* v. *Burns*, are for Brennan the bearable price of having a democracy that concentrates its attention on maximizing individual self-determination for the most constrained party in any competition of adverse interests. In *Metro Broadcasting*, minority competitors for licenses emerged as more constrained, and thus deserving of greater preference, than nonminority competitors.

In a dissent whose tone and language evidenced deep unhappiness with Brennan's reasoning, Justice O'Connor scolded her liberal colleague for playing fast and loose with *Fullilove* in an effort to justify a far lower level of scrutiny than appropriate in racial classification cases. According to O'Connor, not only did *Fullilove* come to the Court under Section 5 of the Fourteenth Amendment, long conceded to be a source of extraordinary federal power, but the program under challenge in that case had the specific purpose of redressing or remedying prior discrimination. Here is the single "compelling" governmental interest that can satisfy the only acceptable test for O'Connor: strict scrutiny. Promoting greater diversity in the dissemination of viewpoints over the airways did not qualify as a "compelling" interest.[69] Brennan's insistence that the Court may employ a more relaxed standard of review than strict scrutiny when the use of racial categories is "benign" elicited what was perhaps the most cutting observation in O'Connor's dissent. Rather than anticipating the end of victimization, she accused Brennan of unleashing reasoning that made it likely that some individuals or groups would always be able to see themselves as victims deserving of preferences: "Divorced from any remedial purpose and otherwise undefined, 'benign' means only what shifting fashions and changing politics deem acceptable."[70] Assuming that fashions and politics are by their nature given to constant change, then Brennan's reasoning supplies an open-ended invitation to award preferences based on racial classification. Not only did she believe that this could not be squared with constitutional principles, O'Connor was convinced that Brennan's approach would be detrimental to the overall health of the society.

If O'Connor disputed the acceptability of the end sought to be promoted by the FCC, she was no more agreeable when it came to the commission's means. In her estimation, the government was guilty of relying on the flawed assumption that insufficient diversity in broadcast viewpoints is tied to underrepresentation of minorities as licensed station operators. This reasoning assumes a nexus between race and behavior that depends on the kind of racial stereotyping and generalizations that O'Connor believed was inherently suspect. Without hard evidence to support the assumed nexus between diversity of viewpoints and the distribution of broadcast licenses, the means employed by the FCC also fail strict scrutiny. In short, she disagreed with Brennan's handling of both the end and the means.

If Brennan appeared to be unconcerned about the things that moved O'Connor to dissent, it was not because he worried any less about governmental regulatory actions in 1990 than in 1970. The explanation has to do with his calculations about the effects of employing or not employing preferences on the freedom enjoyed by people to shape their way of life through some form of expressive activity. It is not insignificant that he included in his *Bakke* opinion the observation that Davis's racial preference program was unlikely to prevent Bakke from having a rewarding career and an enjoyable life. Insofar as Brennan's cost-benefit calculations are intended to free up the most constrained parties in society, they are highly context dependent. His confidence that these calculations are not beyond our capability allows him to downplay the fear that society will inevitably be harmed by the use of racial categories. All this assumes, of course, that the task is manageable and that there is no special danger in using racial categories as long as we can accurately weigh the "costs" borne by all parties in contests having do to with the assignment of preferences. If you have doubts about whether even decent societies are up to this task or whether classifying people according to race may not be inherently dangerous or constitutionally impermissible, then Brennan's victory in *Metro Broadcasting* will not be very comforting. His reasoning clearly tests the limits both of political life and of human nature itself. Significantly, abstracting from these limits was also characteristic of his handling of cases involving the use of gender categories. It will be useful to examine his treatment of gender classification before any final summary is offered of Brennan's Fourteenth Amendment jurisprudence.

Disconnecting Nature and Law: Gender Distinctions as Suspect Classifications

Modern liberal thought was shaped by theorists such as John Locke who understood that civil societies can promote the comfortable preservation of their members only if laws effectively restrain natural impulses. They also understood, however, that laws will be effective only to the extent that they are attuned to these impulses. While they recognized that nature is the source of the problems that make life in the "state of nature" intolerable, they prudently saw that only if civil societies treat human nature seriously can they hope to advance the interests of their members. One explanation for the fall of the communist systems is that Marxism-Leninism cannot be reconciled with natural human drives and desires. In a special way, gender distinctions in American law emerged out of long-standing convictions about what nature intended of men and women, whether in the context of family or occupational responsibilities. Significantly, the traditional norms governing gender classifications were left untouched by the Court until the end of the 1960s. And again Brennan emerged as one of the principal figures responsible for reconstructing the rules that applied to such classifications.

Frontiero v. *Richardson* deserves a high place on the list of cases that supplied evidence in the early 1970s of Brennan's growing impatience with traditional stereotypes and norms that limited expression and self-determination.[71] His plurality opinion contained a "no holds barred" attack on sexual classifications. Using the due process clause of the Fifth Amendment, the petitioner in *Frontiero* brought an equal protection challenge against a federal regulation that automatically treated the spouses of male members of the armed services as dependents for purposes of obtaining allowances and benefits, but required spouses of female members of the services to demonstrate dependency to qualify for the same benefits. Underlying this regulation was the assumption that husbands typically serve as the major breadwinners for families. The government coupled this assumption with an argument based on administrative costs and convenience. Sifting through cases to establish dependency could be time-consuming and costly. But where Brennan would later refuse to subject the assumption that race shapes behavior to the strictest scrutiny in *Metro Broadcasting*, he was not so cooperative in *Frontiero*. He would be as tough on the government in this case as he was when dealing with sovereign immunity in *Bivens* v. *Six Unknown Named Narcotics Agents* and libel regulations in *Rosenbloom* v. *Metromedia*, also early 1970s cases.

Brennan very quickly revealed in *Frontiero* that he was not inclined to negotiate when it came to government use of sexual classifications. In an important break with previous handling of such categories, he announced that reliance on sexual distinctions should be an "inherently suspect" practice.[72] As such, statutory provisions such as the one challenged in this case had to be subjected to "strict judicial scrutiny."[73] With this decided, the task that remained for Brennan was to determine if the regulation could pass muster.

An interesting array of arguments was employed by Brennan to discredit and delegitimize the regulation. Reference was made, for example, to congressional unhappiness with sexual discrimination.[74] By 1973, however, appeals to legislative intent were hardly dispositive for Brennan. By contrast, evidence that people were being disabled by regulations based on factors over which they had no control could establish the kind of "victimization" that would be dispositive:

> Moreover, since sex, like race and national origin, is an immutable characteristic determined solely by the accident of birth, the imposition of special disabilities upon the members of a particular sex because of their sex would be seen to violate "the basic concept of our system that legal burdens should bear some relationship to individual responsibility. . . ."[75]

Interestingly, the personal responsibility argument did not advance Allan Bakke's cause when Brennan reflected on the legality of "benign" uses of racial categories five years later. The difference can be explained in terms of the case-by-case calculations required to free up the most constrained parties in any competition of interests. Nothing less will satisfy the demands of his jurisprudence of libertarian dignity. Where his calculations did not favor Bakke's reverse discrimination claim in 1978, they did favor the attack on gender categories in 1973.

A variation of the "political powerlessness" argument was also made by Brennan in *Frontiero*. Since it was not possible to argue that women constitute a small minority possessing no political power, he emphasized their "underrepresentation" in the "decisionmaking councils" of the country.[76] This observation really exposes the fatal defect in sexual classifications for Brennan. The problem has less to do with any asserted inconsistency with legislative desires or violation of the strict principle of individual responsibility, and more to do with the tendency of regulations such as the one challenged in *Frontiero* to limit the ability of women to freely shape a way of life for themselves, which would include access to careers of their choice. In this regard, underrepresentation in legislative or executive bodies was convincing evidence of the necessity of strict scrutiny. That Frontiero-type regulations might be viewed as beneficial for the female spouses of male members of the military was of no avail. Brennan dismissed this defense of the regulation as reflecting a form of "romantic paternalism" that carried hidden threats to fundamental equality and self-determination.[77] This was the problem, for example, that he found with the Hyde Amendment that limited access to federal funds by women seeking abortions. Dissenting in *Harris* v. *McRae* from a ruling that the Hyde Amendment did not contravene the liberty guarantees of the due process clause, Brennan declared that "the state must refrain from wielding its enormous power and influence in a manner that burdens the pregnant woman's freedom to choose whether to have an abortion."[78] The assertion that natural sexual characteristics should not be employed to limit opportunities for individual expression and autonomy appears throughout Brennan's opinions in gender classification cases.

The extent of Brennan's concern about the effects of even so-called "benign" forms of gender classifications was evident in a dissent submitted a year after *Frontiero* in a case having to do with the constitutionality of a state property exemption available to widows but not widowers. Writing for the Court in *Kahn* v. *Shevin*, Justice William O. Douglas had no difficulty in upholding the exemption as a reasonable policy tailored to the needs of that group (women) most heavily burdened by loss of a spouse.[79] While sympathetic to the aim of the exemption, Brennan dissented on the grounds that the policy could not survive "close judicial scrutiny." There were, in his estimation, less offensive ways of providing relief for needy widows.[80] The stakes in the form of continuing unequal constraints on lifestyle choices required that he play "hard ball" with Florida. As this dissent reveals, Brennan was as prepared to challenge regulations that might put men at a disadvantage as those that might have this effect on women. A man, as well as a woman, can be the principal constrained party in a legal controversy. That *Kahn* was not an anomaly was made evident a year later when he disagreed with the Court's rejection of a male naval officer's challenge to the seemingly more lenient rules that were applied to the promotion of women but not men within that branch of the armed services.[81] Where Justice Stewart could find good reason to give women more time to earn promotion and avoid mandatory discharge, Brennan saw nothing to justify the scheme under either strict scrutiny or even the more deferential rational basis test. The dangers lurking within such schemes were enough to lead him to demand hard evidence of the necessity of the distinctions. The earnestness that characterized his position on gender-based constraints that interfere with lifestyle choices is revealed by the fact that he believed these constraints were no less suspect when men were disabled or disadvantaged than when women were the ones who suffered some disadvantage.

That as elsewhere the goal of reducing inequality in lifestyle pursuits drove Brennan's reasoning in gender classification cases, and not mere subscription to a particular test (for example, strict scrutiny or First Amendment absolutism), was evident in the opinion that he wrote for the Court in *Craig* v. *Boren*.[82] This 1976 Oklahoma case involved a challenge to a statute that prohibited the sale of 3.2% beer to males under twenty-one but only to females under eighteen. Instead of strict scrutiny, Brennan used a two-part intermediate scrutiny test to invalidate the regulation. Anticipating the approach that he would take in later race classification cases such as *Metro Broadcasting*, he declared that to withstand constitutional challenge gender distinctions "must serve important governmental objectives and must be substantially related to the achievement of those objectives."[83] This was much more than Burger and Rehnquist thought the Court should expect by way of justification for public policies of the sort that had been enacted by Oklahoma officials. While Brennan was willing to negotiate to build a winning coalition, his objective dictated a test that still approximated strict scrutiny in practice, even if not identical to it in theory, when government erects obstacles that limit equality and personal freedom.

Although Brennan agreed to accept Oklahoma's characterization of the statute as a regulation designed to promote traffic safety, it is clear from a footnote comment that he really was not inclined to give government officials much benefit of the doubt when gender distinctions are at issue. In a tersely written note, he suggested that the Court might wish to consider at some later date whether the representation of legislative purposes offered by state officials should be accepted at face value or subjected to careful scrutiny to determine if "convenient, but false, *post-hoc* rationalizations" were being employed at the litigation stage.[84] He could dispense with such an assessment in *Craig* because the sex-based distinction being employed by Oklahoma was in his estimation only tenuously related to the advancement of public safety. Pointing to statistical surveys introduced by the appellants, he noted that the percentage of males in the eighteen-to-twenty age group who were arrested for driving while under the influence of alcohol was only slightly higher (2%) than that of females. This disparity was deemed insufficient to justify the disability imposed on males by the law: "Certainly if maleness is to serve as a proxy for drinking and driving, a correlation of 2% must be considered an unduly tenuous 'fit.' "[85] More than this, the very effectiveness of the restriction had not been established to his satisfaction. For Brennan, here was ample cause to set the regulation aside. If not strict scrutiny in name, he showed no interest in letting state officials get away without coming close to dotting every i and crossing every t.

To understand how tough a message was being conveyed in *Craig v. Boren* it is only necessary to reflect on the action taken by Oklahoma. This was not the equivalent of a segregationist policy or a protectionist measure that might threaten the national commercial system. Based on hard statistics that confirmed that males tend to be more reckless and irresponsible when it comes to drinking and driving than females, the state had decided to restrict access by 18-to-20-year-old males to 3.2% beer. Basing the statute on the kind of stereotyping of persons that Brennan considered suspect would seem to be a rational way of responding to the tendency of some persons (in this case males) to believe that prevailing stereotypes (males who drink and drive) are models to be imitated. State officials undoubtedly understood that even a minimal reduction in the threats to public safety posed by drunken drivers would represent an enormous gain for those persons who would be spared serious injuries and/or property loss. Banning consumption of 3.2% beer on the part of 18-to-20-year-old males could be construed as a reasonable form of government action taken to advance the general welfare. In short, it could be seen as a sensible policy enacted in the name of self-defense. Brennan clearly was not oblivious to these arguments. But it is instructive that he could not allow himself to concede that these arguments might be sufficient to justify a policy whose disabling effect on males was hardly dramatic and certainly not pernicious. He could not easily give in to Oklahoma for the same reason that he could not give in to the arguments employed by Rehnquist in the *DeShaney* or *Cruzan* cases or Powell in *Mathews* v. *Eldridge* or Scalia in *Michael H* v. *Gerald D.* It is too easy to find "reasonable" grounds for enacting legislation that restrains the ability of people to express their views or to choose and pursue a way of life with the maximum of freedom. The problem with Oklahoma's law was not that some defense could not be offered of the gender distinctions on which it rested. The law succumbed to Brennan's analysis because the benefits were not great enough and could not be established with sufficient certainty to offset the damage that might be done to individual expression and self-determination.

Brennan's last major opinion in a case involving gender distinctions came in a suit requiring the Court to mediate competing claims raised on behalf of First and Fourteenth Amendment freedoms. Writing for the majority in *Roberts* v. *United States Jaycees*, he found that the constitutional weight of Minnesota's efforts to reduce gender discrimination by targeting the males-only membership practices of the state's Jaycee chapters more than offset any impairment of freedom of association suffered by members of that organization.[86] In reversing the appellate court decision in favor of the Jaycees, Brennan once more revealed that his aims were better advanced by case-by-case calculations than by First Amendment absolutism.

After summarizing the events that provoked the suit, Brennan proceeded to reflect on the weight that should be assigned the First Amendment claims of the Jaycees. In this regard, he noted that the Court had identified two forms of association that merited special protection: "certain intimate human relationships" and activities connected with freedom of speech, assembly, or religion. The first type dovetails closely with the overall aim of Brennan's jurisprudence, that is, "safeguarding the ability independently to define one's identity." This ability, he quickly added, is "central to any concept of liberty."[87] It is surely "central" to Brennan's. The Jaycees, however, gained little from the considerable constitutional weight that this form of association ordinarily carries because of Brennan's conclusion that local chapters tended to be large and membership was "routinely" extended with little consideration of background. What was missing for him was evidence that the associational ties of the Jaycees sufficiently approximated the kinds of "personal bonds [that] have played a critical role in the culture and traditions of the Nation by cultivating and transmitting shared ideals and belief. . . ." These are the forms of association that for Brennan must be carefully guarded by the judiciary because they "foster diversity and act as critical buffers between the individual and the state."[88] As examples of such associations he cited the marriage relationship and activities that go on within families such as the raising and education of children. While acknowledging that other types of relationships also qualify for some protection under this form of associational liberty, he concluded that the Jaycees lacked adequate selectivity or commonality to enable them to get sufficient help from the First Amendment to offset the equal protection claims raised by the state. It is clear that Brennan's goal of freeing up the most constrained parties in this case was assisted by subjecting the arguments of the Jaycees to strict scrutiny while giving the state the benefit of the doubt.

As for the appeal by the Jaycees to freedom of association for expressive purposes, again Brennan found the liberty interest to be weighty but the particular claim of injury to be problematical. This section of the opinion contained his defense of Minnesota's attack on gender discrimination. He commended the state for its efforts to undercut "stereotypical nations" that too often interfere with "equal access to publicly available goods and services."[89] If the state's actions merited considerable weight under the Fourteenth Amendment, the First Amendment charge that expressive activity was seriously impaired by these actions received little weight. Brennan held that the Jaycees had failed to prove that the law "impose[d] any serious burdens on the male members' freedom of expressive association."[90] Any "incidental abridgment" of protected speech was dismissed as "no greater than necessary to accomplish the State's legitimate purposes."[91] Here was a version of the "cost" argument that either implicitly or explicitly is in evidence in his opinions in *Bakke* and *Metro Broadcasting*, among other places. In a brief but revealing comment, Brennan added that for the Court to accept the argument that the admission of women might alter the "content or impact of the organization's speech" would be tantamount to endorsing sexual stereotyping.[92] Having undercut the entire constitutional case offered by the Jaycees, he had no difficulty in awarding the victory to the state.

If Brennan appeared to be tough in his assessment of the First Amendment claims of the Jaycees, and O'Connor in her concurrence made this argument, it clearly is not the result of any hostility to associational rights, either narrowly or broadly conceived. What is especially telling are the declarations that the Jaycee organization is not known for exercising great selectivity when choosing members and that it likely would not have the content of its messages seriously altered by enforcement of the law. After applying "strict" scrutiny to the arguments of the Jaycees, Brennan concluded that conformity to Minnesota's Human Rights Act could come with minimal "cost." At the same time, he believed that the gains in terms of freeing more people to choose their own identities and control their own destinies in a way that had been precluded to them would be significant. This is the kind of cost-benefit analysis, again tied to the maximization of personal expression and self-determination, that by 1986 had become a hallmark of his jurisprudence.

The narrowness of Brennan's focus in *Roberts* can create the impression that there is nothing problematical about the weights he assigned personal and societal or governmental interests when performing his cost-benefit calculations. A broader and more defensible perspective would result in a different assessment of costs and benefits. While there may well be good cause to enforce the Minnesota law against the Jaycees, it is not clear that this should be accomplished by denigrating their status as an association whose activities can "[play] a critical role in the culture and traditions of the Nation by cultivating and transmitting shared ideals and beliefs." If Brennan does not completely overlook the contribution of the Jaycees to American society, his analysis of their claims leaves them vulnerable in a way that may threaten their credentials as an valuable civic organization. This result, in turn, may work against having the kinds of associations that are essential to a healthy democratic polity. It is also noteworthy that his elevated conception of what the First Amendment safeguards (that is, the right to create one's own identity and pursue a way of life of one's own choosing) actually arms the Jaycees to challenge the Minnesota law at the same time that Brennan discredited the arguments offered in defense of their admissions practices. The problem of constitutional confusion aside, good political reasons might be offered for avoiding both sides of his argument. Brennan's tendency to abstract from political concerns simplifies his task but leaves the product of his work open to the kind of Madisonian and Tocquevillean criticism that was considered in connection with his First Amendment opinions and to which we turn once more.

Challenging the Limits of Nature and Society: Brennan's Fourteenth Amendment Jurisprudence

It is hard to fault Justice Brennan for showing sympathy for the plight of Nancy Cruzan or Joshua DeShaney or for attacking racial and gender discrimination. If human beings possess some universal moral sense about what is right or proper or just according to nature, then Brennan's desire to protect the victims of physical abuse or racial discrimination should resonate with all right-thinking persons. At the same time, the emphasis that he gives to taming both the administrative state and nature has an obvious appeal in modernity. The great aim of modern liberal thought, after all, is the conquest of nature or the subjection of natural forces to complete human control. Success in this regard, according to theorists such as René Descartes and John Locke, would translate into greater safety and happiness for the people. As we have seen, the same pursuit of nontragic existence that defines modernity also appears in Brennan's jurisprudence.

The expectation in modernity that the mastery of scientific methodology will enable human beings to conquer nature and control their destiny appears in the weight given to such devices as separation of powers and the legal rules associated with due process of law. Brennan's insistence that additional procedural machinery be available to aggrieved parties in due process and equal protection cases is fully consistent with this tradition. What is not clearly visible in Brennan's opinions is the care that theorists such as Locke took to preserve a capacity for effective political "rule" behind such institutional arrangements as separation of powers and criminal due process guarantees. Considering the emphasis given to individual rights and equality in modernity, there was good reason for theorists to mask political "rule" so as not to provoke dangerous reductions in governmental authority. The risk, however, was that by veiling the tough side of government the impression might be created that strong political rule is dispensable. And, indeed, while Brennan invited assertive governmental action in *Green* v. *County School Board*, his opinions more typically reveal a conviction that political "rule" can and should be relaxed. Accompanying this conviction is his belief that we should aim at relaxing distinctions and norms that derive from society and nature. Witness his unwillingness to have policies governed by prevailing societal norms in *Michael H.*, and his argument that gender distinctions are inherently suspect and ought to be subjected to strict scrutiny in *Frontiero*. The dangers of state-sponsored religion, for example, loomed large in the reasoning offered by Brennan in 1987 for rejecting Louisiana's attempt to legislate equal time for creation science in public school classes that cover evolutionary theory.[93] Significantly, whether the advancement of individual autonomy is productive of good citizenship or civilized behavior did not undergo the same careful scrutiny as regulations based on prevailing opinions and natural distinctions. What is present in his opinions is a hopefulness about the prospect of advancing civilized participation in democratic government through the process of maximizing each person's control over his or her destiny.

Although the responsibilities of a jurist are not those of a founder or legislator, even judicial reflection on the requirements of due process or equal protection should at some point incorporate the distinction between regimes that brutalize human beings and those political orders that may be imperfect but still fundamentally committed to defensible objectives. There is, after all, a difference between the regime that tortured Aleksander Solzhenitsyn and the United States at the end of the twentieth century. It is one thing to create obstacles to effective governance in the case of Stalinist Russia and another thing to invite people to treat the actions of officials in the United States, or the country's prevailing traditions, as inherently suspect. There is also a difference between societies that legitimate the teaching of responsible civic behavior and those that leave this to chance. In this connection, the "costs" and not just the "benefits" of the practice of attaching significance to one's own actions more than to social or political conventions or natural distinctions deserve attention in any serious body of political or judicial thought. Ahistorical existence may permit an immediate expansion of personal freedom, but not without some price. There is good reason to believe that encouraging people to focus on self-expression and the creation of a personal identity is less likely to result in collective action in the advancement of important civic causes, one common version of responsible democratic citizenship, than if adherence to conventions that bind the members of society into a distinctive group is encouraged.

The potentially corrosive effect on responsible conduct of the drive to emancipate people from nature's impulses and social conventions can be seen in the behavior of some of the males who abandon women following conception or the birth of a child. At the same time that the availability of contraceptives gives women greater control over nature, it also permits men to hold their partners responsible for unwanted pregnancies. That is to say, males are positioned to expect women to be able to control the natural effects of sexual intercourse. The failure to exercise such control becomes for some men an excuse to avoid their familial obligations. What this example illustrates is that devices that enable human beings to master or overcome nature do not come without costs.[94] It also reveals the enormous responsibility that accompanies the weakening of natural, social, and political rules and distinctions. For Brennan, this responsibility would have to include a capacity to make the complicated calculations about "costs" and "benefits" relative to the maximization of freedom from all kinds of restraints that supported his own position in cases such as *Bakke*. As we have seen, recitals of the "benign" intentions of governmental institutions in equal protection cases could elicit a sympathetic response as in *Bakke* or a critical response as in *Kahn v. Shevin*. The proper reaction for Brennan depends on the outcome of his version of cost-benefit analysis. Even persons attracted to Brennan's jurisprudence would have to admit that knowing how to weigh the competing claims to achieve the results he desired could strain the capacity of many jurists and certainly most of the lay population.

Brennan obviously would not quarrel with the argument that the great degree of freedom he defends demands a commensurate degree of responsibility and thoughtfulness. It is clear, however, that not everyone is capable of exercising the kind of self-restraint that is required if freedom is to be used responsibly. Brennan provided little direct instruction regarding the necessity of self-restraint while insisting that considerable weight be given to the free choice of an identity or way of life. At the same time that liberation from constraining norms gets plenty of attention in his opinions, minimal emphasis is given to the social, political, or natural duties that are commonly associated with decency and responsible citizenship. While the ideal of a self-regulating system made up of self-defining individuals flows easily from the political writings that helped shape the American founding, also present in modern or "classical" liberal thought is the importance of retaining external sources of support for "right" action or conduct. The importance of seeking such support certainly was not lost on some of the leading figures of the founding period. John Marshall's biography of George Washington, for example, represented an early effort at creating a model of "right" conduct. Washington's use of military force in response to the Whiskey Rebellion is an example of tough governmental action designed to discourage "wrong" conduct and, conversely, encourage "right" behavior in keeping with the limits of political life.

Brennan will properly be remembered for his strenuous and untiring efforts to liberate people to make fundamental choices about the way of life they wish to live. It would be unfair and even mean-spirited to belittle his efforts or his motives. Indeed, his opinions were painstakingly crafted to advance a jurisprudential philosophy that affirmed the dignity of all people. There is nothing untoward, however, in asking whether the political thought that informs the American political system can be reconciled with Brennan's project. Paraphrasing *Federalist* 51, we might ask whether his vision of a community of persons liberated from all manner of restraints can be reconciled with the imperfections that distinguish human beings from angels. If Madison was right in counseling his contemporaries to design a political system for imperfect beings whose world will never be free of tragic elements, then to act on the contrary assumption may be to produce not only unnecessary additional pain for people who witness the tragedies of life but a debilitating cynicism that can easily render people ungovernable. The contemporary appeal of Brennan's arguments in cases such as *DeShaney* or *Johnson v. Santa Clara County* aside, his Fourteenth Amendment jurisprudence cannot be shielded from considerations having to do with the nature of human beings and the limits of political life if his legal thought is to be treated as a serious source of instruction on the fundamental spirit and goals of the American constitutional order.

Notes

1. 16 Wall. 36 (1873).
2. The Black-Frankfurter debate on the meaning of the Fourteenth Amendment, and especially its due process clause, is clearly visible in their opinions in *Adamson* v. *California* (332 U.S. 46 [1947]) and *Rochin* v. *California* (342 U.S. 165 [1952]).
3. 367 U.S. 643 (1961).
4. 372 U.S. 335 (1963).
5. 391 U.S. 145 (1968).
6. 397 U.S. 254 (1970).
7. 424 U.S. 319 (1976) [Brennan dissenting].
8. 381 U.S. 479 (1965).
9. 410 U.S. 113 (1973).
10. 405 U.S. 438 (1972).
11. 497 U.S. 261 (1990) [Brennan dissenting].
12. 489 U.S. 189 (1989) [Brennan dissenting].
13. 438 U.S. 265 (1978).
14. 480 U.S. 616 (1987).
15. On the application of the equal protection principle to open housing requirements in property transfer cases see, for example, *Reitman* v. *Mulkey* (387 U.S. 369 [1967]). Brennan joined White's opinion that struck down an attempt in California to repeal open housing laws on the grounds that the only objective could have been to legitimize discrimination in the sale of property. In dissent, Harlan argued to no avail that the people only sought to return the state to a position of neutrality in this field. Harlan clearly understood the enormous significance of the Court's broad view of illegal state action. Classic decisions upholding the application of the Civil Rights Act to private establishments can be found in *Katzenbach* v. *McClung* (379 U.S. 294 [1964]) and *Heart of Atlanta Motel, Inc.* v. *United States* (379 U.S. 241 [1964]).
16. 360 U.S. 423 (1959).
17. 367 U.S. 1 (1961) and 367 U.S. 203 (1961).
18. 380 U.S. 51, 58 (1965).

19. 397 U.S. 254.

20. Ibid. at 273–74.

21. Ibid. at 265. The "general Welfare" and "Blessings of Liberty" language comes from the Preamble of the Constitution. Invocation of this language has become increasingly common in political rhetoric since the 1960s. Significantly, in his dissent in *San Antonio Independent School District* v. *Rodriguez*, Brennan argued that the fundamentality of a right for equal protection analysis should not depend only on whether it is "explicitly or implicitly guaranteed" by the Constitution. 411 U.S. 1 (1973).

22. 397 U.S. at 264–65.

23. Ibid. at 265.

24. Brennan's comments on the need for added procedural safeguards due to the absence of any assurance that administrative action would result in a just disposition of cases appeared in a footnote. Ibid. at 264, n. 12.

25. 405 U.S. 208, 223 (1972).

26. Ibid. at 227. See also his opinion in *Goldberg*, 397 U.S. at 266. The insistence that government agencies employ pretermination or posttermination procedures designed to safeguard rights and significant personal interests continued to occupy Brennan until the very end of his time on the Court. See, for example, his majority opinion in *McKesson Corporation* v. *Florida Alcohol and Tobacco Division*, 496 U.S. 18 (1990). Another 1990 case in which Brennan emphasized the importance of arming people to check on regulatory action that might deprive them of benefits was *Wilder* v. *Virginia*. Here, he wrote for the majority in a 5–4 Medicaid rulemaking case (496 U.S. 498).

27. 422 U.S. 749 (1975); 424 U.S. 319 (1976).

28. 422 U.S. 749, 804.

29. 424 U.S. 319, 349.

30. Ibid. at 350.

31. 489 U.S. 189, 212 (1989).

32. 491 U.S. 110 (1989).

33. Ibid. at 144–45. A decade before *Michael H.* v. *Gerald D.* came to the Court, Brennan had emphasized the "natural" character of traditional family units defined by blood ties in his majority opinion in *Smith* v. *Organization of Foster Families for Equality and Reform*, 431 U.S. 816 (1977). While giving special weight to the traditional definition of family units in this case, he acknowledged that significant relationships can exist in the absence of blood ties. Anticipating his opinion in *Michael H.*, Brennan stressed the need to accord special weight to the interests of "natural parents" in cases having to do with the care and up-bringing of children (see ibid. at 846). It is also noteworthy that he defended judicial restraint in cases such as *Organization of Foster Families* that he believed involved "issues of unusual delicacy." Ibid. at 855.

34. 491 U.S. at 141.

35. Ibid.

36. 497 U.S. 261 (1990).

37. Ibid. at 303.

38. Ibid. at 314.

39. Ibid. 313, n. 13; also see 315–16.

40. Reference to Brennan's commitment to a "right to be let alone" appears

in Stephen J. Friedman, "William J. Brennan," in *The Justices of the United States Supreme Court 1789–1969*, Leon Friedman and Fred L. Israel, eds. (New York: Bowker, 1969), 2855. On the state of nature in modern natural rights theory see Leo Strauss, *Natural Right and History* (Chicago: University of Chicago Press, 1953), 169, 222–24.

41. 384 U.S. 641 (1966); 391 U.S. 430 (1968).

42. 384 U.S. at 650. In the same year as *Katzenbach* v. *Morgan*, Brennan argued for a broad reading of the rights "secured" to the people by the Constitution in *United States* v. *Guest* (383 U.S. 745, 779 [1966] {Brennan concurring and dissenting}).

43. 4 Wheat. 316 (1819).

44. 384 U.S. at 656 (emphasis added). Brennan also made a strong argument for judicial deference in his dissent in *National League of Cities* v. *Usery*, a 1976 commerce clause case (426 U.S. 833). Pointing to Marshall's opinion in *McCulloch* v. *Maryland*, Brennan insisted that the political process constituted the proper vehicle for restraining Congress's use of the commerce power. His resistance to judicial activism in this case, specifically judicial activism linked to Rehnquist's understanding of the constitutional system, can be reconciled with his more characteristic defense of judicial activism when *National League of Cities* is considered against the backdrop of the use that had been made of the commerce power to attack racial segregation in legislation such as the Civil Rights Act of 1964. Brennan's insistence in *Katzenbach* v. *Morgan* that the Court only determine if Congress could have believed that a problem existed that necessitated use of its remedial powers was reminiscent of the deferential handling of regulations in the economic rights area after 1937 that led some scholars to argue that judicial abdication and not just self-restraint had replaced the activism of the pre-1937 period. See, for example, Douglas's opinion for the Court in *Williamson* v. *Lee Optical*, 348 U.S. 483 (1955).

45. 384 U.S. at 670.

46. 391 U.S. 430 (1968); see in addition his majority opinions in two companion cases, *Raney* v. *Board of Education* (391 U.S. 443) and *Monroe* v. *Board of Commissioners* (391 U.S. 450).

47. 391 U.S. at 439 (emphasis in the original).

48. 400 U.S. 112 (1970).

49. Ibid. at 278. The period of the drafting of the Fourteenth Amendment is described as a time of "constitutional confusion." Ibid. at 252.

50. Ibid. at 269.

51. Ibid. at 264.

52. Ibid. at 275. The argument that the principal advocates of the Fourteenth Amendment intended to accomplish more than they admitted publicly at the time is commonly referred to as the "Bickel Thesis." See Alexander Bickel, *The Least Dangerous Branch* (Indianapolis: Bobbs-Merrill, 1962).

53. 438 U.S. 265 (1978).

54. Ibid. at 378. In *Swann* v. *Charlotte-Mecklenburg Board of Education*, Burger upheld the use of busing as a remedy for dismantling dual school systems that owed their existence to government action (402 U.S. 1 [1971]).

55. 438 U.S. at 375.

56. Ibid. at 337.

57. 443 U.S. 193 (1979); 480 U.S. 616 (1987).

58. 443 U.S. at 205 (emphasis in original).

59. Ibid. at 219.

60. Ibid. at 209.

61. 480 U.S. at 642.

62. For Scalia's comments on the importance Brennan assigns to Congress's failure to respond to the interpretation of Title VII offered in *Weber*, see ibid. at 671.

63. Ibid. at 629, n. 7.

64. Ibid. at 630, n. 7.

65. 497 U.S. 547 (1990).

66. 448 U.S. 448 (1980).

67. 497 U.S. at 564-65.

68. Ibid. at 597.

69. Ibid. at 612.

70. Ibid. at 615.

71. 411 U.S. 677 (1973).

72. Ibid. at 686.

73. Ibid. at 688.

74. Ibid. at 687.

75. Ibid. at 686. The quoted portion of the passage was drawn by Brennan from *Weber* v. *Aetna Casualty and Surety Co.* (406 U.S. 164, 175 [1972]). A related "victimization" argument appeared in *Plyler* v. *Doe*, where Brennan defended the interests of children of illegal immigrants who were threatened by loss of educational opportunities (457 U.S. 202, esp. 223 [1982]).

76. 411 U.S. at 686, n. 17.

77. Ibid. at 684. Considering the attack on practices that smack of "romantic paternalism," it is not surprising that the government did not get very far with its argument based on administrative convenience (see ibid. at 688–691). Brennan again attacked the "old notion" that women can be assumed to be dependents within the home in his opinion for the Court in *Orr* v. *Orr*, an Alabama case that involved a challenge to laws which authorize state courts to impose alimony obligations on husbands but not wives (440 U.S. 268 [1979]).

78. 448 U.S. 297, 329 (1980). A related dissent in a case having to do with statutory exclusion of pregnancy benefits from California's disability insurance program appears in *Geduldig* v. *Aiello* (417 U.S. 484 [1976]). The insistence that policies that add to "the burdened role of the contemporary working woman" should be subjected to searching analysis also marked Brennan's dissent in *General Electric Co.* v. *Gilbert*, a 1976 case in which the Court ruled that without violating Title VII of the Civil Rights Act of 1964 a private employer could adopt a disability plan that excluded pregnancy from its list of temporary disabilities subject to compensation. Writing for the Court, Rehnquist declared that the plan was based on an acceptable use of "gender neutral" risk assignment processes (429 U.S. 125, esp. 158 and 160 for Brennan's comments on the need to be attentive to the burdensome effect of policies on women).

79. 416 U.S. 351 (1974).

80. Brennan was able to write a plurality opinion striking down a provision of the Federal Old-Age, Survivors, and Disability Insurance Benefits program

(OASDI) that favored widows over widowers in *Califano* v. *Goldfarb* (430 U.S. 199 [1977]). The argument that the government could save money and effort by writing the presumption of wives' dependency into the statute was dismissed as an unacceptable justification for gender-based distinctions in government benefits programs. Rehnquist, joined by Burger, Stewart, and Blackmun, wrote a dissent in *Goldfarb*. Also see Brennan's opinion for the Court in *Weinberger* v. *Wiesenfeld*, a case involving the use of a widows-widowers distinction in the awarding of survivors' benefits under the Social Security Act (420 U.S. 636 [1975]). Brennan relied on a tough assessment of the government's purposes in *Wiesenfeld* and concluded that the gender distinction could not be squared with what he considered to be the principal purpose of the provision, that is, enabling the surviving parent to remain at home to care for dependent children.

81. *Schlesinger* v. *Ballard*, 419 U.S. 498 (1975).

82. 429 U.S. 190 (1976).

83. Ibid. at 197.

84. Ibid. at 200, n. 7. This same skepticism about the reliability of state characterization of laws reappeared in a dissent by Marshall that Brennan joined in *Personnel Administrator of Massachusetts* v. *Feeney*, a 1979 case that challenged the constitutionality of a state veterans preference statute. Where Massachusetts claimed to be doing nothing more than rewarding persons for service to the country, Marshall found clear evidence of "purposeful gender-based discrimination" (442 U.S. 256 [1979]).

85. 429 U.S. at 201–2.

86. 468 U.S. 609 (1984). Members of the Minneapolis and St. Paul chapters of the Jaycees had invoked the terms of the state's Human Rights Act against the membership restrictions of the national organization after being told that the charters of both chapters were in danger of being revoked as a result of their admission of women as regular members.

87. Ibid. at 619.

88. Ibid. at 618–19.

89. Ibid. at 624.

90. Ibid. at 626. Interestingly, Brennan conceded that organizations also possess a right to "self-definition" in his concurrence in *Corporation of Presiding Bishop of Church of Jesus Christ of Latter-Day Saints* v. *Amos*, 483 U.S. 327 (1987).

91. 468 U.S. at 628.

92. Ibid.

93. *Edwards* v. *Aguillard*, 482 U.S. 578 (1987). Brennan held the Louisiana law to be in violation of the First Amendment's establishment clause "because it seeks to employ the symbolic and financial support of government to achieve a religious purpose." Ibid. at 597. Writing in dissent for himself and the Chief Justice, Scalia argued that there was sufficient evidence in the record to rule that the state's Balanced Treatment Act possessed a secular purpose and therefore could be reconciled with the principles of the establishment clause.

94. Interestingly, the modern administrative state represents a significant device that Wilsonian liberals, among others, believed had the potential for improving the degree of control that people had over their lives. Brennan, like Max Weber before him, understood the threats that accompany the creation of bureaucratic apparatus. In short, at least some of the "costs" associated with the

conquest of nature were visible to Brennan. For a thoughtful commentary on the importance of connecting government action with the natural "moral sense" of the people so as to restrain social irresponsibility, see James Q. Wilson, *The Moral Sense* (New York: Free Press, 1993).

Chapter Five

BRENNAN'S MADISON AND MARSHALL: A CASE STUDY IN DECIPHERING LANGUAGE AND THOUGHT

[The] government of the United States has been emphatically termed a government of laws, and not of men. It will certainly cease to deserve this high appellation, if the laws furnish no remedy for the violation of a vested legal right.

> —John Marshall, *Marbury* v. *Madison* (1803)

In the extended republic of the United States, and among the great variety of interests, parties and sects which it embraces, a coalition of a majority of the whole society could seldom take place on any other principles than those of justice and the general good. . . .

> —James Madison, *Federalist* No. 51 (1788)

What the constitutional fundamentals meant to the wisdom of other times cannot be their measure to the vision of our time. Similarly, what those fundamentals mean to us, our descendants will learn, cannot be the measure to the vision of their time.

> —William J. Brennan, Jr., Georgetown Address (1986)

C onsidering the emphasis given in the United States to accountability in government, the common law tradition and the conviction that policy making is properly the preserve of elected officials, it is not surprising that judicial officials go to great lengths to base their decisions on constitutional and statutory language and precedent. Respect for language and precedent serves the dual function of promoting continuity and predictability in the law, important considerations in connection with the principle of due process, while simultaneously serving to limit the discretionary authority of unelected officials in a democratic order that boasts of its belief in the sovereignty of the people. When it comes either to deciphering the language of the Constitution or to reliance on prior

137

reasoning for guidance and legitimacy, two figures clearly dominate the constitutional landscape: James Madison and John Marshall.

First for his work at the Constitutional Convention of 1787 and then for his labors on the Bill of Rights, Madison earned the title of "father" of the American Constitution. He is, as it were, our premier Founder. As for John Marshall, his reputation can hardly be exaggerated in American constitutional history. The weight that his opinions carry remains unmatched. Conspicuous references to his opinion in *Marbury* v. *Madison*, the first major defense of a general power of judicial review by the Supreme Court, abound in American case law. Considering the weight assigned to precedent and especially to the views of Madison and Marshall, the interpretation given to their writings has important implications for the way of life of the American people.

This chapter examines the use made by Justice William Brennan of Madison and Marshall. It would be sufficient to point to Brennan's unrivaled influence over three decades on the Supreme Court to justify paying special attention to the implications of his appeal to the speeches and writings of both men. An added and perhaps more weighty justification for this project, however, can be found in the fact that his opinions are likely to exercise a shaping influence over American constitutional law for decades to come. And in this connection, Brennan's version of Marshall and Madison constitutes for many jurists the only interpretation of Marshall and Madison they will acknowledge. For this reason, the task of uncovering Brennan's view of what these figures represent in American constitutional history constitutes more than mere esoteric historiography.

Brennan's credentials as the leading liberal member of the modern Court are indisputable. As we have already seen, whether the focus is the First Amendment or the Fourteenth, or the range of permissible national action under the commerce clause or the requirements of due process of law, he either led the way or freely endorsed expansive readings of constitutional and statutory language. From his majority opinion in *Baker* v. *Carr* in 1962 that opened up judicial oversight of electoral districting to his controversial decision in the 1989 *Texas* v. *Johnson* case that treated flag burning as protected expression, his entire tenure was marked by opinions that introduced new approaches to handling constitutional questions (e.g., application of strict scrutiny to gender distinctions in *Frontiero*) or nontraditional extensions of personal liberties and interests (protection against patronage practices in *Elrod* v. *Burns* and broad extension of protection against libel in *Rosenbloom* v. *Metromedia*) to the end of supplying greater judicial protection for rights and redress for grievances. At the risk of being excessively repetitive, it is worth noting once more that Brennan was the principal Warren Court spokesman for the comprehensive constitution doctrine, that is, the claim that the Constitution provides comprehensive protection for all rights and redress for all injuries. Precisely because of his status in American constitutional law, the use made of Madison and Marshall by Brennan warrants serious attention.

A Mirror View of Madison and Marshall

There is little doubt that the dominant post-Bicentennial view of Madison's work is that it represents an uncompromising defense of individual rights against potentially threatening political power. There is, in short, a decidedly rights-oriented quality to most contemporary characterizations of Madison's political thought. Marshall's legacy is no different. His *Marbury* decision is celebrated as legitimating not only the primacy of individual rights but the dominance of the courts as the principal institutions for protecting rights. Although he carefully avoided a direct collision with Thomas Jefferson over the president's refusal to deliver commissions to several Federalist appointees named to judicial posts by John Adams in the closing hours of his administration, Marshall's *Marbury* opinion is commonly associated with the claim that the judiciary not only is the major guardian of rights, but is the organ of government responsible for continuously ratcheting up protection for individual rights.[1] In light of what has been said of the jurisprudence of libertarian dignity, it is not surprising that this is also the way Madison and Marshall are cast in Brennan's opinions.

Brennan's Marshall is above all an exponent of judicial protection for the private rights of all persons. Here is the essential message of *Marbury* for Brennan. This view of *Marbury* is coupled with the common claim that in cases such as *McCulloch* v. *Maryland,* Marshall legitimated an expansive reading of the Constitution that served the ends of magnifying both national power and individual rights. Such an interpretation of Marshall complements Brennan's jurisprudence of libertarian dignity that looks to the realization in the modern state of the maximum of autonomous individualism under the protection of the judiciary.

To repeat a point developed in chapter two, Brennan repeatedly reminded judicial officials that they are oath-bound to exercise what powers they have to the end of protecting rights. It is in connection with this construction of the judicial task that he made heavy use of passages from Marshall's decision in the *Marbury* case. In Brennan's majority opinion in *United States* v. *Raines* in 1960, a voting rights case brought under the Civil Rights Act of 1957, he returned to *Marbury* to gain support for the claim that the Court has an inescapable constitutional "duty" to review government actions that endanger rights. Indeed, Brennan drew directly on Marshall's assertion that this is the Court's "gravest and most delicate duty."[2] While acknowledging that the Court should avoid "unnecessary pronouncements" on constitutional issues, Brennan left no doubt about his conviction that the judiciary is "duty" bound to protect individual rights. It is, indeed, incomprehensible to him that the Constitution may have left some rights without protection or that the judiciary might legitimately sidestep protecting rights. Hence, his repeated recurrence to the passage in *Marbury* where Marshall proclaims that "The very essence of civil liberty certainly consists in the right of every individual to claim the protection of the laws, whenever he receives an injury."[3] Among other places, Brennan incorporated this argument in his majority opinion in *Baker* v. *Carr,* the 1962 case that opened the doors to judicial review of state electoral districting schemes over the objections of Felix Frankfurter and John Marshall Harlan who insisted that the Constitution is not a comprehensive document providing protection for all rights and redress for all injuries.[4] For Brennan, the position of Frankfurter and Harlan at the least amounted to judicial abdication, if not to outright judicial heresy. It is to the above-cited passage from *Marbury* on the connection between true civil liberty and dependable legal redress for all injuries that Brennan also recurred in his majority opinion in *Bivens* v. *Six Unknown Named Narcotics Agents,* a decision that led the way in weakening the principled basis of the sovereign immunity doctrine. The objective in *Bivens* was to guarantee redress for people claiming abuses of authority by public officials.[5] Insofar as the sovereign immunity doctrine shielded agents of the government from suits for damages when real injuries were either alleged or could be established, it could not be squared with the principles of Brennan's Constitution or his interpretation of Marshall.

While Brennan is not alone in utilizing *Marbury* to supply legitimacy for something like a comprehensive constitution doctrine, the breadth and influence of his jurisprudence lend special significance to his reading of Marshall. As the preceding chapters have sought to establish, there is considerable evidence that Brennan consciously sought to construct a body of legal thought that would supply a corrective to the remaining blemishes of Holmesian and New Deal-style liberalism. These blemishes appear in actions by interest groups or legislative coalitions or administrative agencies that confine individual freedoms or equality, for example, malapportioned electoral districts or laws and regulations that perpetuate traditional racial or gender stereotypes. Marshall's assertion in *Marbury* of a broad power of judicial review fit well with the formidable tasks that Brennan saw falling to the Court. In this connection, it is not surprising that besides reliance on *Marbury*, he found Marshall's reasoning in *McCulloch* to be a valuable source of support.

To achieve the full results that he desired, Brennan argued for a reading of the Constitution that accommodates the demands of a "progressive" society. In *McCulloch*, Brennan believed he could find support from Chief Justice Marshall for a type of constitutional construction that dovetailed with his own aims. In the course of rebuffing Maryland's attempt to tax the operations of the Second Bank of the United States, Marshall forcefully distinguished between the nature of a constitution and mere legal codes by emphasizing the grand ends and permanence associated with the former and the more particular objectives typically identified with the latter. He carefully reminded the competing parties, especially Maryland's legal counsel, that they "must never forget that it is a *constitution* we are expounding."[6] For Marshall, it would be inconsistent with the nature of the Constitution to subject its language to unduly narrow or strict interpretation. Hence his association with the "loose constructionism" school in constitutional law.

As loose construction of the Constitution served Marshall's goal of assisting the national government in gaining the powers it needed to achieve the great ends set out in the Constitution, so loose constructionism served Brennan's end of perfecting the American republic as a rights-oriented society. Brennan returned to *McCulloch*, for example, to legitimize an expansive interpretation of the Constitution in *Paul* v. *Davis,* a federal case that turned on giving a broad reading to the "liberty interests" protected under the Constitution.[7] Frustrated with the majority, Brennan used *McCulloch* in dissent in this case to rebuke William H. Rehnquist for holding that the respondent should seek redress under state laws. Following a dismissal of the charges against him, Edward C. Davis III had brought suit alleging that his reputation had been damaged by the inclusion of his photo in a flyer that purportedly identified active shoplifters. It was inconceivable to Brennan that the federal Constitution could not be construed to supply relief for persons who had been stigmatized in the manner alleged by the respondent.[8] Again in *United States* v. *Leon,* a 1984 exclusionary rule case, Brennan cited *McCulloch* in dissent to remind the majority that "many of the Constitution's most vital imperatives are stated in general terms and the task of giving meaning to these precepts is therefore left to subsequent judicial lawmaking in the

context of concrete cases."[9] In this statement Brennan combined the
themes of ambitious judicial review and the legitimacy of loose constructionism that he associated with both *Marbury* and *McCulloch*.

An additional use made of Marshall's reasoning in *McCulloch* by
Brennan was to justify a broad reading of the powers of the national
government, especially the important commerce power that became the
basis for legitimizing much significant federal legislation such as the Civil
Rights Act of 1964. In *National League of Cities* v. *Usery*, a 1976 commerce clause case that saw the Court using federalism and Tenth
Amendment arguments to limit the regulation of state activities under
the national commerce power, Brennan in dissent reminded the Rehn-
quist-led majority of Marshall's exceedingly generous interpretation of
legislative authority in *McCulloch*.[10] Seemingly at odds with his often
repeated claim that the justices are duty-bound by their oath to meticulously review all allegations of abuse of governmental power, Brennan
counseled judicial restraint in federal commerce clause cases in *National
League of Cities*.[11] It is just such general counsel regarding court review
of congressional action that Marshall provided in *McCulloch* with the
result of broadening the reach of the national legislative power.[12] Considering Brennan's refusal to treat appeals to federalism or separation of
powers or democratic proceduralism as having a dispositive quality, a
good case could be made for concluding that his invocation of judicial
self-restraint in *National League of Cities* rested mostly on the fact that
the national government had acted under the federal Constitution to
advantage or improve the situation of a whole class of people. As noted
in an earlier discussion of *Katzenbach* v. *Morgan*, congressional action
that has the effect of ratcheting up rights was especially welcomed by
Brennan.[13]

The use made of Madison's political thought by Brennan closely
paralleled his construction and application of Marshall's opinion in *Marbury*. What is especially noteworthy for Brennan in Madison's writings
and speeches is the weight assigned individual freedoms, especially the
right of the people to express their views on government action, and the
role of the courts as guardians of the liberties of the people. In *United
States* v. *Leon*, Brennan quoted at length from Madison's defense of incorporating a set of guaranteed rights, a "Bill of Rights," into the Constitution. His arguments seemed tailor-made for a defense of Brennan's
jurisprudence of libertarian dignity:

> If [these rights] are incorporated into the Constitution, independent
> tribunals of justice will consider themselves in a peculiar manner the
> guardians of those rights; they will be an impenetrable bulwark against

every assumption of power in the Legislature or Executive; they will be naturally led to resist every encroachment upon rights expressly stipulated for in the Constitution by the declaration of rights.[14]

Brennan made reference to this same argument from Madison in a dissent in *United States* v. *Calandra*, a case having to do with a witness's refusal to answer questions on the grounds that they were based on evidence obtained from an illegal search and seizure. For Brennan, Lewis Powell's favorable ruling for the government violated the Madisonian position that the courts are entrusted with a special responsibility to protect rights, especially in cases involving allegedly deviant action by public officials. In *Calandra*, Brennan drew attention to the Supreme Court's obligation both to uphold individual rights and to ensure that public officials obey the laws.[15]

Madison also appeared in Brennan's opinions as an uncompromising defender of the democratic bona fides of the political order. In *New York Times* v. *Sullivan*, where Brennan sets out the "malice rule" in his majority opinion, Madison's defense of "free public discussion of the stewardship of public officials" was connected to the principle that the people are the true sovereign body under the Constitution.[16] The "father" of the Constitution was thus enlisted in the cause of highly participatory democratic government. This use of Madison fit well with Brennan's counsel in *CBS* v. *Democratic National Committee* that special attention be given to protecting the people in the expression of personal views to the end of permitting them to secure "some measure of control over their own destinies."

Another way in which Brennan used Madison to validate an activist judiciary was by drawing attention to his thoughts on the structural separation of powers among three coordinate departments of government. It is with respect to this matter that Brennan drew attention to Madison in his opinion for the Court in *Nixon* v. *Administrator of General Services*. Congressional action authorizing archival custody of former President Richard Nixon's papers, seen by Chief Justice Warren Burger and Rehnquist as a potential threat to presidential independence and power, was upheld by Brennan as an acceptable action in the context of the doctrine of separation of powers. Although the check on Nixon's invocation of presidential privilege was anchored explicitly in references to the interests of the people and Congress, it certainly fit with Brennan's defense of a broad judicial review power that extends to overseeing and refereeing disputes that are highly political in nature, including matters that involve the internal affairs of the political departments. For Brennan,

Madisonian separation of powers legitimated not only the imposition of limitations by the political branches on one another, but the activism of the judiciary.

When all the pieces of Brennan's Madison are assembled, the image that emerges is strikingly close to the characterization that Brennan provided of his own jurisprudence. His jurisprudence of libertarian dignity amounted to an effort to supply maximum protection not only for self-expression but for self-definition, hence the claim that only Nancy Cruzan, the central figure in the Missouri right to die case of 1990, should decide what could be done with her body and his insistence that people should be free to burn the American flag if they believe this is the best way to express themselves or "define their own identity"—to borrow a phrase from his opinion in *Roberts* v. *United States Jaycees*. Long before *Cruzan* v. *Missouri* and *Texas* v. *Johnson*, Brennan asserted that Madison held just such convictions. In some 1961 reflections entitled, "The Bill of Rights and the States," Brennan declared that "[for Madison], the suppression of individuality was the deadly enemy of the spirit, making a mockery of the dignity of man."[17] Here is a characterization of Madison that fits neatly with the view of the constitutional order that informed Brennan's work over a period of more than three decades.

In both Marshall and Madison's work Brennan believed could be found undeniable support for a rights-oriented jurisprudence that legitimates broad-ranging decision making by judicial officials. Here as well are the two crucial elements that he thought were needed to perfect the American republic: a judiciary empowered to act forcefully to redress grievances and an expansive view of the liberties subject to redress. It is noteworthy that many of the appeals to Marshall and Madison appear in dissenting opinions where Brennan was especially frustrated with the reasoning of his brethren. Recourse to Marshall and Madison in these opinions was clearly intended to verify the soundness and accuracy of his own position on the means and ends of a true republic of rights. It is to the persuasiveness of his interpretation and application of their constitutional thought that this chapter now turns.

The Statesmanship of Madison and Marshall

That Justice Brennan accurately identified some of the major fragments of the constitutional thinking of James Madison and John Marshall is not in doubt. It is the sufficiency of Brennan's characterization of their thinking that warrants close attention. In this connection, perhaps as good a beginning point as any when examining Madison's and Marshall's constitutional thought is to remember that both of these Founders gained a reputation for their statesmanlike appreciation of the practical difficulties that had to be addressed for the United States to be a decent and strong democratic republic. Their principal achievements were in the field of practical governance or, more specifically, in the merging of theory and practice. They sought out ways to ensure that private rights and the pursuit of individual interests were accorded the most reasonable protection in practice, which meant reconciling appeals to individual freedoms and liberties with the real demands of domestic and international politics.

From his work on the famous "Memorial and Remonstrance" on religious liberty in 1785 to his pivotal role in shaping the Bill of Rights in 1789, there is no question that Madison understood that to be considered legitimate, according to modern natural rights theory, a republic must respect the rights of the people. He also recognized that the government must be almost inconspicuous with regard to some matters, such as religion, if it is to be successful. To the greatest extent possible, the people ought to be free to articulate and pursue their interests and ideals. Madison does not equivocate in *Federalist* 10 when it comes to setting out what we should desire of government. In language that is as bold as it is blunt, he asserted that "The protection of [the] faculties [of men] is the first object of government." This observation is followed by another that is equally critical to understanding the constitutional order that Madison fathered: "From the protection of different and unequal faculties of acquiring property, the possession of different degrees and kinds of property immediately results; and from the influence of these on the sentiments and views of the respective proprietors ensues a division of the society into different interests and parties."[18] For Madison, it is not only necessary that the government protect persons in the exercise of their faculties if it is to be legitimate, but such protection is essential if we are to have a vibrant and prosperous society. For a society whose members will be driven by interest and ambition more than angelic virtue, protecting the right of people to acquire and enjoy property can be an effective way of advancing the common good. The competition of interests turns out to be good as a prod to economic development and scientific and technological innovation as well as good for societal stability. Stability results from the cooperation that is required for groups to exercise real influence. Coalitional politics involving a large number of groups was Madison's answer to factional politics. Hence the significance he attached to getting the American people to go along with the creation of a large republic that could support a multiplicity of interests.

It is to the checking and balancing and coalescing of competing interests that Madison looked for assistance in limiting governmental tyranny and in moderating civic behavior. He was confident that government protection for the exercise of the faculties along with institutional provision for the checking and balancing of interests of all kinds would serve as an effective control of the distinctive ill of democratic orders: factious violence.[19] In keeping with this reasoning, he urged generous judicial protection for individual liberties. It is Madison's reflections on the utility of judicial attention to governmental encroachments on protected rights and on the importance of supplying institutional encouragement for persons to pursue their varied interests and ideals that Brennan incorporated into cases such as *Calandra.* What must be appreciated, however, is Madison's careful attention to the connection between the enjoyment of private rights and the proper maintenance of the requisites of effective government. It is revealing of Madison's thinking that when he summarized in *Federalist* 51 the task faced by the delegates who attended the Constitutional Convention of 1787, he did not shy away from admitting that the first problem was to ensure that the new political system should be capable of controlling the people: "In framing a government which is to be administered by men over men, the great difficulty lies in this: you must first enable the government to control the governed; and in the next place oblige it to control itself."[20] In this same vein, when introducing his version of a bill of rights in Congress two years later, Madison pointedly warned his colleagues that any additional clauses must be "of such a nature as will not injure the constitution."[21] The Constitution he was intent on protecting created a framework for a strong national government. The principal lesson of the period between 1776 and 1787 for Madison was that weak and inconsistent governance is bad for rights and, hence, bad for democracy.

Among other things, getting a government that is equal to Madison's goal of controlling the governed means seeing that the different departments of the government are poised to discharge the responsibilities with which they are entrusted by the Constitution. As excessive restraints on the executive would be dangerous so also would be a judiciary that seeks to expand its powers beyond their intended limits. It is significant, for example, that when describing the Convention's final judgment on the scope of the review powers of the national judiciary, Madison approvingly noted that the delegates had decided to limit the court to reviewing "cases of a Judiciary nature."[22] This was in clear contrast to the endorsement by some delegates of a general power of judicial review. For his part, Alexander Hamilton acknowledged in *Federalist* 81 that his own defense of a general power of judicial review, a defense adopted by John Marshall in *Marbury*, was not supported by the specific language of the Constitution but rather by the theory of limited government. The point here is not to set Madison up as an opponent of judicial review, which would be erroneous. It is, rather, to highlight his understanding that we must not overlook the practical demands of effective governance, among which is the need to allow the political departments to do their work free of excessive judicial intrusion, even in the name of protecting rights. Madison understood that a healthy balance must be maintained between concern for rights and attention to the requirements of effectiveness in government. Hence his reservations about placing the Bill of Rights in too prominent a position, for example, at the front of the Constitution.[23]

Madison's fear that the Anti-Federalists or old Confederalists would use a bill of rights to weaken the national government accounts in large part for his eagerness to play a leading role in shaping the first amendments added to the Constitution. The fact that Madison urged inclusion of a provision that would have specifically restrained state interference with fundamental rights lends added credibility to the claim that he understood the importance of supplying considerable protection for individual liberties. But his opposition to including anything in the Bill of Rights that would have impaired the ability of national officials to govern effectively deserves no less emphasis and, indeed, warrants heightened attention in the face of the contemporary inclination to constantly broaden protection for personal freedoms while reducing the constitutional weight of political and governmental interests. Madison's concern that the Bill of Rights might unduly weaken the national government represents an important key to understanding his constitutional thought. That it was not merely a passing product of the experiences of the nation under the Articles of Confederation is confirmed by the reappearance of a similar fear in the face of Jefferson's argument that no generation should be permitted to shift its debts to succeeding generations, thereby seriously limiting their descendants' freedom to act as they wish. For Madison, such reasoning abstracts from the realities of political life and may leave government helpless in the face of political necessities that might require extraordinary action, including occasional deficit spending. Though he understood that deficit spending constrains the freedom of future generations to control their own affairs as they please, such constraints represent part of the cost of equipping the government to protect national interests. He added that the kind of action he was defending ultimately would be to "the benefit of posterity."[24] Leaving an opening for one generation to bind another through, say, deficit spending represented for Madison a concession to political necessity that is not incompatible with republican principles of government. Nor can it be overlooked that this argument rests on the important assumption that society is something greater than the individual members who compose it at any single historical moment.

Madison never lost sight of the connection between effective government and protection for rights. Thus, for example, the same system of separated and divided powers that serves the end of shielding individuals from tyrannical government also facilitates effective government by dividing the duties of government among a number of public officials who are positioned to provoke each other to engage in more thoughtful deliberation and action. By using the veto power, the president can compel Congress to rethink all or part of some piece of legislation. By masking the full authority of political officials behind the appearance of divided powers and then making this authority tolerable by entrusting it to the representatives of the people, the arrangement set out in the Constitution also serves to deter undesirable public meddling that might be occasioned by alarmist concerns for the protection of individual liberties. The judiciary contributes to the results desired by Madison not only by protecting private rights when appropriate, but by exercising self-restraint so that appeals to rights do not end up overwhelming effectiveness in government. He understood that the habitual practice of championing rights claims against problematical political action could endanger effective government by provoking the people to insist on damaging curbs on governmental authority, a danger made all the more real if the people are naturally inclined to question the actions of political and administrative officials.

The same attention to affording adequate protection for private rights while giving political officials room to govern effectively appears in the legal opinions of John Marshall. Not unlike Madison, Marshall's credentials as an advocate of modern natural rights are indisputable. His forceful defense of property rights in *Fletcher* v. *Peck*, an 1810 case arising out of a challenge to state action revoking a prior land deal on the grounds that it was marred by improprieties on the part of some Georgia legislators, continues to stand as a classic example of natural rights reasoning.[25] His *Marbury* opinion contains as crisp a statement on the centrality of rights in the American republic as appears anywhere in American constitutional law: "[The] government of the United States has been emphatically termed a government of laws, and not of men. It will certainly cease to deserve this high appellation, if the laws furnish no remedy for the violation of a vested legal right.''[26] *Marbury* as well stands as the preeminent precedent for the principle that the judiciary has a special responsibility to protect private rights. In one of the most cited passages in American constitutional law, he announced that ''[it] is emphatically the province and duty of the judicial department to say what the law is. . . .''[27] For Marshall, this high responsibility in turn necessitated that judges enjoy real independence in the discharge of their duties.[28]

If *Marbury* stands as the great precedent for the principle that courts have a special obligation to redress violations of vested rights, it likewise contains an early reminder of the limits of judicial review of governmental action. Immediately following his observation that the protection of vested rights occupies a special place in the American republic, Marshall acknowledged that there are considerations that might properly ''exempt [a case] from legal investigation, or exclude the injured party from [legal redress].'' There are, for example, political duties that Marshall conceded fall within the discretionary powers of the president: ''By the constitution of the United States, the president is invested with certain important political powers, in the exercise of which he is to use his own discretion, and is accountable only to his country in his political character, and to his own conscience.''[29] That is to say, there are matters of a political nature that may defy judicial review. This significant observation from Marshall paved the way for later justices, such as Frankfurter in malapportionment suits, to insist that oversight of so-called political questions is not a proper judicial activity. Marshall understood not only that judicial self-restraint was constitutionally sound in keeping with the doctrine of separated and divided powers, but that it had the practical value of protecting the judiciary from the dangers likely to arise even from well-intentioned ventures into what Frankfurter called the ''political thicket.''[30] In short, it is good for both government in general and the judiciary in particular for the courts to circumscribe their review of political decision making.

Marshall's commitment to protecting natural rights that are associated by him with ''principles of natural justice,'' as well as to sustaining the requisites of effective government, appears in classic form in his opinion in the Aaron Burr treason case.[31] Considering Marshall's careful attention to Burr's rights, it is surprising that his opinion is not more frequently cited by rights–oriented jurists. One explanation for this may be the problem that some jurists have in drawing support from reasoning that benefited as unpalatable a historical figure as Burr. Another explanation may be found in the belief that the *Burr* opinion represented a partisan effort by the Federalist Marshall to embarrass Jefferson, leader of the Democratic Republican Party. Only a cursory reading of Marshall's reasoning is needed to confirm that his opinion is solidly grounded in a painstaking review of common law principles and the language of the Constitution. This is a meticulously crafted opinion that incorporated a response by Marshall to those critics who would have him engage in end-oriented reasoning rather than language-based and principles-driven reasoning. Marshall's articulation of his duty to adhere to the latter rather than the former type of reasoning is fully in keeping with his defense of judicial review in *Marbury*.

Few passages in American case law rival Marshall's summation in the *Burr* opinion of the high responsibilities that fall to members of the judicial department:

> That this court dares not usurp power is most true. That this court dares not shrink from its duty is no less true. No man is desirous of placing himself in a disagreeable situation. No man is desirous of becoming the peculiar subject of calumny. No man might he let the bitter cup pass from him without self-reproach, would drain it to the bottom. But if he have no choice in the case, if there be no alternative presented to him but a dereliction of duty or the opprobrium of those who are denominated the world, he merits the contempt as well as the indignation of his country who can hesitate which to embrace.[32]

Here is a classic defense of duty or political virtue above personal interests, including concern for one's immediate reputation. His characterization of what is to be expected of courts of law, together with the extensive protection he afforded Burr's rights in the face of extreme political pressure, makes Marshall's opinion an attractive precedent for jurists holding Brennan's convictions. What must also be appreciated, however, is Marshall's acknowledgment in the *Burr* case that the interests of the government "ought to be treated with respect" and that the privileges of the chief executive enjoy constitutional protection alongside protection for personal rights.[33] Hence in response to the request for a subpoena duces tecum directed to President Jefferson, which he admittedly consented to issue, Marshall carefully reminded the parties that courts are not "to proceed against the president as against an ordinary individual."[34]

Marshall's careful treatment of governmental interests needs to be highlighted because it has been obscured by the overwhelming attention given his defense of judicial review and natural rights. Thus, for example, while *McCulloch* v. *Maryland* represented for Brennan a vindication of broad national powers that are most ideally used when put in the service of advancing protection for individual rights, a more balanced reading of Marshall's opinion includes the preceding concern plus an intent to make available to the central government the powers required to ensure strong and effective governance. This is the point of the famous passage in *McCulloch* on the scope of the powers of the national government:

> We admit, as all must admit, that the powers of the government are limited, and that its limits are not to be transcended. But we think the sound construction of the constitution must allow to the national legislature that discretion, with respect to the means by which the powers it confers are to be carried into execution, which will enable that body to perform the high duties assigned to it, in the manner most beneficial to the people. Let the end be legitimate, let it be within the scope of the constitution, and all means which are appropriate, which are plainly adapted to that end, which are not prohibited, but consist with the letter and spirit of the constitution, are constitutional.[35]

This observation is followed by the equally important statement that the "degree of the necessity" of the means is to be determined by the political departments and for the Court to inquire into such matters "would be to pass the line which circumscribes the judicial department, and to tread on legislative ground." Marshall curtly added that "This court disclaims all pretensions to such a power."[36] Here is another example of his recognition that the judiciary's power is to be understood in terms of the larger system of separated and divided powers and the requisites of competent democratic republican government. Marshall's judiciary would be prepared to defer to legislative judgments about how Congress might best carry out its constitutional duties. Presumably these judgments would involve efficiency calculations of the sort Brennan challenged in *Mathews* v. *Eldridge*.

In sum, Marshall understood that natural rights are not well protected if government officials are left with insufficient powers or are placed in a situation that discourages reasonable use of those powers.[37] His careful insertion of a defense of the discretionary powers of the president in *Marbury* followed from his understanding of the importance of preserving an effective executive and not from any desire to conciliate Jefferson or to soften the effect of his endorsement of a general power of judicial review. Striking evidence of Marshall's acknowledgment that practical politics has a protected place in the Constitution can be found in the great commerce case of 1824, *Gibbons* v. *Ogden*. In his opinion for the Court, Marshall went so far as to suggest that the appropriate use of the commerce power is typically to be determined through political and not judicial processes. In words that have received too little attention, he reminded his contemporaries of how the affairs of the people are principally to be managed in a representative democracy:

> The wisdom and the discretion of congress, their identity with the people, and the influence which their constituents possess at elections, are, in [the regulation of commerce], as in many other instances, as that, for example, of declaring war, the sole restraints on which they have relied, to secure them from abuse. They are the restraints on which the people must often rely solely, in all representative governments.[38]

This observation stands as both an important concession to governmental and political interests and a significant limitation on judicial review. The contrast with Brennan's insistence that the judiciary has a moral obligation *to do* whatever it *can do* to advance the cause of individual expression and autonomy could hardly be more dramatic.

It is only when passages such as the ones above from *McCulloch* and *Gibbons* are combined with Marshall's well-documented commitment to protecting natural rights that the full grandeur and teaching of his jurisprudence can properly be appreciated. He never forgot that political existence is not unidimensional, and especially not simply rights-defined. Government must of necessity impose duties on the citizen body. Instructive in this connection is a passage found in his opinion in *Providence Bank* v. *Billings*: "However absolute the right of an individual may be, it is still in the nature of that right, that it must bear a portion of the public burdens; and that portion must be determined by the legislature."[39] Hence his defense of George Washington's harsh actions in suppression of the Whiskey Rebellion and his conviction that persons in the military might not claim the full benefits of the jury trial provision of the Bill of Rights. His views on the latter issue reflect his understanding of the complexities, and perhaps the tragic side, of governance. Full extension of the jury trial provision to crimes committed by members of the armed forces, according to Marshall, "would probably have prostrated the constitution itself, with the liberties and the independence of the nation, before the first disciplined invader who should approach our shores. Necessity would have imperiously demanded the review and amendment of so unwise a provision."[40] His reference to "necessity" is a reminder that practical political considerations have a place in constitutional jurisprudence as do appeals to explicitly protected rights. At the center of the statesmanship of Marshall and Madison is a body of constitutional thought that respects natural rights and accommodates the real difficulties involved in administering the domestic and foreign affairs of modern democratic states.

Distilling Lessons (and Law) from Constitutional History

There is good reason for Brennan to associate Madison and Marshall with the spirited defense of individual rights and a strong and independent judiciary. But it also bears repeating that for both Madison and Marshall, constitutional republicanism looks to achieve reasonable goals by making reasonable demands on the citizen body. Neither Madison nor Marshall associated liberal republican constitutionalism with utopian ends or enormous human sacrifice. This does not mean, however, that they believed it would be easy either to construct or to administer a modern state based on liberal republican principles. They did believe, however, that achieving the proper balance between the pursuit of rights and effectiveness in governance was within the grasp of the American people. Among other things, this would require that the enjoyment of individual rights could not come at the expense of having a government capable of controlling the governed. On the other hand, effectiveness in government could not come at the expense of due process of law. The Constitution represented for Madison and Marshall the best framework devised by their time for achieving both decent and competent democratic government.

Brennan clearly is more idealistic, and hence more ambitious, than Marshall and Madison. Brennan's ambition is born of a generous or expansive interpretation of the ends of the modern liberal republic (i.e., protection for life, liberty and the pursuit of happiness), and a belief that democratic states are much more resilient than they were thought to be by Madison and Marshall. In fact, it is the inextricable linkage of these convictions in Brennan's thought that helps explain his virtually one-dimensional reading of Madison's and Marshall's constitutional thought. Undergirding his commitment to "libertarian dignity" is the conviction that government can function in the face of robust and uninhibited criticism and that the people are fundamentally governable because they are fully capable of protecting their mores and conduct from being corrupted as a direct or indirect result of their own actions or the actions of others. In this same connection, he concluded that it is permissible to limit what the government can do in the name of self-preservation. If democratic government possesses great resilience and the people can be presumed to be reasonable, then why should there be any objection on practical or theoretical grounds to expanding individual liberties or freedoms; especially when the founding philosophy of the republic proclaimed the primacy of individual rights? In short, for Brennan we have reached a historical point where practice can satisfy the high ends of political theory.

The vision of a perfected American republic presented by Brennan and supported by his construction of Madison's and Marshall's constitutional thought contrasts not only with traditional conceptions of the republic but even with the dominant liberal positions of this century. Both Holmesian judicial liberals and New Deal political liberals left openings for political action that might significantly confine individual freedom; witness Oliver Wendell Holmes's decision to uphold a Virginia sterilization law in *Buck* v. *Bell* and the perpetuation by New Deal coalitions of practices that did not always advance minority interests.

Brennan's jurisprudence addresses the deficiencies of twentieth-century judicial and political liberalism by giving a radically progressive construction to the ends of modern liberal republican thought and by treating the democratic state and citizenry as capable of almost Herculean self-defense. For their part, Marshall and Madison gave what might be characterized as a moderate or temperate reading to the ends of the modern liberal state and viewed decent and competent democratic government as something that should never be taken for granted. They took seriously the age-old teaching that civilized orders are constantly threatened by the forces of barbarism, in the form of either anarchy or tyranny. Consider in this connection the attention given by Madison to the problem of factious violence in *Federalist* 10 and to governmental tyranny in *Federalist* 51. Fear of the latter danger, however, did not prevent him from arguing for a government that was active in giving proper scope and direction to the way the citizens exercise their faculties. Providing the people with attractive incentives to use their faculties in the proper pursuit of economic interests, for example, was important in his mind to limiting the threat of factious activity. Marshall as well understood the need to entrust political officials with sufficient authority to govern the people, and direct their collective energy, while always insisting that these officials respect the overarching natural rights principles of the republic. Hence Marshall's generous construction of legislative

power in *Gibbons* and *McCulloch* on the one side, and his uncompromising defense of due process of law and property rights in *Burr* and *Fletcher*
on the other.[41] Finally, Madison and Marshall understood that effectiveness in democratic republican government depends on a prudent veiling,
but not elimination, of the harsher side of political rule. At one and the
same time, the threatening side of government cannot be dispensed with
if rights are to be protected, but that side cannot be too fully enlarged
because of the dangers of governmental tyranny. It is also important not
to tempt the people to strip political officials of authority out of fear of
tyranny. When entrusted to persons who understand the teaching left
by Madison and Marshall, the system of separated and divided powers
moderates the use of governmental authority without denying officials
the wherewithal to govern effectively.

While not without problems, the American constitutional system
has functioned in a manner not far removed from what was desired by
Madison and Marshall. With its amplification of individual rights, its
depreciation of the constitutional weight of political interests, and its
emphasis on exposing public action to full view, Brennan's jurisprudence
seemingly leaves government institutions vulnerable to the degenerative
forces of individualism that invite both anarchy and then tyranny. At the
least, his jurisprudence shrinks what society might do in the name of
self-defense while making almost unlimited temptations available to
many people who may not be capable of dependable self-restraint and
self-control. The Constitution fathered by Madison and forcefully defended by Marshall represented a response to the experience of weak
government under the Articles of Confederation that was still faithful to
the American commitment to natural rights as proclaimed in the Declaration of Independence. It is the sufficiency of the balance that leading
Founders such as Madison struck between the commitment to individual rights and competence in government that Brennan's jurisprudence
effectively calls into question.

Notes

1. See, for example, Harry H. Wellington, *Interpreting the Constitution* (New
Haven: Yale University Press, 1990). Wellington served as the dean of Yale's
Law School from 1975 to 1985.

2. 362 U.S. 17, 20 (1960). Among other "duties," Brennan traced back to
Marshall the judiciary's responsibility to protect freedom of the press. See *Rosenbloom* v. *Metromedia*, 403 U.S. 29, 51 (1971).

3. 1 Cranch 137, 163 (1803).

4. 369 U.S. 186, 208 (1962).

5. 403 U.S. 388, 397 (1971).

6. 4 Wheat. 316, 401 (1819) [italics in the original].

7. 424 U.S. 693, 732 (1976).

8. In a strongly worded passage, Brennan accused the Burger Court in *Paul* v. *Davis* of allowing a "frightening" situation to arise by failing to provide adequate protection for people threatened with "arbitrary" uses of authority by police officials. 424 U.S. at 721.

9. 468 U.S. 897, 932 (1984).

10. 426 U.S. 833, 857 (1976).

11. Ibid. at 876–78. Nine years after *National League of Cities*, Blackmun used the argument that Congress is entrusted with the principal responsibility for setting the limits of the commerce power in a case that overturned Rehnquist's majority opinion. *Garcia* v. *San Antonio Metropolitan Transit Authority*, 469 U.S. 528 (1985).

12. 4 Wheat. at 423.

13. Brennan specifically distinguished between congressional action that extends protection for rights and action that has the effect of "dilut[ing]" rights in *Katzenbach* v. *Morgan*, 384 U.S. 641, 651–52, n. 10 (1966).

14. 468 U.S. 897, 930. The quote is taken from Madison's speech to Congress of June 8, 1789, on the utility of incorporating additional guarantees for rights into the body of the Constitution. *The Papers of James Madison*, Charles F. Hobson and Robert A. Rutland, eds. (Charlottesville: University of Virginia Press, 1981), XII: 206–7. In this same connection see Brennan's address on "The Role of the Courts—The Challenge of the Future," in *An Affair with Freedom: William J. Brennan, Jr.*, Stephen J. Friedman, ed. (New York: Atheneum, 1967), 332.

15. Ibid. at 356–57, 366.

16. 376 U.S. 254, 274–76 (1964).

17. Brennan, "The Bill of Rights and the States," in *An Affair with Freedom*, 27.

18. *Federalist* 10, 78.

19. See *Federalist* 10 and Madison's speech to Congress of June 8, 1789, on the occasion of his defense of a bill of rights.

20. *Federalist* 51, 322.

21. *The Papers of James Madison*, XII: 198.

22. Max Farrand, *The Records of the Federal Convention of 1787* (New Haven: Yale University Press, 1966) II: 430.

23. Herbert J. Storing, "The Constitution and the Bill of Rights" (unpublished paper delivered at Utah State University, December 5, 1975), 26.

24. "Letter of James Madison to Thomas Jefferson," February 4, 1790, in *The Papers of James Madison*, XIII: 23.

25. 6 Cranch, 132–36, 139 (1810).

26. See 1 Cranch at 163, 166.

27. Ibid. at 167.

28. See *Cohens* v. *Virginia*, 6 Wheat. 264 (1821).

29. 1 Cranch at 165, also 166.

30. *Colegrove* v. *Green*, 328 U.S. 549, 556 (1946).

31. *United States* v. *Burr,* 25 Fed. Cas. 55, 77 (1807). Reference to the principles of natural justice also appears in Marshall's opinion in *Cohens* v. *Virginia* (6 Wheat. 420 [1821]).

32. 25 Fed. Cas. at 179.

33. 25 Fed. Cas. at 85.

34. This quote was used to good effect by Burger in *United States* v. *Nixon,* the Watergate Tapes case (418 U.S. 683 [1974]).

35. 4 Wheat. 316, 421 (1819).

36. Ibid. at 423.

37. See John Marshall, *Life of Washington* (Philadelphia: Wayne, 1804), III: 582–84, 588, 590–92.

38. 9 Wheat. 1, 197 (1824).

39. 4 Peters 514, 563 (1830). Marshall adds an observation in *Providence Bank* regarding the exercise of state powers that complements what he had earlier said in *McCulloch* about federal legislative power: "This [legislative power] may be abused; but the constitution of the United States was not intended to furnish the corrective for every abuse of power which may be committed by the state governments." Ibid. at 563. Again in keeping with his argument in *McCulloch,* he noted in his 1830 opinion that the principal check on "unwise" legislation is the "wisdom and justice" of representatives and the relationship of legislators to their constituents. Ibid. at 563.

40. Cited in Robert K. Faulkner, *The Jurisprudence of John Marshall* (Princeton: Princeton University Press, 1968), 79.

41. Although generally associated with the amplification or enlargement of legislative authority, even *McCulloch* includes a warning to Congress not to employ its powers to "[accomplish] . . . objects not entrusted to the government." This is the so-called "pretext" argument that has been used with varying degrees of success by justices who have objected to federal regulatory actions. See, for example, Chief Justice Melville W. Fuller's dissent in *Champion* v. *Ames,* 188 U.S. 321 (1903).

Chapter Six

CONCLUSION

*W*illiam Brennan, Jr., a Catholic Democrat from New Jersey, carefully crafted through his opinions a legal philosophy that sought to bring about a truly catholic and democratic (meaning universally egalitarian and individual rights-oriented) nation-state. His project amounted to a concerted and lifelong exercise in liberating individuals to enjoy the maximum of self-expression and self-determination. His jurisprudence of "libertarian dignity" might appropriately be labeled the jurisprudence of authentic individualism. Prevailing traditions, distinctions rooted in nature, appeals to governmental efficiency, and democratic majoritarianism, among a great many other things, are all subject to limitation to the end of expanding the realm of individual choice and self-construction in a highly egalitarian society. Here was Brennan's understanding of what was meant by modern liberalism's pledge to conquer necessity and nature and, thereby, fear itself. Whether measured by his vision of a completed republic of rights or his labors on behalf of this project, Brennan ranks with Woodrow Wilson, Franklin Roosevelt and Oliver Wendell Holmes as one of the major liberal figures of the twentieth century.

By addressing the difficulties that remained under New Deal-style coalitional politics and the modern bureaucratic state, Brennan's jurisprudence can reasonably be viewed as an effort to complete the work of the political and judicial liberals who preceded him. There is clear evidence in his writing that he saw himself assisting the country in completing what was initiated with the American Revolution and Constitution. The grandness of the task was not underestimated by Brennan, and he understood that the brunt of the burden for carrying out this project would fall to the judiciary. He never tired of reminding lawyers and jurists of their great responsibilities. Nor did he hold back public criticism when he believed that his colleagues were failing to advance the cause of libertarian dignity, for example, when the Court permitted states and localities to display manger scenes at Christmas, impose gender-specific requirements on access to benefits or services, or regulate unorthodox lifestyles. For Brennan, such practices threaten social pluralism and stifle freedom of choice. The fact that the Court might rely on history or the traditions of the society to support such practices only compounded the sin being committed. Antonin Scalia's recurrence to tradition to defeat Michael H.'s demand to intrude on a marriage relationship in order to gain the right to visit his natural daughter was not really distinguishable for Brennan from reliance on tradition to defend racial segregation. In all such instances, he believed that the Court's obligation was to neutralize history, tradition, and prevailing norms as constraints on human behavior and, thus, as threats to self-satisfaction. Here is the explanation as well for Brennan's refusal to go along with Warren Burger's bow to Georgia's asserted interest in protecting the morality of the people in *Paris Adult Theatre* and William Rehnquist's declaration that Missouri's clear and convincing evidence standard as applied to persons in Nancy Cruzan's condition need only pass the rational basis test. Nor were John Marshall Harlan's defense of federalism in *Baker* v. *Carr* and Lewis Powell's acceptance of the government's efficiency calculations in *Mathews* v. *Eldridge* any less dangerous. In Brennan's mind, the positions taken by Burger, Rehnquist, Harlan, and Powell in these cases protected obstacles to perfecting the United States as an egalitarian and rights-oriented democracy or, more to the point, as a constitutional order that permits people to define a way of life for themselves as self-constituting beings.

Brennan's conviction that the nation could only satisfy its historical destiny when it was fully reconciled to being a "facilitative, pluralistic" society, and not an "assimilative, homogeneous" one, was matched by the belief that the country had reached the point in its development when practice might be expected to fulfill the high demands of theory. Hence his assertion that government appeals to economy, efficiency, and self-defense should be expected to pass strict scrutiny rather than the rational basis test, and the same was true of appeals to majoritarian sentiments. For Brennan, the concessions of Progressive and New Deal liberals that had perpetuated restraints on personal liberty and delayed the achievement of true racial and gender equality had become both constitutionally and morally indefensible. His opinions make clear that he believed the time had come to insist on government action that liberates the human "will" by removing or weakening anything that constrains or determines behavior while also compensating the "victims" of such constraints, for example, indigents or illegitimate children.

If Wilsonian liberalism identified the perfectly efficient democracy as the last stage of historical development, and New Deal liberalism set out to ensure through political and administrative means that fundamental wants no longer marred human existence, Brennan pointed to a society that successfully neutralized all manner of constraints, including those associated with "rational" governance, in order to afford people the greatest possible opportunity to shape their own identities. As "reason" could not be conceded a right to rule, so neither could the "general will" be given this power. Significantly, where leading Founders such as James Madison spoke of the sovereignty of a citizen body whose pursuit of personal interests has been moderated and restrained by institutions and practices that balance private rights and the requisites of effective government, Brennan celebrated the sovereignty of each individual over his or her own way of life. In this connection, he insisted that reason make its peace with the passions or desires. Appeals to "necessity" or the "rationality" of government action were unpersuasive for Brennan precisely because they commonly open the door to government constraints on personal lifestyle choices. As he recognized that significant constraints on human behavior result when the desires are compelled to submit to the dictates of reason, so he recognized that reliance on nature or natural distinctions also imposes serious constraints on conduct. If the conquest of nature for John Locke meant learning how to channel natural impulses and forces, for Brennan it meant nothing less than the "overcoming" of nature. His was a paradigm for not merely ahistorical existence, but for existence in rebellion against the constraints and alienation from personal "authenticity" that tradition and attention to nature unavoidably produce. After all, self-consciousness rooted in an awareness of death, or of our nature as mortal beings, can exercise a considerable constraint on conduct. In sum, Brennan's legal writing points to a society composed of free traders in ideas and lifestyles whose forays in one direction or another are truly robust and uninhibited. It might be added that within such a society honor most likely would come to be associated with the successful advancement of self-satisfaction freely defined and not with, say, a Lincolnesque commitment to holding the republic together. Human good really becomes the "pursuit of happiness" understood as the continuous process of making and remaking ourselves. In this indeterminate phrase from the Declaration of Independence can be found the fundamental creedal principle of Brennan's jurisprudence of libertarian dignity.

Whether construed in light of the interpretation that Brennan gave to the judicial oath or the nature of the project to which he was committed, his task involved nothing less than active judicial involvement in shaping a way of life for the American people. There can be no more "political" undertaking than this. As we have seen, he was far less concerned than his colleague Felix Frankfurter about the dangers of getting the Court involved in "political thickets." If anything, Brennan labored to make the political thicket obstacle to judicial decision making disappear so as to magnify opportunities for the courts to "dialogue" with political officials on both the proper ends and the procedures of democratic government. It was just such a "dialogue" that he believed had vindicated his liberal construction of Title VII of the Civil Rights Act of 1964 in *United Steelworkers v. Weber.*

Brennan also subscribed to a far more expansive view of what the Constitution protected and demanded of government than did Frankfurter. Believing that government has a moral obligation *to do* whatever it *can do* to ensure comprehensive protection for all rights and redress for all grievances, with special attention to freeing up the most constrained parties in society, Brennan had no difficulty in concluding that government officials can be guilty of sins of omission as well as of commission. In this way he could find constitutional protection for persons such as Joshua DeShaney as well as for Gregory Lee Johnson. As was evident in *Oregon v. Mitchell* and *Johnson v. Santa Clara County,* employing ambiguity to create openings for offering new constructions of constitutional or statutory language represented just one of the means he employed to advance the ends he associated with the Constitution.

As noted throughout this study, Brennan saw no reason to compromise with the ideal of a nontragic democratic state. The time had come in his estimation to make good on the Enlightenment promise of greater freedom and comfortable preservation for everyone, but without the stultifying effects of scientific or economic rationality. Importantly, his appreciation of scientific rationality's promise of a demythified world did not represent a concession that "rationality" constitutes the sole or even the best test of legitimacy. Brennan understood that freedom in the form of self-definition requires, among other things, the reduction of speech to mere expression as compared to the equation of speech with reasoned discourse. There is little evidence that he perceived there to be any significant "cost" to this form of human existence or that the possibility that there may be some "costs" led him to temper his goals.

Brennan's vision of the ends of the American constitutional order and the resilience of decent democracies and their people is in sharp contrast to the teaching left by Founders such as James Madison and George Washington. Where they carefully guarded the capacity of the government to "govern" the people and defended institutions and practices that pointed the people in the direction of socially and politically constructive forms of conduct, Brennan shrank what government might do in the name of self-defense or self-preservation while dangling almost unlimited temptations in front of people whose capacity for self-control was not taken for granted by Madison and Washington. For Madison's heavy reliance on institutional arrangements and procedures to check tyranny and promote governmental competence, Brennan emphasized rights-based claims directed by private parties at government action. Nor is this all that separates Brennan from these Founders. Madison clearly thought that some things are right or proper or just by nature and other things wrong or unjust and that people should have the good sense and good taste not to be too extreme in using the freedoms they enjoy. He defended self-government as a viable political alternative because he believed that people possess a natural moral sense that can restrain and direct willfulness in the pursuit of personal interests. Brennan also assumed a capacity for responsible behavior and valued good sense. But when he posits the making and remaking of ourselves through expressive activity as the decisive human action, he transforms us into beings whose lives are abstracted from any fixed standards that permit judgments to be made about what is just or good which are not merely subjective judgments or the product of power politics.

For Madison, decent and competent democratic government necessitates not only knowledge of the distinction between reasonable and unreasonable action, but the advancement of what is reasonable and the discouragement of what is unreasonable. He understood that this double task could be advanced by attaching law to the deepest convictions of the people that are consistent with "right reason." It is not mere hopefulness that led Madison to declare in *Federalist* 51 that "Justice is the end of government [and] . . . the end of civil society. It ever has been and ever will be pursued until it be obtained, or until liberty is lost in the pursuit." It would be a mistake to conclude that his willingness to rely on private interest and not pure reason to drive the American republic was evidence that his sights were set on something other than the advancement of justice and the common good. Madison's convictions about the "end" of a defensible democratic order fit with the teaching that rights must be bounded to some not insignificant degree by the requisites of effective government and decency in society. All of this becomes problematical for Brennan because it is constraining. His insistence in *Texas* v. *Johnson* that no "reasonable" person would allow himself or herself to be incited to act violently in response to the burning of the American flag facilitates challenges to state regulations of the kind used against Johnson. When "reasonableness" is equated with toleration, and "reason" is seen to be at its best when fully domesticated and stripped of its cunning side, then it becomes much easier to argue that people may be emancipated from regulations (e.g., whether involving school prayers or access to pornography or bans on flag burning) designed to encourage decent or "reasonable" behavior.

For the very reason that the human condition is fundamentally unproblematical for Brennan, the imposition of governmental regulations regarding proper lifestyle choices on human beings such as Johnson *is* problematical. Libertarian dignity necessitates great opportunities for creative expression rather than a Lincolnesque admonition that law-abidingness must be ingrained in persons such as Gregory Lee Johnson. Insofar as a transcendent standard exists for Brennan, it takes the form of toleration of each person's right to pursue a preferred way of life. Toleration on this scale requires the reduction of all opinions to mere preferences or prejudices. It also necessitates acceptance of almost universal self-assertiveness without either submission or conflict whatever the lot nature has cast for us. That such a life would be productive of much satisfaction and progress, or would even be acceptable to most people, is assumed but never seriously explored or proven by Brennan.

When examined in its totality, Brennan's jurisprudence points us to a community of self-regarding individuals engaged in shaping themselves through expressive activity defined in the broadest terms. The traditional argument that a civil society has to be grounded in some substantial common values beyond the mere commitment to self-expression if it is to constitute a true community disappears from sight. That every society must be capable of collective action in the advancement of important causes, or that rules based on good sense and good taste help distinguish civilized free societies from "states of nature," clearly are not the principal messages of Brennan's legal writing. He cannot admit to any great transformation or sublimation of preferences being required for his "good man" or "woman" to become a "good citizen." The pursuit of individual dignity through uninhibited expression, which is at the heart of his jurisprudence, requires that persons such as Johnson be left as dislocated selves who are neither fundamentally sustained nor restrained by the institutions, traditions, and dominant opinions or mores of the society. The absence of serious attention in his opinions to the corrosive potential of radical pluralism and self-regardingness, and even self-conscious existence is not mere oversight. As he presumed that it is possible to maintain a community in the face of heterogeneous opinions about preferable ways of life, so he assumed that government can sustain order and protect the interests of the whole society with minimal regulation of individual activities and with modest constitutional support for much government action. As a result, even regulations that might be acceptable to Brennan often are left without good principled support in his legal thought. To take one example, his tentative acceptance of governmental regulations designed to protect minors from exposure to obscene material in *Paris Adult Theatre* can be dismissed by critics as merely representing an expression of personal preference or sentiment, a difficulty cheerfully pointed out by Burger in his majority opinion.

If Brennan disagreed with the leading Founders on how best to govern people, he also defended a grander view of the role of the judiciary than held by Madison and Marshall. Brennan looked to justices such as himself to possess a heightened understanding of the essential elements of the fully consummated state and of the kind of cost-benefit calculations that are required to reach this end. He relied on just such calculations to check the appeal to associational freedom in the Minnesota Jayceees case in order to advance gender equality. Once language, history, and majoritarian preferences are rendered suspect as decisive guides for judicial decision making, virtually all that remains is the judgment of the members of the judiciary regarding proper and improper public and private action. The judgment of the justices must trump the reasoning of all other persons, according to Brennan, since the courts are entrusted with the final determination of what is acceptable in all significant public matters that bear on the way of life of the people. And these judgments are to rest on the "reason and passions" of the times more than on the original thinking that informed the Constitution. The judiciary emerges as the institution that can best be trusted to mediate disputes in a rights-oriented society where willfulness is an extension of authentic personhood and where moral truths have the status of personal claims. The end result of this reasoning, however, is to depreciate the status of the Constitution as the defining document of the political community and to assign the greatest weight at any moment to what is needed to permit people the widest possible freedom in the pursuit of a preferred way of life. Liberty is left as a principle into which meaning can be "poured" by different persons. But since common opinion, history, language, and nature are rendered suspect as guides for assessing claims, it is difficult to see how the burden of sifting through competing views of what is desirable can be discharged without engaging in subjective decision making or inviting divisive disputes. Indeed, it is not clear that Brennan can protect his whole jurisprudence of libertarian dignity against a charge of subjectivity.

A sophisticated understanding of American constitutional history is not needed to recognize that Brennan's opinions capture and develop some of the major impulses of modernity. When we dissect his opinions, we are dissecting part of the modern mind, especially the hatred of alienation and the longing to be a complete self. In this regard, his writings should enable us to better understand ourselves, but still only a part of ourselves. Brennan's jurisprudence represents that side of modernity that wishes to believe that political existence is not necessarily tragic. Contained in this body of thought is the conviction that nothing is superior to human will, conceived in a heterogeneous and particularistic fashion. Hence the necessary defense of wide-open and uninhibited freedom of expression. The practical implications for governance are significant. Governmental action is restrained by the limitless variety of claims that can be raised to maximize individual autonomy, for example, First and Fourteenth Amendment challenges to the management of institutions such as prisons, police departments, hospitals, and schools or to policies governing the distribution of public benefits and services.

Brennan's jurisprudence represents the side of the modern psyche that rejects as flawed, or at least as dated, the teaching about the tragic dimensions of the human condition and the limits of political life found in William Shakespeare's *King Lear,* Herman Melville's *Billy Budd,* and much earlier in Plato's *Apology* and the teachings of the Old and New Testaments. These works point to the problematical side of human existence that is perhaps best reflected in the inability of even reputable communities to satisfy the highest yearnings and demands of the best of people, represented in *King Lear* by Cordelia. Evidence that the thought of the Founding Fathers reflected this sober teaching can be seen both in *Federalist* 10, where Madison defended a representative form of government that assumes the necessity of devices for enlarging and refining the views of the people, and in *Federalist* 51, where he declared that the "first object" of the Constitutional Convention was to frame a government that was sufficiently strong to control the people. Madison understood that popular government, whether it be a direct or a representative democracy, carries costs, for example, the constant threat of majority tyranny and the predictable inefficiencies of coalitional politics. These were assumed to be inescapable but, under proper management, tolerable costs. To a large degree, both the Holmesian juridical and New Deal political liberals made their peace with these costs. Brennan invites us to inquire into the necessity for such compromise.

William Brennan combined the utopianism of modern scientific thought with the aims of twentieth-century liberalism in a jurisprudence that compels government to find common ground with "uninhibited and robust" expression and self-definition. His was a good faith effort to advance the dignity of all persons, and his labors on behalf of this task can best be described as Herculean. Brennan's lifelong commitment to this project is one of the remarkable events in American constitutional history. There is no doubt that he was not blind to many of the difficulties left unresolved by his jurisprudence. He understood at the same time that the achievement of his objectives depended to no insignificant degree on his willingness to abstract from these problems. There is reason to fear, however, that his failure to make concessions to "necessity," whether in the form of the demands of political life or nature, leaves the intended beneficiaries of his legal thought vulnerable to the disintegrative forces of the radical individualism that is at the heart of his perfected republic of rights. At the least, even people sympathetic to his project must ask not only whether he is demanding a better world than political life can offer, but also whether the insistence on limiting the ability of political orders to meet the everyday costs of governing imperfect beings might end up shaking the foundations of even decent communities. For not only is it the case that history, tradition, and political calculations disappear as decisive guides for individual action for Brennan, he does not leave even nature for us to use to guide our conduct once the imperfections of governmental institutions and practices have been exposed to full view. It is, however, precisely the purity of Brennan's defense of the side of the modern psyche that values the ideal of authentic individualism that makes the serious examination of his jurisprudence an appropriate exercise for all who are interested in the cultural implications of modernity.

Bibliography

Basler, Roy, ed. *The Collected Works of Abraham Lincoln*. New Brunswick: Rutgers University Press, 1953.

Bickel, Alexander. *The Supreme Court and the Idea of Progress*. New York: Harper, 1970.

Bloom, Allan. Politics and the Arts. New York: Cornell University Press, 1960.

Brennan, William J., Jr. *Modernizing the Courts*. New York: Institute of Judicial Administration, 1957.

———. "Reason, Passion, and 'The Progress of the Law'." 10 *Cardozo Law Review*, 1988.

———. "The Bill of Rights and the States." In *An Affair with Freedom: William J. Brennan, Jr.*, ed. Stephen J. Friedman. New York: Atheneum, 1961.

———. "The Role of the Court—The Challenge of the Future." In *An Affair with Freedom: William J. Brennan, Jr.*, ed. Stephen J. Friedman. New York: Atheneum, 1967.

———. "Address to the Text and Teaching Symposium." In *The Great Debate: Interpreting Our Written Constitution*. Washington, D.C.: Federalist Society, 1986 [The Georgetown Address].

Brennan, William J., Jr. "Color-Blind, Creed-Blind, Status-Blind, Sex-Blind." 14 *Human Rights,* No. 1, 30–37 (Winter 1987).

———. "How Goes the Supreme Court?" 36 *Mercer Law Review* 781–94 (1985).

———. "The Constitution of the United States: Contemporary Ratification." 27 *South Texas Law Review* 433–45 (1986).

Cardozo, Benjamin. *The Nature of the Judicial Process*. New Haven: Yale University Press, 1921.

Croly, Herbert. *The Promise of American Life*. New York: Macmillan, 1909.

Douglas, William O. *The Court Years 1939-1975: The Autobiography of William O. Douglas*. New York: Random House, 1980.

Farrand, Max. *The Records of the Federal Convention of 1787*. New Haven: Yale University Press, 1966.

Faulkner, Robert K. *The Jurisprudence of John Marshall*. Princeton: Princeton University Press, 1968.

Freedman, James O. *Crisis and Legitimacy*. Cambridge University Press, 1978.

Friedman, Stephen J. "William J. Brennan." In *The Justices of the United States Supreme Court 1789–1969,* ed. Leon Friedman and Fred L. Israel. New York: Bowker, 1969.

Frisch, Morton J. *Franklin D. Roosevelt: The Contribution of the New Deal to American Political Thought and Practice*. Boston: Twayne, 1975.

Fukuyama, Francis. *The End of History and the Last Man*. New York: Avon Books, 1992.

Gunther, Gerald. *Cases and Materials in Constitutional Law*. Mineola, N.Y.: Foundation Press, 1980.

Hall, Kermit L. *The Magic Mirror*. New York: Oxford University Press, 1989.

Hobson, Charles F., and Robert A. Rutland, eds. *The Papers of James Madison*. Charlottesville: University of Virginia Press, 1981.

Ickes, Harold. *The New Democracy*. New York: Norton, 1934.

Levy, Leonard W. *Against the Law: The Nixon Court and Criminal Justice*. New York: Harper and Row, 1974.

———. *Original Intent and the Framers' Constitution*. New York: Macmillan, 1988.

Link, Arthur S., ed. *The Papers of Woodrow Wilson*. Princeton: Princeton University Press, 1966.

Lowi, Theodore J. *The End of Liberalism*. New York: Norton, 1969.

Lowi, Theodore J., and Benjamin Ginsberg. *Poliscide*. New York: Macmillan, 1976.

Mansfield, Harvey C., Jr. *Taming the Prince: The Ambivalence of Modern Executive Power*. New York: Free Press, 1989.

Marshall, John. *Life of George Washington*. Philadelphia: Wayne, 1804.

Murphy, Paul L. *Constitution in Crisis Time: 1918–1969*. New York: Harper and Row, 1972.

O'Brien, David. *Storm Center*. New York: Norton, 1986.

Pangle, Lorraine, and Thomas Pangle. *The Learning of Liberty*. Lawrence: University of Kansas Press, 1993.

Report of the President's Committee on Administrative Management. Washington: U. S. Government Printing Office, 1938 [The Brownlow Report].

Rohr, John. *To Run a Constitution*. Lawrence: University of Kansas Press, 1986.

Storing, Herbert J. *What the Anti-Federalists Were For*. Chicago: University of Chicago Press, 1981.

Strauss, Leo. *Natural Right and History*. Chicago: University of Chicago Press, 1953.

Wermiel, Stephen. "The Nomination of Justice Brennan: Eisenhower's Mistake? A Look at the Historical Record." 11 *Constitutional Commentary* 515–537 (Winter 1994–95).

Wilson, James Q. *Bureaucracy*. New York: Basic Books, 1989.

———. *The Moral Sense*. New York: Free Press, 1993.

Wilson, Woodrow. *Constitutional Government in the United States*. New York: Columbia University Press, 1911.

———. *The New Freedom*. Englewood Cliffs, N.J.: Prentice Hall, 1961.

Index of Cases

Subject Index

About the Author

$\mathcal{D}$avid E. Marion is Elliott Professor of Political Science and Director of the Center for Leadership in the Public Interest at Hampden-Sydney College in Virginia. His research and writing span the fields of constitutional law, American political thought and public administration. He has been an educational consultant at Montpelier, James Madison's plantation home in Orange County, Virginia.